Wallace Stevens' Poetics

Wallace Stevens' Poetics:
The Neglected Rhetoric

Angus J. Cleghorn

palgrave

WALLACE STEVENS' POETICS
Copyright © Angus J. Cleghorn, 2000.
All rights reserved. No part of this book may be used or reproduced in any manner whatsoever without written permission except in the case of brief quotations embodied in critical articles or reviews.

First published 2000 by
PALGRAVE™
175 Fifth Avenue, New York, N.Y. 10010 and
Houndmills, Basingstoke, Hampshire, England RG21 6XS.
Companies and representatives throughout the world.

PALGRAVE™ is the new global publishing imprint of St. Martin's Press LLC Scholarly and Reference Division and Palgrave Publishers Ltd (formerly Macmillan Press Ltd).

ISBN 0-312-23101-6 hardback

Library of Congress Cataloging-in-Publication Data
Cleghorn, Angus J.
    Wallace Stevens' poetics : the neglected rhetoric / Angus J. Cleghorn.
        p.   cm.
    Includes bibliographical references and index.
    ISBN 0-312-23101-6
    1. Stevens, Wallace, 1879–1955—Criticism and interpretation.   2. Stevens, Wallace, 1879–1955. Owl's clover.   3. English language—20th century—Rhetoric.   4. Poetics.   I. Title.

    PS3537.T4753 Z6228 2000
    811'.52—dc21   00-036910

A catalogue record for this book is available from the British Library.

Design by Westchester Book Composition

First edition: December, 2000
10 9 8 7 6 5 4 3 2 1

Printed in the United States of America.

For Julie

Contents

Acknowledgments   ix

Preface   xi

Chapter 1   Introduction: Strike the Pose   1

Chapter 2   *Ideas of Order:* Compos(t)ing the romantic   27

Chapter 3   *Owl's Clover* I & II: "How clearly that would
             be defined!"   55

Chapter 4   *Owl's Clover* III, IV, V: "The civil fiction,
             the calico idea"   85
             Coda: A Defense of *Owl's Clover* by
             "The Noble Rider"   113

Chapter 5   The Neglected *Parts of a World* &
             Transport to Summer's Confrontations   123

Chapter 6   Lyrical Dialogues with Epic Narratives   167

Chapter 7   Conclusion: The Necessary Abstracts of
             Market Belief and Social Democracy   189

Notes   209

Bibliography   225

Index   233

Acknowledgments

I would like to thank Kathryn Chittick for initiating my interest in Stevens; Tom Grieve for patient, thorough supervision, as well as a memorable trip to Scotland; William Doreski for enthusiastic feedback; and John Serio for fostering scholarship on Stevens. Jacqueline Vaught Brogan is a ghost writer here whose influential work I had to put aside while writing my book. Glen Lowry, George Bowering, David Stouck, and Miriam Nichols offered valuable insights on the manuscript. I would also like to thank my family of readers: Amanda and Laura, Mom and Dad. *The Wallace Stevens Journal* published parts of chapters 2, 3, and 6 as articles; thanks for permitting me to include this material here.

Excerpts from COLLECTED POEMS by Wallace Stevens. Copyright © 1954 by Wallace Stevens. Reprinted by permission of Alfred A. Knopf, a division of Random House, Inc.

Excerpts from OPUS POSTHUMOUS by Wallace Stevens. Copyright © 1957 by Elsie Stevens and Holly Stevens. Reprinted by permission of Alfred A. Knopf, a Division of Random House Inc.

Excerpts from LETTERS OF WALLACE STEVENS by Wallace Stevens. Copyright © 1966 by Holly Stevens. Reprinted by permission of Alfred A. Knopf, a Division of Random House Inc.

Preface

One of the main suggestions in this book is that Wallace Stevens' long poem of the Depression, *Owl's Clover,* is central to understanding his poetry overall. It has been rejected by critics as a failed political satire, and as an abandoned terminus in Stevens' poetics.

The publication of the Library of America *Collected Poetry and Prose of Wallace Stevens* in 1997 continued the trend of marginalizing the poem. Editors Frank Kermode and Joan Richardson placed the full version of *Owl's Clover* at the back of the book in a section entitled "Uncollected Poems," which includes Stevens' juvenile poems. However, *Owl's Clover* was published as a volume by Alcestis Press in 1936, and Stevens revised it to a shorter poem for 1937's *The Man with the Blue Guitar.* The editorial decision made by Kermode and Richardson has been criticized by Milton Bates in *The Wallace Stevens Journal.* Also, in *The New York Review of Books,* Helen Vendler says the poem "deserves a prominent and uncut place in any comprehensive scheme of Stevens's moral and poetic evolution."[1] My study rebuts typical reductions of *Owl's Clover* as a failure in political satire or in aesthetics and demonstrates its literary and cultural relevance in two core chapters. I argue that *Owl's Clover* reveals Stevens' polemical underpinnings in a well-developed rhetorical style that continues into late great poems such as "Esthetique du Mal" and "Description without Place."

Crucial studies of the poem by Alan Filreis and James Longenbach show that *Owl's Clover* reveals more about Stevens' attitudes to socio-political culture than any other work.[2] However, their zeal for historical definition sometimes leads them to arrest the poetry's dynamic rhetoric. My book investigates Stevens' language as it maneuvers in and manipulates history through poetry's rhetoric.

Wallace Stevens' Poetics

Chapter 1

Introduction: Strike the Pose

Throw away the lights, the definitions,
And say of what you see in the dark
That it is this or that it is that,
But do not use the rotted names.
   —*The Man with the Blue Guitar* (*Collected Poems* 183)

Wallace Stevens fulfills an unusually casual prophesy made by Ezra Pound about literature, in 1936: "the transition may have been from literary to rhetorical."[1] Stevens' poetry displays an increasing commitment to the power that language has to shape the world, and "rhetoric" is the best way to characterize such potency. In contemporary vernacular, the word "rhetoric" often refers to language that is somehow tainted or untrue, but Stevens' poetry makes us realize that truth is relative at best, that "It is a world of words to the end of it" (*CP* 345), going so far as to say: "The world is at the mercy of the strongest mind in it whether that strength is the strength of sanity or insanity, cunning or good-will" (*Opus Posthumous* [*OP*] 199). These words reveal that although Stevens was skeptical about truth and justice, he nevertheless thought that clever wordsmiths carried influence.

Stevens' conviction reveals some historical differences in culture between now and then: in the time and place Stevens published poetry—from 1914 to 1955 in America—there remained a public optimism for the power of democratic progress. The world wars did not deter the United States from ascendancy; they allowed the United States to become the dominant superpower. In this context of empire building, the public, including Stevens, was generally confident about the power of their leaders, which meant that rhetoricians' words carried weight. From our skeptical turn-of-the-century vantage point this is remarkable because we have little faith in the words of power. This distrust of language means that poets today face a huge challenge in uttering rhetoric able to break apart popular media veneers.

Stevens explored the limits of linguistic power, often keeping his ears tuned to contemporaneous political rhetoric. The Wallace Stevens that I am writing about has been made possible by recent historical scholarship, primarily by Alan Filreis and James Longenbach. By making use of Stevens' letters, which daughter Holly Stevens provided, scholars have recently modified the old view of the dandy poet to instead envision a poet thoroughly responding to "the pressure of the contemporaneous" (*OP* 230). These words are taken from a talk Stevens gave in 1936, entitled "The Irrational Element in Poetry." As the title suggests, Stevens confronts society and politics by looking into the "irrational" power of language. Rhetoric, specifically its musical and evocative qualities—Stevens gives an example of a cat running on the roof overhead—supplies the irrational element that registers with people. Stevens brings together the categorically divided worlds of politics, rhetoric, music, and imagery. The poet and the lawyer are no longer *The Strange Case of Dr. Jekyll and Mr. Hyde*. Stevens suggests that irrational, or simply, not yet understood, rhetorical concoctions dominate language, thought, and consequently Western culture. His poetry often depicts supposedly rational historical figures making decisions according to transient desires. Philosophers and rulers are "subjects of desire," as Judith Butler argues in her book of that name. Butler and Stevens deconstruct Western cultural foundations, such as Reason and Imperialism, by showing that Western power manipulates human fear and desire through rhetorical power and seduction.

Stevens' poems manifest "irrational" rhetoric in illustrative, dramatic, and reflexive ways. Readers of Stevens sometimes complain that he writes poetry about poetry, which is true. He must, because Stevens constantly brings language to the surface of the poem; he makes language's material construction an issue in poems in order to teach readers to be aware of language's craftiness. Stevens stresses that language *must be abstract:* that is, the material properties of language enact, direct, inflect, distort, and seduce. Observing language's abstract processes entails that we notice words in dynamic physical motion, effecting surrounding words and contexts; this emphasis on the material abstract opposes the view that language transparently describes things as if they were fixed in space and time. Stevens' abstract language directs his rhetoric. This material textuality also opposes the opinion of the abstract as a far-off intellectual tangent. Critics such as Marie Borroff, Charles Altieri, Glen MacLeod, and Alan Filreis have thoroughly shown Stevens' similarity to the materially emphatic Abstract Expressionist painters.[2] In general, modern art moves away from referential realism and toward the materials of paint, shape, and color, so explicit in the Abstract Expressionism of Jackson Pollock, Robert Motherwell, and Willem deKooning.

Stevens' abstract technique presents a material language that displays its rhetorical, hence political, character. For example, *Owl's Clover* asks us to

> Conceive that marble men
> Serenely selves, transfigured by the selves
> From which they came, make real the attitudes
> Appointed for them and that the pediment
> Bears words that are the speech of marble men.   (*OP* 83)

Transformative verbs emphasize the evolution of these patrimonial "marble men." Their dynamism is both described and more forcefully enacted by the poetry's alliteration: "the pediment / Bears [Appointed] words. . . ." Readers hear "attitudes / Appointed" on "pediment." Nouns are swept into verbal action, then stamped onto hard stone tablets, which present and represent "the speech of marble men." Our hypothetical conception of the marble men is "transfigured" by the concurrent dynamic processes of verbs, by sounds producing sense, and by a series of crystallizations (from conception to intrinsic "selves," from ancestry to legacy, from "attitudes" to pediment, then to speech). The plastic materiality of the language fastens an elastic hold. The language's grasp is connected with its utterance so that rhetoric is heard and comprehended simultaneously. Stevens' rhetoric conflates our understood divisions between abstract/material, aesthetic/political, creative/polemical. The patrilineal political stance of these "marble men" is caught up in their automated monumental aesthetic. When *Owl's Clover* was published in 1936, critics did not receive the long poem favorably, and this opinion has persevered. In the 1990s, however, Filreis and Longenbach have demonstrated that *Owl's Clover* reveals more about Stevens' politics in history than any other poem. However, their historical empiricism sometimes overlooks the epistemological challenges made in *Owl's Clover*: Stevens' rhetorical poetry invalidates taxonomic divides between politics and aesthetics by demonstrating their symbiosis.

Binary oppositions function significantly in the Stevens critical legacy.[3] To take a recent example, Filreis suggests that in *Owl's Clover,* the poet was "trying to create when he *should* have been arguing." Filreis counters Joseph Riddel's previous reading that opts for creation over argument.[4]

Riddel represents the vast majority of Stevens' critics, as recent as Eleanor Cook in 1988, who deem Stevens' political satire, especially *Owl's Clover,* "a dead end."[5] This critical oscillation makes room for my position that Stevens' rhetorical poetry collapses the division, evidenced by Riddel and Filreis, between *creation* and *argument.*

This partition is a taxonomy that has been ingrained in human minds since Descartes' "I think, therefore I am." Cartesian Reason has estranged humans from themselves by instituting an impossible objective power to know thyself. Objective reason as such is manifest in egotistical aesthetics: monuments, for example, claim huge representative status. Monumental art's permanent iconography is an aesthetic commonly found in military states. Stevens' thirties poems often depict statues that represent the inflated statures of state leaders. For Stevens, this aesthetic–political–philosophical–social problem (it is epistemological, a problem of how knowledge works) resides in the everyday world, as well as in international politics, history, and poetry. It extends beyond Descartes to epic models of literature from Homeric Greece, which were revitalized in the modernist work of Ezra Pound, T. S. Eliot, and James Joyce.

Stevens places the epic's authorial power to represent whole cultures in the contexts of monumental aesthetics and philosophical Reason. Stevens' late poetry especially realizes the masculinity of these dominant forms of representation. Poems such as "The World as Meditation," "The Sail of Ulysses," and "Prologues to What Is Possible" problematize masculine egotistical control. Several critics, such as Jacqueline Vaught Brogan, Lisa Steinman, Melita Schaum, Bonnie Costello, and Michael Beehler have interpreted Stevens' oeuvre as a criticism of the "man-locked set" of the West that is "almost feminist in its impulse."[6] The curative aspects of Stevens' verse—whether in terms of gender, politics, aesthetics, semiotics, or philosophy—demonstrate potential for improving cultural ethics. Necessary for the cure, Stevens' rhetorical poetry deconstructs the divisions made in the interests and habits of power, displaying language as it forces culture.

Accompanying Stevens' social critique is an enduring optimism in the poetry. It is a trust in the ability to recreate experience through art, to make artful experience into provisional orders for readers to discern. This poetic capability can be considered Romantic, much like Wordsworth's "eye made quiet by the power / Of harmony, . . . / We see into the life of things," or Coleridge's Primary and Secondary Imaginations, in which sensual reception is followed by a reconstituted perception. We might also consider Stevens' recreations as indicative of American revolution: this mentality persists through nineteenth-century frontier poetry, notably in Emerson and Whitman, who roam endlessly in mind and body.

To recreate anew as Americans love to do, things first have to be taken apart. Between Stevens' death in 1955 and the present, linguistic and literary theory has been revolutionized by deconstruction, the text-based theory developed by Jacques Derrida in 1960s Paris. Terry Eagleton writes that the task of Derrida's "deconstructive criticism . . . is to show how texts come to embarrass their own ruling systems of logic . . ." (*Literary Theory* 133). Critics such as J. Hillis Miller, Paul Bove, Michael Beehler, and Melita Schaum have applied deconstruction to Stevens.[7] Schaum's overview, *Wallace Stevens and the Critical Schools,* includes a chapter entitled "Preferring Text to Gloss: From Decreation to Deconstruction in Stevens Criticism," which clearly conceptualizes these theoretical developments. I utilize Paul de Man's "rhetoricity" in order to show the playful "confusion between sign and substance" in Stevens' poems. "Thirteen Ways of Looking at a Blackbird" enables readers to observe paradoxes between textual language and what it refers to:

I
Among twenty snowy mountains,
The only moving thing
Was the eye of the blackbird.

II
I was of three minds,
Like a tree
In which there are three blackbirds.

III
The blackbird whirled in the autumn winds.
It was a small part of the pantomime.
. . . .
XIII
It was evening all afternoon.
It was snowing
And it was going to snow.
The blackbird sat
In the cedar limbs.

These lines "embarrass their own ruling systems of logic" by contrasting statements and images in each sequence of the poem.[8] "The only moving thing," the eye of the singular blackbird, is contrasted by "three blackbirds," and, next, a whirling blackbird. This poem denies that language can be definitive and that an image can be effectively represented in stasis. The poem especially deconstructs when, following the birds that whirl through the middle of the poem, the thirteenth sequence returns the blackbird to its singular static position that it had in stanza I. This return to the initial narrative position throws into question the haphazard events in between. The diverse images are out of whack, and they also appear to be completely illusory because the first and final static images enclose the poem in an unsettling unity denying the various plots in between. Besides teasing the reader's mind for the fun of it, Stevens undermines the confident logics with which we see, comprehend, write, and narrate. In the 13 stanzas, narrative refuses linear progression, and therefore challenges the prevalent view that stanzas are consequential. Unsettling these functions that produce knowledge is one of the few constants in Stevens' poetry.

Simone Weil's metaphysical concept of "decreation" was used by Stevens long before deconstruction came about. While Weil originally used the term in *Gravity and Grace* to describe a renunciation of the self in search of God, in "The Relations between Poetry and Painting," Stevens uses decreation as a form of human access to secular invention:

> [Weil] says that decreation is making pass from the created to the uncreated, but that destruction is making pass from the created to nothingness. Modern reality is a reality of decreation, in which our revelations are not the revelations of belief, but the precious portents of our own powers. (*Necessary Angel* 173–4)

An example of decreation fundamentally opens "Notes Toward a Supreme Fiction":

> Begin, ephebe, by perceiving the idea
> Of this invention, this invented world,
> The inconceivable idea of the sun.
>
> You must become an ignorant man again
> And see the sun again with an ignorant eye
> And see it clearly in the idea of it.
>
> Never suppose an inventing mind as source
> Of this idea nor for that mind compose
> A voluminous master folded in his fire.

How clean the sun when seen in its idea
Washed in the remotest cleanliness of a heaven
That has expelled us and our images . . .

The death of one god is the death of all.
Let purple Phoebus lie in umber harvest,
Let Phoebus slumber and die in autumn umber,

Phoebus is dead, ephebe. But Phoebus was
A name for something that never could be named.
There was a project for the sun and is.

There is a project for the sun. The sun
Must bear no name, gold flourisher, but be
In the difficulty of what it is to be.   (*CP* 380–1)

This decreative poem disassembles concepts in a more patient teacherly manner than does the disjointed deconstructive play of "Thirteen Ways of Looking at a Blackbird." A fundamental difference between decreation and deconstruction is that the decreative process first denies present concepts and consequently entails promise in recreating innovative names for future usage. Deconstruction dismantles known structures by showing how language manipulates contexts. An everyday example is the word "peacekeepers," used by American leaders to describe the military. In this case, a paradox exists between the signifier "peacekeepers" (meaning people who prevent war) and the signified reality of military force. We can learn about how socio-political power works in history via deconstruction. However, the disjointed structures (between signifiers and signifieds, between peace and war in this instance) remain scattered: there is no unifying impulse or central source of agency in deconstruction; whereas in a decreated world the poet plays the active creative role that for Weil was divinely receptive.

Abandoning the realist tendency to transparently copy the external world allows a new multi-perspectivism. The poet explains in a letter that "Thirteen Ways of Looking at a Blackbird" is "a collection . . . of sensations" (*Letters* 251) composing the multi-perspective poem, which neatly returns to an unmoving blackbird at the end, suggesting that each materially abstracted image was, after all, imaginary. Confusion arises from this poem because Stevens emphasizes material language comprising its own reality, while highlighting mental processes involved in creating language, and yet he describes the poem's basis in the senses. He writes "I do not know which to prefer, / The beauty of inflections / Or the beauty of innuendos, / The blackbird whistling / Or just after" (*CP* 93). Perception ("inflection") and reflection ("innuendo") entail sense, then thought. Stevens fabricates "a collection . . . of sensations" so that we think about the many ways in which thought is generated, particularly by poetic language that markedly differs from the original lost inflection of the whistling blackbird (of which there may have been none).

Brogan cites Stevens' "Thirteen Ways of Looking at a Blackbird" as Cubist. Perspectivism in the Western art world coincides with the growing field of psychology in Freud's time. Where Freud built a science of psychoanalysis, artists stretched limits unbounded by scientific concerns such as treating patients. Surrealism grew out of modern art and dream psychology. Surreal art allows the artist to act as the fantastical patient while at the same time the artist's controlled medium puts him in the analyst's interpretive mode. Surrealism emphasizes dreamy perceptions more than the geometry of composition displayed in Cubism. In Cubism, the artist depicts the compositional process, including disjunctions between perception and representation. For Stevens, perception occurs between "imagination and reality," which was the subtitle of his book of essays entitled *The Necessary Angel*. I dislike Stevens' broad polarization because each pole appears extreme, therefore practically unreachable. The poems, on the other hand, lead readers between reality and imagination into perception's created ground: in the role of host Stevens shows us his inhabited world:

THE GLASS OF WATER
That the glass would melt in heat,
That the water would freeze in cold,
Shows that this object is merely a state,
One of many, between two poles. So
In the metaphysical, there are these poles.

Here in the centre stands this glass. Light
Is the lion that comes down to drink. There
And in that state, the glass is a pool.
Ruddy are his eyes and ruddy are his claws
When light comes down to wet his frothy jaws

And in the water winding weeds move round.
And there and in another state—the refractions,

The *metaphysica,* the plastic parts of poems
Crash in the mind—But, fat Jocundus, worrying
About what stands here in the centre, not the glass,

But in the centre of our lives, this time, this day,
It is a state, this spring among the politicians
Playing cards. In a village of the indigenes,
One would have still to discover. Among the dogs and dung,
One would continue to contend with one's ideas.   (*CP* 197–8)

This poem from *Parts of a World* (1942) illustrates the logic of Stevens' modern art that I've so far outlined, which states that we live in a perceptually recreated world that cannot be considered a truthful representation of the three-dimensional world our eyes see. "The *metaphysica,* the plastic parts of poems / Crash in the mind." Representation, as with all communication, involves filtration, and the extracted materials are words, paint, talk.

Because Stevens emphasizes perception, readers must be willing to allow his words to provide fresh sight. As Charles Altieri says, "we should be more willing to listen to Stevens before we allow ourselves the pleasures of trying to be superior to him . . ." (Gelpi 87). The phenomenologist Maurice Merleau-Ponty speaks further on the intricacies of communication in an essay entitled "The Primacy of Perception," which offers an outlook that works for reading Stevens:

I will never know how you see red, and you will never know how I see it; but this separation of consciousness is recognized only after a failure of communication, and our first movement is to believe in an undivided being between us. There is no reason to treat this primordial communication as an illusion, as the sensationalists do, because even then it would become inexplicable. And there is no reason to base it on our common participation in the same intellectual consciousness because this would suppress the undeniable plurality of consciousness. It is thus necessary that, in the perception of another, I find myself in relation with another "myself," who is, in principle, open to the same truths as I am, in relation to the same being as I am. And this perception is realized. From the depths of my subjectivity I see another subjectivity invested with equal rights appear. . . . Just as my body, as the system of all my holds on the world, founds the unity of objects which I perceive, in the same way the body of the other—as the bearer of symbolic behaviours and of the behaviour of true reality—tears itself away from being one of my phenomena, offers me the task of true communication, and confers on my objects the new dimension of intersubjective being, or in other words, of objectivity. Such are, in a quick resume, the elements of the perceived world.[9]

This belief in open communicative dialogue and perception Stevens shares with us. As with Stevens' process of decreation, Merleau-Ponty's notion of the "primacy of perception" enacts innovative recreations. These concepts do not depend on origins; they decreate original ground in an effort to recreate thoughts, which may or may not be our own, as they are often given to us by others. Recall Stevens making this point in "Notes Toward a Supreme Fiction":

> Never suppose an inventing mind as source
> Of this idea nor for that mind compose
> A voluminous master folded in his fire.   (*CP* 381)

Merleau-Ponty's "primacy of perception" involves decreation in its reception of truth through communication, but it also acknowledges the contextual limitations of each talker "as the bearer of symbolic behaviours." Merleau-Ponty's phenomenology displays a deconstructive awareness (this essay and this man are contemporaneous with Derridean deconstruction), but he foregoes deconstructive social analysis for recreative mending.

> By these words, the "primacy of perception," we mean that the experience of perception is our presence at the moment when things, truths, values are constituted for us; that perception is a nascent *logos;* that it teaches us, outside all dogmatism, the true conditions of objectivity itself; that it summons us to the tasks of knowledge and action. (25)

Reading this in 1986 for the first time, I linked it to Wordsworth and Coleridge. I now find the Romantic idealism of "when things, truths, values are constituted for us" overdetermined because "constituted" assumes a static registration of an "objective" idea. However overassertive Merleau-Ponty's objective conclusions may be, his continual returns to processes of *logos* and dialogue curb my skepticism because provisional truths are always tested in action, thus modified:

> This leads us . . . to draw certain conclusions from what has preceded as concerns the realm of the practical. If we admit that our life is inherent to the perceived world and the human world, even while it re-creates it and contributes to its making, then morality cannot consist in the private adher-

ence to a system of values. Principles are mystifications unless they are put
into practice; it is necessary that they animate our relations with others. . . .
If we admit that sensibility is enclosed within itself, and if we do not seek
communication with the truth and with others except on the level of a dis-
embodied reason, then there is not much to hope for. (25–6)

This re-creative dialogic agency is exactly what I read in Stevens' poetry.
Stevens' detractors often think that the poet's "sensibility is enclosed within
itself." They refuse to be reached despite the many invitations expressed in
the poems. Merleau-Ponty's phenomenology is ethically hopeful, and it is
interesting that the similar philosophy of Emmanuel Levinas is increasingly
being read with Stevens. Even though Stevens says in *Adagia,* "Ethics are
no more a part of poetry than they are of painting" (*OP* 191), the poet
does state that "Poetry is a means of redemption," (*OP* 189) and scholars
such as Michael Beehler and Krzysztof Ziarek have recently studied ethical implications.[10]
The illustration of philosophical practices such as decreation and deconstruction in Stevens' poetry make it possible to connect Stevens with a
wide range of Western metaphysical thinkers. B. J. Leggett has written
about *The Nietzschean Intertext;* Paul Bove about Heidegger and Stevens
sharing a *Destructive Poetics;* Riddel has applied Heidegger, Nietzsche, and
Foucault to Stevens' work; and Judith Butler has written an excellent article on "'The Nothing That Is': Stevens' Hegelian Affinities." Butler sees
social and philosophical promise in the deconstructions by Stevens that
Hillis Miller often stressed as nihilistic. A typical Stevens' poem proceeds
by displaying opposites as needlessly destructive, thereby identifying violence in divisive and hierarchical systems. Unlike Hegel, Stevens tends not
to synthesize discordance; his poems, especially in the thirties, implode
opposites in symbiotic destruction. Gloomy forecasts occur when Stevens
demarcates philosophical, ontological, aesthetic, and political contradictions. But the optimism observed by Butler and others arises from many
of Stevens' poems that present cohabitations without sacrificing differences. Butler's essay moves toward this conclusion, referring to the end of
The Man with the Blue Guitar: "Significantly, the poem does not remain
rooted in a nostalgia for the ontological harmonies of the past but moves
to the meditation of difference as the very condition of a postmodern
affirmation" (286):

> . . . a wrangling of two dreams.
> Here is the bread of time to come,

> Here is the actual stone. The bread
> Will be our bread, the stone will be
>
> Our bed and we shall sleep by night.
> We shall forget by day, except
>
> The moments when we choose to play
> The imagined pine, the imagined jay.   (*CP* 184)

In Stevens' poetry "the imagined jay" is written. It is the character we concoct, not reality, which is explained as "faster than / Any character. It is more than any scene" (*CP* 192). For Stevens, language refuses to represent reality as truth; representation may temporarily suffice, a metaphor might work, but it is never a final copy. This semiotic principle is not mere tentativeness; it is a way of keeping the world in motion as it is, of keeping change alive through ever-evolving difference.[11] Butler affirms this epistemological liquidity whereas Miller previously feared its lack of secure order. Butler writes near the end of her essay:

> Although Hegel is figured as the philosopher who subordinates all difference to Being, he is also the philosopher, defended by Wahl, Jean Hyppolite and others, who proclaimed the impossibility of language to fix the negative with a name . . . who sought a mode of thinking that would not capture its object but let it live. (287)

Letting difference live and living with difference sounds like a tiresome postmodern catchphrase, but Stevens' poetry painstakingly achieves as much, and delves into difficult and varied subjects to forge possibilities. "Re-statement of Romance" is an exemplary poem chosen by Butler, which I will soon turn to. She also cites Gilles Deleuze in a slightly confusing way that I will modify: "Recently, Deleuze has argued that the description of the world outside of totalizing metaphysics ought not to rely on the copula at all, that one must 'substitute the AND for the IS. A *and* B'" (Butler, *Theorizing American Literature*, 286). To be and not to be, that is.

   The challenge of getting away from totalizing metaphysics—of letting the object or text live—is that acknowledging and understanding are forms of thought that require classification. To name is to objectify. Since I am going to communicate my perspective upon Stevens' presentations of difference, I need to describe these vital relations exhibited in the poems. I am in a secondary position to Stevens' poetry, as the poetry is to the external world that we perceive. Stevens never forgets the primacy of the physical world, although he repeatedly asserts language's capacity to form perceptions of it. Language possesses transformative power, yet the physical world is immanently independent as well. Gyorgyi Voros writes in *Notations of the Wild: Ecology in the Poetry of Wallace Stevens*, "Unlike Emerson, Stevens knew from the start that the condition of humans in the universe was a condition of unrequited love, since Nature can never answer to human longing in human terms" (3).

By viewing and describing some poems, I will illustrate how Stevens' poetry revolutionizes epistemology (how we know things, such as nature, aesthetics, politics, philosophy, society, knowledge itself). Stevens consistently explores how we know things, but this concern is not limited to epistemology; it always moves toward ethical implications. "Poetry is a response to the daily necessity of getting the world right" (*OP* 201). Such a project means that Stevens takes on huge systems of knowledge and power, which I pursue in this study. For now, here is an example of "getting the world right" in the case of two people, which serves as a base for all else:

> The night knows nothing of the chants of night.
> It is what it is as I am what I am:
> And in perceiving this I best perceive myself
>
> And you. Only we two may interchange
> Each in the other what each has to give.
> Only we two are one, not you and night,
>
> Nor night and I, but you and I, alone,
> So much alone, so deeply by ourselves,
> So far beyond the casual solitudes,
>
> That night is only the background of our selves,
> Supremely true each to its separate self,
> In the pale light that each upon the other throws.   (*CP* 146)

This poem preserves difference while esteeming communication, much like Merleau-Ponty's "primacy of perception." Judith Butler writes that "Re-statement of Romance" resembles the philosophy of Hegel, "who sought a mode of thinking that would not capture its object but let it live" (*Theorizing American Literature* 287). Butler also argues that the poem succeeds beyond Hegel as a "postmodern affirmation." The figures of the poem (two people, light, night) do not exert symbolical or hierarchical claims upon each other. While each figure is "Supremely true each to its separate self," each overcomes isolation and achieves potency from "what each has to give." As a result "pale light" shines, which sounds like a divine or enlightened trope, except that this light is grounded in the domestic locale of the duo's mutual perception. This light is physically part of its context and is shared by the figures in a metaphysically suggestive way. Each figure exists in its own night in the same respect, without claiming the night as its own metaphor.

Because these differential relations are maintained, in choosing a term to describe their linguistic figuration, I propose metonymy, which occurs when "a person or thing or action is replaced by one of its attributes, or by something closely associated with it" (*Modern Poems* xliv). However, Stevens' use of metonymy differs because "a person or thing is [not] replaced by one of its attributes. . . ." Instead of replacement, which makes metonymy a figure close to synecdoche, these figures exist "Merely in living as and where we live" (*CP* 326):

> That night is only the background of our selves,
> Supremely true each to its separate self,
> In the pale light that each upon the other throws.   (*CP* 146)

Stevens' metonymies preserve close-knit associations and attributes; they *aggregate* more than they replace.[12] In "That night is only the background of our selves," "night" and "our selves" share a collective compositional context. There is no symbolic interchange, no replacement between these figures, as is common in metonymy. Stevens' figures are composed as apparent metonymies, but replacement (one thing representing another) is forsaken for the sake of preserving each figure's potency. Because Stevens' metonymies aggregate rather than replace, this means that difference can be sustained between figures, such as night and self, self and other.

Eleanor Cook also observes the preservation of difference in Stevens' volume, *Parts of a World*. In her chapter on this volume of poetry, entitled "Against Synecdoche," she cites Paul de Man's criticism of synecdoche's figural ability to stand for the whole. Stevens' use of metonymy emphasizes attributes that do not stand for or replace wholes but instead emphasize parts. Part III of "Connoisseur of Chaos" from *Parts of a World* makes the argument:

> After all the pretty contrast of life and death
> Proves that these opposite things partake of one,

At least that was the theory, when bishops' books
Resolved the world. We cannot go back to that.
The squirming facts exceed the squamous mind,
If one may say so. And yet relation appears,
A small relation expanding like the shade
Of a cloud on sand, a shape on the side of a hill.   (*CP* 215)

The "small relation" of aggregating metonymy—"the shade / Of a cloud on sand"—works in opposition to synecdoche. Instead of making the cloud an ominous indication of Thor or the symbol of Wordsworth's personally sublime thunderstorm, Stevens leaves such looming inferences for the reader, and compresses the cloud-sand relationship to a material "shape on the side of a hill."

This material emphasis can also be visualized in the Cubist painting of Cezanne, Braque, and Picasso, as well as the Cubist writing of Gertrude Stein. As Jacqueline Brogan has shown in *Part of the Climate*, Stein's work, especially "Three Portraits of Painters" (1912), displays a Cubist style of writing in which fragments of syntax are repeated and layered so that with each repetition, differences are introduced upon previous sentence fragments, as in "Picasso":

Something had been coming out of him, certainly it had been coming out
of him, certainly it was something, certainly it had been coming out of him
and it had meaning, a charming meaning, a solid meaning, a struggling
meaning, a clear meaning" (*Stein* 333–4).

"Three Portraits" is an exemplary piece of Cubist writing that conveniently includes Cezanne (the forerunner of Cubist painting) and Picasso (the champion of it). In Stein's writing and in Cubist painting the representation of a unified external world becomes formally fragmented (in syntax, in geometrical shapes). The viewer of Cubist work sees a two-dimensional picture that does not pretend to stand for the three dimensional reality perceived through our eyes. Shape and color dominate the paintings; repeated syntax and sound command Stein's literature. I think of such representation as the *material abstract* because the painter or writer's abstract composition displays its materiality. Cubist works do not escape their plastic artificiality by attempting to copy external phenomena in a realistic manner.

The material presentation of a two-dimensional plastic poetry may appear at odds with "real world" applications. As Stevens writes in *Adagia*,

"There are two opposites: the poetry of rhetoric and the poetry of experience" (*OP* 187). However, language's rhetorical function unifies the written and social worlds: language, and rhetoric in particular, influences listeners, as well as those people who do not hear it but are effected inadvertently. For instance, legislation affects citizens regardless of their exclusion from lawmaking. Stevens knew legal implications firsthand from his training in law, and his poetics increasingly work through the statutes of language in order to set precedents.

After rejecting law and journalism, careers that involve rigid linguistic structures, Stevens wrote *Harmonium,* which demonstrated a vital poetry of experience. However, the spontaneity of that 1923 volume took the wind out of the poet's sails until *Ideas of Order* was written ten years later and published in 1935. In order to achieve a vital mature experiential poetry, Stevens needed to show how the contemporary spirit (his and his country's) could no longer be uplifted by ineffectual romantic rhetorics of the past. The search for effective artforms was especially desperate and frantic in the Depression. My second chapter will investigate *Ideas of Order* as a volume of poetry largely involved with cleansing Stevens' romantic view of poetry and searching for "some harmonious skeptic soon in a skeptical music" to respond to the difficult thirties. My argument, that Stevens attempts to wash his hands of old romantic tropes, counters some established interpretations. I suggest that "The Idea of Order at Key West" is not "a Wordsworthian crisis poem, in its American modification," as Harold Bloom argues. Instead, this beautiful poem manages to display the artificial nature of the romantic muse, the singer on the beach, transforming her into a material abstraction, rather like a stage prop, that is shown to be a container for the poet's lyrical spirit. The muse is portrayed as an artificial other, a dialectical demon manifesting poetic desire. Stevens' point is that poetic figures should not require the pathetic fallacy of an otherly ether, and that poetry can come a little bit closer to the mystery of the muse without the muses being used as its tool shed—a signified trope to house the poet's signifiers.

A question raised about the muse in "Key West," "Whose spirit is this?" persists for Stevens throughout the 1930s as he says "Farewell to Florida," and to exoticism in general. My chapters 3 and 4 investigate the poet's civic responsibility to his native North in the Depression, deemed "a slime of men in crowds." More broadly asking "Whose sprit is this?" Stevens' long poem, *Owl's Clover,* features an Old Woman, the Marxist reviewer Stanley Burnshaw, a public park full of immigrant Americans, as well as the European colonizers of Africa. The poem casts these figures amid the rhetorics they are deemed to speak and the rhetorics they are imagined encountering. By fashioning a series of highly stylized dictions, Stevens draws the reader's attention to the ideals posed in varying rhetorics.

For example, the first poem in the series of five, "The Old Woman and the Statue," sets an old destitute woman in a public park at the foot of a marble statue of glory-bound horses. In this contrast Stevens fabricates the Old Woman as a symbol of the depressed thirties, at the foot of a glorious state artifact that blatantly ridicules her destitution. Stylized rhetorics accompany the Old Woman, the Statue, and the poet or other viewers as witnesses. The poem begins, for instance, grandiloquently describing the statue from the sculptor's perspective:

> So much the sculptor had foreseen: autumn,
> The sky above the plaza widening
> Before the horses, clouds of bronze imposed
> On clouds of gold, and green engulfing bronze,
> The marble leaping in the storms of light.
> So much he had devised: white forelegs taut
> To the muscles' very tip for the vivid plunge . . .
> The heads held high and gathered in a ring
> At the centre of the mass, the haunches low,
> Contorted, staggering from the thrust against
> The earth as the bodies rose on feathery wings,
> Clumped carvings, circular, like blunted fans,
> Arranged for phantasy to form an edge
> Of crisping light along the statue's rim.
> More than his muddy hand was in the manes,
> More than his mind in the wings. The rotten leaves
> Swirled round them in immense autumnal sounds.   (*OP* 75)

In the depiction of the sculptor's vision we hear the rhetoric of his romantic view. In the poem's hyperbolic depiction, glory and militaristic victory are vividly defined in the marble, bronze, and gold of this monument. We might be rhetorically seduced by this monumental drum roll; perhaps we even buy into the sculptor's transcendent union with his statue, and then with nature, by god, until we read the next line: "But her he had not foreseen: the bitter mind / In a flapping cloak" (*OP* 76). The sculptor's party is crashed by the Old Woman, and so a drama ensues between State art and social hardship. From this juxtaposition of social contexts and rhetorics, readers become attuned to a new political criticism in Stevens' innovative satire. Stevens makes romantic vision rhetorical and often ironic.

By listening to this rhetorical poetry, readers grow accustomed to tropes, for example, of glory, brilliance, and definition to the extent that we question the efficacy of these monumental aesthetics, especially when they affect citizens such as the Old Woman. Stevens "unmasks the construct" of State art by drawing our attention to the "rhetoricity" of the Statue in the poem. Paul de Man describes his term: "Accounting for the 'rhetoricity' of its own mode, the text also postulates the necessity of its own misreading. . . . The rhetorical character of literary language opens up the possibility of the archetypal error: the recurrent confusion of sign and substance" (*Blindness and Insight* 135–6). *Owl's Clover* displays "rhetoricity" by showing that the substance carried in a linguistic sign (the Statue's militaristic glory) does not mesh with its context (a park that's home to the homeless). The elevated civic sculpture becomes a pejorative enforcer of an Old Woman's vagrancy. Stevens portrays this injustice through excessive rhetoric; the poem's language is so hyperbolic that ironies arise with surrounding circumstances. These contradictions arise between art and context, thereby suggesting that the artful rhetoric of monumentalism is wrong for the 1930s. Chapters 3 and 4 of my book address Stevens' rhetorical deconstruction of monumental aesthetics and politics. "Monumentalism" refers to rigid artforms such as the Statue, and more extensively points to the human habit of forging definition and mastery upon dynamic phenomena that cannot be fixed. Stevens' poetry teaches us to perceive the moving world, which sounds like a simple concept, until we try to practice it in all thinking and communication.

A poem entitled "Add This to Rhetoric" illustrates clearly and in detail Stevens' use of rhetorical language to teach us how the poet thinks with words:

> It is posed and it is posed.
> But in nature it merely grows.
> Stones pose in the falling night;
> And beggars dropping to sleep,
> They pose themselves and their rags.
> Shucks . . . lavender moonlight falls.
> The buildings pose in the sky
> And, as you paint, the clouds,
> Grisaille [to paint grey], impearled, profound,
> Pfft. . . . In the way you speak

> You arrange, the thing is posed,
> What in nature merely grows.

Every image of the poem is layered by the additions that follow. As one pose is layered upon another we compare and contrast differences between lines that refuse to offer easy metaphors or much narrative continuity. The poem begins with an indefinite "It," which may refer to the inconclusive "This" of the title, which could mean the poem ("Add This [Poem] to Rhetoric"). Or, "It" might be the elusive vitality that the poet wants to capture, but can only pose, since "in nature it merely grows." The mystery of "It" contributes to the general question of how things are arranged here. Nature grows, stones pose, and beggars pose too as they drop to sleep. The poet composes each of these occurrences in a poem entitled "Add This to Rhetoric." The title frames a theoretical poem, which then presents a series of images directly, appearing nontheoretical.

The question of rhetorical theory is then tripped up in a contrast between nature and artifice. In midverse the "moonlight falls" as a "lavender moonlight," affected by the "Shucks" of the poetic voice who hollows out nature. So nature (even if it just grows) is always colored by the observer: this fact is emphasized by the painted clouds. The fabrication of phenomena is reiterated by the intrusive personification of the "buildings pose in the sky." All of this is clearly *spoken, arranged, posed,* as the poet tells us, in contrast to "What in nature merely grows." Because the poem is called "Add This to Rhetoric," I think it points to the impossibility of representing nature or achieving a naturally organic art, and the consequent inevitability of making nature rhetorical. There is no realistic mimesis, and so nature as it is represented here needs to be added to rhetoric too. Every little posture, even how we see "Stones pose in the falling night," is rhetorical. Every figured form belongs to a complex matrix of poses that constitute expression.

The sources or agents of expression are indeterminate though. "It is posed" indefinitely declares a universal statement; the beggars are objectively described but actively pose; "Shucks" presents a poetic voice in a character who disturbs nature; then "you paint" and "you speak" further beg the question of who is involved in this questionably romantic, definitely rhetorical composition. The mystique of this poem is maintained because many unknowns persist, and yet the poem's images "merely grow" in clear demarcations. The poem is much like a Picasso collage because its images pose with significance yet readers are left to concoct connections between images, perhaps implying that the "you" in the poem is each reader, the arranger. The poem continues:

> To-morrow when the sun,
> For all your images,
> Comes up as the sun, bull fire,
> Your images will have left
> No shadow of themselves.
> The poses of speech, of paint,
> Of music—Her body lies
> Worn out, her arm falls down,
> Her fingers touch the ground.
> Above her, to the left,
> A brush of white, the obscure,
> The moon without a shape,
> A fringed eye in the crypt.
> The sense creates the pose.
> In this it moves and speaks.
> This is the figure and not
> An evading metaphor.
>
> Add this, it is to add.   (CP 199)

The last line stresses the aggregating technique of this poem, which adds to rhetorical theory. Simple "adding" forwards rhetoric in a composed series of one word (image, metonymy, metaphor) after another, so that we readers think about how we assemble data. Do we construe metaphors between things? Do we look for metonymical contiguity (shared contexts in time and space)? Do we expect causal relationships? or, Do we listen for the most persuasive linguistic spell, whatever sounds good? If "it is to add," and surely reading is an accumulative process, then how do we add it up?

The dilemmas of representation, difficult as they are on their own, are trivialized by language's subordination to nature. The immanent sun outshines the previous day's artistic images. And yet in the poem, Stevens uses "bull fire," creating another metaphor that vividly recasts the supposedly immanent one. The "project for the sun," from "Notes," and the refusal "to use the rotted names," from *The Man with the Blue Guitar,* are at work here. Although natural immanence had been denied representability, the sun nevertheless outshines the poetic images that leave "No shadow of themselves." This dilemma of representation is manifested and condensed into the "poses of speech, of paint, / Of music"—a list of materials. And then the materials become representative in the (apparently) painted image of a reclining female figure.

This alternation between artistic matter and artistic representation enlivens the compositional process, the posing. In this case, the female figure is complemented "to the left" by "A brush of white," which is then addended by "A fringed eye in a crypt." This powerful metaphor of the reflective moon as a source of vision in mystery is contrasted by "The sense creates the pose." The final line, "Add this. It is to add," downplays the content, asserting that the major point of the poem is simply compositional: every image of the poem is layered by the additions that follow; some poses seem purely visual, some metaphorical, some theoretical. As one pose aggregates upon another we read comparisons, perhaps metaphors such as "A fringed eye in the crypt." However, Stevens carefully states, "This is the figure and not / An evading metaphor," because each image is a newly added figure, which is completely another scripted figure, whether it happens to register as a metaphor in the reader's consciousness or not.

The point Stevens wants to add to rhetoric is that metaphor, paint, speech, architecture are all posed material figures. No form of representation can securely fix itself in context, or be immanent for any length of time. "What in nature merely grows" acts as the running joke of the poem because that riddle cannot be represented. Adding to the mystery, Stevens employs the moon as the romantic trope that traditionally illuminates; the actual moon reflects light as the poet wants to and can only do so in the lavender fringes of his work. Against the possibility of mimetic realism, this poem posits rhetoric's posture as the only alternative. Rhetoric in the Aristotelian sense is meant to persuade, which remains the challenge in a representative domain where all an artist can do is compose by addition.

The metonymies of "Add This to Rhetoric" begin to paint a pretty symbolist picture. However, the metonymies never stop aggregating, and thereby continually point to their artificial construction (or rhetoricity). The metonymic aggregates deconstruct while they construct and therefore the poem remains perpetually creative. Brogan's book, *Stevens and Simile*, makes a similar point about how this poem simultaneously enables readers to compose and dissemble it. Brogan emphasizes Stevens' use of "as if" to form conditional hypotheses that enable readers to turn up fictions.

The poem's concluding stress on figural addition over "evading metaphor" suggests that there are no inherent references being evaded, no central figural icons at the center of a symbolic order. By instead emphasizing the way rhetorical postures accumulate in a given composition, Stevens provides an aesthetic that counters symbolism. By this I mean that in symbolist art there are constant tropes that factor in interpretation, be they Wordsworth's Nature, van Gogh's yellow light, or Mallarme's fulfillment of the void (the blank page, nothingness). These tropes belong to prevalent "symbolic orders," to use Kenneth Burke's terminology. The most common symbolic order in the West, or "doxa," as Roland Barthes would say, is Christianity. Stevens more than any other English-speaking modernist poet rejected the Christian doxa. This is not to say that his poetry is not replete with Christian images, but as Stevens does with romanticism, he likewise criticizes Christianity as a symbolic order incapable of helping people in the twentieth century. His first major poem of 1915, "Sunday Morning," asks of the lounging protagonist, "Why should she give her bounty to the dead?" Later in the poem, Stevens spoofs resurrection in a mock-revelation, "'The tomb in Palestine / Is not the porch of spirits lingering. / It is the grave of Jesus, where he lay'" (*CP* 70). Christianity is a worn-out trope, as stated in 1944's "Esthetique du Mal": "The death of Satan was a tragedy / For the imagination" (*CP* 319). The poet bluntly claims in *Adagia,* "Christianity is an exhausted culture" (*OP* 202).

Christianity and other ruling symbolic mythologies have icons at their center. As the last great Symbolist poet W. B. Yeats wrote in "The Second Coming,"'"the centre cannot hold."This poem anticipates the death of one symbolic order, Christianity, on the eve of millenial mystery; "And what rough beast, its hour come round at last, / Slouches towards Bethlehem to be born?" In Symbolist art or any aesthetic that's part of a ruling doxa, there always remains an "evading metaphor" tied to representation. In Yeats's poem, Christ's birth pervades as much as it evades. Persistent metaphors inform all ideological art, which is a point Stevens makes about Marxism in *Owl's Clover.* Ideological doctrines assume a fixity that is inflexible to new ideas. To combat such rigidity, Stevens practices what is now known as the postmodern enterprise of parodying (satirizing, deconstructing, decreating, ironizing) established ideologies, forms, and tropes. "To live in the world but outside of existing conceptions of it" (*OP* 190) is a maxim of Stevens' that betrays both his attention to "existing conceptions," which are commonly parodied in postmodernism, and also his modernist optimism that something else could rise from the ashes.

The alternative, "it is to add," is not a specifically concrete proposal because if it were, it would be symbolic, it would pose an icon at center. Instead, "it is to add" stresses composition as the-universal-if-there-has-to-be-one of his poetry. Attending to the process of adding means that readers, alongside the poet, assemble the forms (language) of poems. Stevens' poems are most often conditional (in syntax and setting) so that we think about contexts and agents. The evading metaphors of symbolic orders are "the rotted names" no longer used; "the mind, to find what will suffice, destroys / Romantic tenements of rose and ice" (*CP* 239). The (re)created figures tend to be posed through the metonymical addition of parts, rather than more symbolic totalizations.

After my third and fourth chapters on Stevens' rhetorical critique of fixed Western paradigms in *Owl's Clover*, I turn to the poet's response to the Second World War. As the war loomed and began, Stevens wrote *Parts of a World*. Chapter five will look at a few poems Stevens omitted from *Parts of a World*. "Life on a Battleship" and "The Woman That Had More Babies Than That" successfully employ rhetoric as a form of criticism. Since *Owl's Clover* was received poorly, it is not surprising that these poems were omitted from *The Collected Poems*. "Life on a Battleship," especially, confronts the militaristic mentality that Stevens sees as the worst of monumentalism. The protagonist of the poem captains a ship entitled *The Masculine*. The strong nomenclature fits with the captain's sublime megalomania, which Stevens traces back to Cartesian philosophical reason.

The rhetorical techniques of these thirties poems continue through some of Stevens' most ambitious and successful 1940s poetry provoked by World War II, namely "Esthetique du Mal" and "Description without Place." Even though Stevens neglected to include rhetorical poems from the 1930s in *The Collected Poems*, the poet's satirical techniques and socio-political objectives persevere in "Esthetique du Mal's" portraits of an American soldier, politicians in Geneva, a Mediterranean monk-assassin, and Konstantinov, an insubordinate Russian deemed traitor. "Esthetique du Mal" examines how people confront and represent the sublime. This poem displays human figures overwhelmed by larger forces such as a volcano, war, political systems, and death. Our tendency to order imposing experience by classifying it, by monumentalizing it, is shown to be a faint attempt to elevate the human ego. This confrontation with human malaise is set, from the outset of the poem, in the context of a soldier who is "reading paragraphs / On the sublime" (*CP* 313). The soldier employs his scholarly text as a shield to do battle with the sublime, but his reasoned resistance negates the presence of Vesuvius grumbling nearby. The poem counters this intellectualized sensual deprivation by confronting psychosomatic reactions, incorporating body and mind in a physical metaphysics. Stevens admits human frailty and reaches toward others rather than glorifying the self to do battle with sublime immanence. These ethical imperatives, as always in Stevens' poetry, depend upon how we represent ourselves linguistically.

Also found in the wartime *Transport to Summer* volume, "Description without Place" is Stevens' strongest theoretical poem, and perhaps his most political. The title refers to the poem's contention that "we live in a description of a place and not in the place itself," (*Letters of Wallace Stevens* [*L*] 494) and "what we say of the future must portend" (*CP* 346). The poem grants rhetoric additional power in Stevens' poetics, generally saying that language has the capacity to make what it will of the world. Because there is no fixed underlying or overarching order of things, communicators have the capacity for instigating immense change. This power holds the potential for huge destruction as much as good, but Stevens' responsibility as a poet is to teach readers to be attentive to the powers of language so that when rhetorical power is wielded, people can understand the contexts and motives of words in order to judge them. As a poet, Stevens' role is ideologically elusive, although he consistently undermines ideas he deems destructive. He prefers to play the pedagogue, the rabbi, the necessary angel enabling his countrymen to see clearly. Although he refuses to be a partisan, this choice does not prevent political activity. In June 1945 Stevens read "Description without Place" at Harvard's Phi Beta Kappa convocation, sharing the podium with Sumner Welles, a United Nations diplomat spreading the word on American global expansion following World War II. While it must be said that the complexity of "Description without Place" is best appreciated with careful study, Stevens' act nevertheless deconstructed Welles' far-reaching, typical American foreign policy rhetoric, entitled "A Vision of the World at Peace." In chapter 5 I will juxtapose Welles' speech with "Description without Place" in order to demonstrate the poem's deconstruction of expansionist rhetoric.

Chapter 6 pursues the larger issue of epic scope in language and culture, of which Welles' American imperial rhetoric served as a local example. Stevens writes many post–World War II poems that navigate the boundaries of epic and lyric poetry. Stevens continues to implode binary oppositions, as in the thirties and forties when he attended to romance and rhetoric, state and citizen, left- and right-wing ideology, good and evil. Several poems look back to Homer's *Odyssey* as an epic model, as had the earlier modernist work of Joyce, Eliot, and Pound. Stevens' main interest in the epic is in questioning the authority of the quest. Stevens' late poems retrace aspects of *The Odyssey* in order to propose alternative scenarios to this established tale of the tribe. Stevens questions narrative tradition by fabricating the thoughts, motives, and desires of the captain in "Prologues to What Is Possible"; he recounts the final leg of the *Odyssey* from Penelope's domestic feminine perspective in "The World as Meditation"; and "The Sail of Ulysses" questions the whole epic paradigm in a thinly veiled autobiography of the poet's progress. These poems about narrative all undercut epic mastery by appealing to the reader as a "coproducer" (Michael Davidson's term) of the poetic tale.[13] In versions of the necessary angel persona, Stevens posits the poet as "a half-figure" who helps public perception but requires readerly civilians to consummate the dialogic requests uttered in the poems.

This inscription of the dialogic other challenges the mastery implicit in the epic, and breaks the insularity of the lyric. The outward reach of the late poetry culminates another narrative impulse running throughout Stevens' poetry. Stevens' early verses were written to his future wife Elsie Kachel Moll. When Stevens began to write publicly, resentment crept into their marriage because the solitary object of Stevens' affection, Elsie, was supplanted by poetry in general. Without a fixed beloved object in mind, Stevens developed a wide focus and consistently questioned approaches to writing. The numerous subject matters include the muse, Florida, the Depression, political ideology, power itself, World War II, the role of poetry, epic/lyric, and semiotics. All of these topics comprise and contribute to Stevens' ever-present desire for consummation in poetry. His countless recreations are a form of this, as is the persistent trope of marriage that brings harmony to an oeuvre most concerned with discord. The main marriage Stevens writes about is between the sexes. Sexual cohabitation informs Stevens' coproductive late poetry, and is pursued as a paradigmatic imperative for culture. Stevens' version of the androgynous ideal most commonly undercuts the monumental art of the "man-locket set." For instance, in the masculinely titled essay, "The Figure of the Youth as a Virile Poet," Stevens varies Greek myth by asserting "The Sister of the Minotaur" as "the intelligence that endures." This sister variously inhabits the poetry as a lover, a mother, the earth, the soldier, "ephebe," a sibyl, an "interior paramour." In this final "single shawl" this consummate other unfolds as the reader that Stevens evokes and talks to in the late poems. Stevens' primarily lyric poetry breaks the solitary confinement of its genre while questioning the epic mastery that dominated Western aesthetics into the twentieth century.

I propose that Stevens' poetry grants perceptions of the world that meld the physical and psychic in order to challenge our ethical communications. The poems awaken us to an ambitiously diverse range of human experience innovatively and honestly. They take on all the intellectual, political, and emotional issues that press upon Stevens in his time. First, we will look at Stevens' deconstruction of romantic muses in the 1930s, primarily manifest in the music of "Key West."

Chapter 2

Ideas of Order:
Compos(t)ing the romantic

. . . we must somehow cleanse the imagination of the roman-
tic . . . (NA 138)

The poetry dramatizes the desire for a metaphorical
redemption of difference only to withdraw from the con-
ceit and thematize—poetically—its inevitable failure. The
poems become, in par, a curative for Romantic symbolism,
engaging the illusion only to dispel it all the more fully.
(Judith Butler, " 'The Nothing That Is': Stevens' Hegelian
Affinities," *Theorizing American Literature,* 270)

1935's *Ideas of Order* was the first new volume of poetry
Stevens published since *Harmonium* in 1923. It was
the beginning of Stevens' larger project, *The Whole
of Harmonium,* which became *The Collected Poems.* Responding to the
social, intellectual, and political upheaval of the thirties, Stevens reevaluated
the role of the poet in society. This meant questioning the assumptions
behind the spontaneous poetry in *Harmonium.* The secular philosophy in
"Sunday Morning" and "The Snow Man" creates earthy hedons that continue to be possible throughout Stevens' poetry. The interdependence of
sound, image, and reference in "Thirteen Ways of Looking at a Blackbird,"
"Anecdote of the Jar," "Le Monocle de Mon Oncle," and "The Comedian
as the Letter C" continues to be foundational in the ongoing operations of
Stevens' poetics. However, the poetry of the thirties is specifically directed
toward social responsibilities as they are ordered by ideas in language. Just
after writing "Mr. Burnshaw and the Statue" in 1935, a poem responding
to a Marxist review of *Ideas of Order,* Stevens explains the manner of his
work to his publisher, Ronald Lane Latimer:

> This leaves two questions: Whether I accept the common opinion that my verse is essentially decorative, and whether my landscapes are real or imagined. . . . I did not agree with the opinion that my verse is decorative, when I remembered that when *Harmonium* was in the making there was a time when I liked the idea of images and images alone, or images and the music of verse together. I then believed in *pure poetry,* as it was called.
>
> I still have a distinct liking for that sort of thing. But we live in a different time, and life means a good deal more to us now-a-days than literature does. In the period of which I have just spoken, I thought literature meant most. Moreover, I am not so sure that I don't think exactly the same thing now, but, unquestionably, I think at the same time that life is the essential part of literature. (*L* 288)

Because "life is the essential part of literature," Stevens looked at the way his life as a poet had been formed by the traditions of poetry and the customs of living. The only way he could be socially responsible was to take stock of himself first. "Farewell to Florida," written with the hindsight of having finished most of *Ideas of Order,* narrates the departure from *Harmonium's* South, which for Stevens was a romantic sojourn that took the place of what other American modernists found in Europe.[1] The poem's function as both introduction and coda to *Ideas of Order* not only provides a convenient frame of reference, but also suggests the intricacy of Stevens' approaches to romance. The romantic traditions and customs that Stevens inherits are the fulcrum upon which this volume tilts. Stevens' efforts at change depend upon discarding the past for a "freshening of life." Several poems exhibit such performances, as we will see shortly, the most difficult and successful of these being "The Idea of Order at Key West," on which "Farewell to Florida" comments:

> Key West sank downward under massive clouds
> And silvers and greens spread over the sea. The moon
> Is at the mast-head and the past is dead.
> . . . .
> Her mind had bound me round. The palms were hot
> As if I lived in ashen ground, as if
> The leaves in which the wind kept up its sound
> From my North of cold whistled in a sepulchral South,
> Her South of pine and coral and coraline sea,
> Her home, not mine, in the ever-freshened Keys,
> Her days, her oceanic nights, calling
> For music, for whisperings from the reefs.
> . . . .

My North is leafless and lies in a wintry slime
Both of men and clouds, a slime of men in crowds.   (*CP* 117–18)

"Farewell to Florida" operates knowing the accomplishment of "The Idea of Order at Key West," therefore enabling a view of the dead figure (the Floridian muse). Images of apocalypse, sacrifice and voyage precede "Her mind had bound me round."[2] "Her mind" personifies the poet's use of Florida as muse. "[B]ound me round" describes the tropical environment's seizure of the poet's Keatsian negative capability. Yet Florida's Nature is not quite the muse here; perhaps the poet's sensory perception of it is. "As if I lived in the ashen ground" hypothesizes the subjective involvement that is made distant by "Her South," "Her home, not mine, in the ever-freshened Keys." In contrast, Stevens' "North of cold" is a subjective metaphor describing how his temperate temper is shaped by his native landscape, here in polyphony with the South.

Unlike the harmonic Romanticism of Wordsworth in "Tintern Abbey," for example, Stevens tries to rid himself of the muse's possession. In "Farewell to Florida,' the other preoccupies the poet, but he realizes that he can only imagine his experience of the other: the repetition of "as if" indicates hypothetical involvement. This conditional simile allows empirical objects to remain separate: "The palms were hot." Even the identification of his "North of cold" is conditioned by "as if." This simulacra is not the symptom of an indeterminate mind; the conditional simile emphasizes the readiness of a mind in–determinacy: that is, a mind that is in a perpetual state of determination. Stevens reiterates the importance of flux in "The Well Dressed Man with a Beard": "It can never be satisfied, the mind, never" (*CP* 247). As Jacqueline Brogan demonstrates in *Stevens and Simile*, the poet often uses simile to make comparison relative as opposed to final, and the conditional sentence brings contextual accuracy to linguistic representation. The relationship between subject and object is maintained in an economy of difference: "Her home, not mine." The condition of the other is "calling / For music, for whisperings from the reefs." The reef-music is its own entity, as the poet's music is, until the reef whispers in the poet's poem—an example of the condition of indeterminacy. In Stevens' poem, the words on the page are the only determination.

The desire for music here speaks for the poet's "rage for order" of the outside world. This rage is carefully navigated in *Ideas of Order,* and "Farewell to Florida" is framed by the words "go on, high ship." For Stevens the epic becomes his local North, and the vehicle becomes the poem. His initial begrudging responsibility to "a slime of men in crowds" quickly consumes Stevens to the extent that public need in the 1930s takes the role of muse. The anomalous title "Mozart, 1935" introduces the demand for "Some harmonious skeptic soon in a skeptical music" proclaimed in that poem. The nexus of muse, music, and social responsibility indicates Stevens' determination to equip language with social power. Rhetoric develops a prominent role in his poetics at this time, as I mentioned in chapter 1. As an approach to language, Stevens' rhetoric is more de Manian than Machiavellian; his poetry displays the power of language to determine human action, rather than attempting to acquire power through poetry. Although the rhetorical poetry of the 1930s esteems teaching over dogma, its pedagogy often points to rhetoric's capacity to determine society.

In the figures of language Stevens sees society determined. This large stride between figuration and social constitution is enacted in the poetry's particular brand of logic: "Thought tends to collect in pools," Stevens writes in "Adagia" (*OP* 196). Because of Stevens' tendency to collect similar figures into recurring motifs, or "pools," it is worthwhile to make a distinction between figures as scripted signifiers in a poem, and tropes as a domain of figures. Tropes are a collection of similar figures, or ideas patterned into trope. This poetic trait takes shape most clearly in the portrait of Nietzsche studying "the deep pool" (*CP* 342) in "Description without Place," to which I return in chapter 5. The strength of a trope depends upon its persuasive ability; it becomes rhetorically dependent upon its means of persuasion—music, image, logic. Poetry's rhetoric, then, depends upon composition, and Stevens makes the composition of the poem its subject matter. Recall the accumulative process of "Add This to Rhetoric": "It is to add." By drawing attention to rhetoric, Stevens gets readers involved in composition, even if we are persuaded or moved by the music of rhetoric. Composition is also compost, as its etymology suggests. The poem is composed of tropes fermented and worn through time. The last three words of *Ideas of Order* are "Of wormy metaphors": the digestion of old poetic soil for a regenerative ground is an apt, if crude, metaphor for Stevens' project.[3]

As a site of dramatic configuration, the poem engages the reader as "maker." In "Idea of Order at Key West," this drama is enacted on several levels. The poet questions the muse's role in the formation of the poem itself. In questioning this traditional inspiration, Stevens makes the reader think about where music comes from. The poem's narrator solicits help from his companion on the beach, but the identity of the companion is uncertain for most of the poem so that the questions are first posed to the reader. This indeterminacy is dramatized so that the reader becomes complicit in determining mysteries unanswered by ghostly "pale Ramon." In this dramatic manner, readers are coaxed into an epistemological game, which is most powerfully swayed by the "music" that sound and image make together.

Florida is not the only romance at stake in this volume. I have alluded to Keats and Wordsworth because they are part of Stevens' Romantic inheritance. However, Stevens' romanticism does not rigorously study the traditions of his forbears; there is no "anxiety of influence" (in the words of Harold Bloom) in his work. Stevens is more interested in the effect that music has as a form of (romantic-rhetorical) persuasion, and so he works at transforming outdated romantic tropes into vital signifiers. In *Ideas of Order*, Stevens carefully combs romantic traditions so as to dispose of all the past intonations that have become brittle and outdated assumptions. In "The Irrational Element in Poetry," Stevens writes: "The slightest sound matters. . . . We no longer like Poe's tintinnabulations. You are free to tintinnabulate if you like. But others are equally free to put their hands over their ears" (*OP* 226). Birdsong is an unrelenting trope in Stevens, and one of traditional efficacy, but "Autumn Refrain" does not resuscitate the nightingale; the poem wonders at its power as a linguistic construct, especially since no said birds can be found in America. In "Sad Strains of a Gay Waltz" Stevens uses the waltz as an image for the outworn dance of romantic poetry. In "Mozart, 1935," the anomaly of the title represents the gap that the poet must fill. Brahms and Mozart are called up by Stevens as composers whose music moved audiences in the past, as Stevens wants to do for the present. But the thirties requires a "harmonious skeptic soon in a skeptical music" to intone society. Increasingly, Stevens' poems point to the worlds of social and political action in order to demonstrate how they are determined by rhetoric. *Owl's Clover* will portray figures of the Old Woman, Marxists, imperialists, and immigrants who are all bound by cultural composition. As images themselves, these figures are "Impassioned seducers and seduced" moved by society's impositional chords. Romance, then, is useful to Stevens because it performs the musical seduction that is required of poetry in order to move people:

> The music of poetry which creates its own fictions is one of the "sisterhood of the living dead" [*CP* 87]. It is a muse: all of the muses are of that sisterhood. But then I cannot say, at this distance of time, that I specifically meant the muses; this is just an explanation. I don't think that I meant anything definitely except all the things that live in memory and imagination. (*L* 297: Nov. 26, 1935)

In these poems, sound creates sensual rhythms and it carries echoes of tropes "that live in memory and imagination." Romantic harmonies of the past, such as Wordsworth's, have married the music of Nature with the human heartbeat. Such techniques have helped produce transcendental harmonies such as Truth, Beauty, and Joy, which were said to be located within a divine Nature. The master tropes of Romanticism are so effective at seducing readers that they continue to inform the reverential view of nature that many people hold. Stevens is less interested in questioning these aesthetics themselves than he is in questioning the way these tropes have become accepted values, which he sees as dead symbols.

In the thirties, Stevens uses the figure of the Statue to signify the monumentality of figural acceptance—tropes become landmarks in poetry, Nature, and the city-state. Stevens looks at the ways in which figurations become fixtures, and attempts to find figurations that work indeterminately. To achieve as much, Stevens' figures engage readerly participation by reflecting their own inception so that metaphors become known as comparisons that we imply, rather than comply with, like fixed statues.

Stevens' 1936 lecture, "The Irrational Element in Poetry," discusses the difficulty of defining the poet's choice of words and sounds. Following his discussion of "Poe's tintinnabulations," Stevens links the irrationality of knowledge with rhetoric's music:

> You have to know the sound that is the exact sound; and you do in fact know, without knowing how. Your knowledge is irrational. . . . What is true of sounds is true of everything: the feeling of words, without regard to their sound, for example. There is, in short, an unwritten rhetoric that is always changing and to which the poet must always be turning. (*OP* 226)

Sound, words, rhetoric, and knowledge are inextricably linked through composition. Because of this potent concoction, Stevens' poetry dramatically assembles language's epistemology in its progression. While Stevens goes to great lengths to guide the reader, the "unwritten rhetoric" is the irrational element of the poet's choosing. Reasons for authorial choices are impossible to discern, but Stevens' compositions make critical recreation more possible because the poetry dramatizes its bricolage.

Other modernists felt similar pressures of the contemporaneous, and wrote about the social role of the poet as it takes effect in composition. In Pound's estimate, "the most intense form of criticism" is "[c]riticism in new composition."[4] He qualifies this claim by saying that "the man who formulates any forward reach of co-ordinating principle is the man who produces the demonstration," and cites Eliot as one whose criticism in his poetry is "infinitely more alive, more vigorous than" that of his essays. "Tradition and the Individual Talent" proposes the artist's "continual extinction of personality," wherein the poet is analogous to a catalyst in a chemical experiment.[5] Eliot's scientific formulation is vastly different from Stevens' irrational element, which enlists the reader within the poem's sensibility. Eliot regards the artist as a cultural transmitter lacking egotistical inclusion, and he criticizes *Hamlet* for its abundance of emotion not contained within the play's structure. Eliot admonishes the sensibility that spills out from *Hamlet,* whereas I suspect that Stevens would consider the play's rhetorical excess successful. Stevens realizes the presence of the poet's will in the work: "We say that we perfect diction. We simply grow tired. Manner is something that has not yet been disengaged adequately. It does not mean style; it means the attitude of the writer, his bearing rather than his point of view" (*OP* 220). In recognizing the writer's bearing, Stevens is not proclaiming a song of autonomous self, but a rhetorical pose implemented for the poem's purpose. Stevens' distinction from his more objectivist modern contemporaries lies in his honesty regarding poetry's pose, the abstraction of "subject-matter." The poet admits irrational choice over scientific exactitude; Stevens does not admonish this abstract process for the sake of artistic authority:

> One is always writing about two things at the same time in poetry and it is this that produces the tension characteristic of poetry. One is the true subject and the other is the poetry of the subject. The difficulty of sticking to the true subject when it is the poetry of the subject that is paramount in one's mind, need only be mentioned to be understood. In a poet who makes the true subject paramount and merely embellishes it, the subject is constant and the development orderly. If the poetry of the subject is paramount, the true subject is not constant nor its development orderly. This is true in the case of Proust and Joyce, for example, in modern prose. (*OP* 221)

I am surprised that in 1936 Stevens concedes that anybody could make "the true subject paramount." Stevens argues in his work of this time that "the poetry of the subject is paramount," since that is its rhetorical force. From this quotation we can discern some distinctions among modernists. Stein and Stevens refuse the transcendent leap that claims "poetry of the subject" as "the true subject." Eliot and Pound forward their "poetry of the subject" as "the true subject." Williams manages to enlist the reader within his sensibility's "poetry of the subject." His seductive verse appears to be the "true subject" because, as with Pound, "the poetry of the subject" is undisclosed—"no ideas but in things." Williams succeeded to the extent that Stevens called his work "anti-poetic," a compliment some mistake for insult.[6] However, readers of Williams need only look at his prose writings on imagination to confirm his use of an abstract poetic technique so precisely American in its time that it appears to present the true subject. Marianne Moore used similar precision to create a clear poetry of the subject. On the other side of the Atlantic, Gertrude Stein utilized abstract composition in compelling rhythms that persuade readers through sensual repetition, thus making irrational knowledge in a manner akin to Stevens. Stein and Stevens forward the irrational elements of poetry in new urgent manners that, for the first time in the history of poetry, do not attempt to posit their irrationale as true.

All of these modernists perform "criticism in new composition," and Pound describes how their essays are merely supplemental to their poetic concretions. Pound's second "most intense form of criticism" is "[c]riticism via music, meaning definitely the setting of a poet's words"—a description that collides with Stevens' "Irrational Element." The compositions of poems are *Ideas of Order.* Pound and Stevens emphasize music as the poem's vehicle of persuasive order. For Stevens, music is also a metaphor bridging romantic harmony and socio-political rhetoric.

The equivalence between ideas of order and the composition of music is the main project for this volume of poetry, and consequently the basis of this chapter's thesis. Stevens' poetry uses music, the irrational element, as subject matter and a method of persuasion. And since for Stevens "the theory of poetry is the theory of life" (*OP* 202), his new techniques/subject matter/theory inform the poetry's new inspiration: "the pressure of the contemporaneous." The social (dis)order of the thirties becomes the muse.

For a harmonious and skeptical music to influence people, the past's stale music must be weeded out. The last three words of *Ideas of Order,* "Of wormy metaphors" (*CP* 162), refer to how Stevens burrows in old poetic soil, and regenerates fertile ground (good manure). Stevens' critique of the past's romantic ways refers not only to poetic and musical tradition, but also a personal turn of mind. Several poems exhibit Stevens' romantic deconstructions. Using Brahms as a metaphor of his earlier spirit's vitality, he ends "Anglais Mort à Florence" this way:

> He was that music and himself.
> They were particles of order, a single majesty:
> But he remembered the time when he stood alone.

> He stood at last by God's help and the police;
> But he remembered the time when he stood alone.
> He yielded himself to that single majesty;
>
> But he remembered the time when he stood alone.
> When to be and delight to be seemed to be one,
> Before the colors deepened and grew small.   (*CP* 149)

Not his most rousing verse, it certainly is a painful elegy of youth as the thrice repeated line emphasizes. The subject's dissipated autonomy and/or solipsism is supplanted by the first line in the middle stanza. The only part of the poem that almost arrives in the present, and it sticks out like a sore thumb: "God's help" for the writer of *Harmonium?* The suggestion of faith is surprising for a poet who usually writes about the eccentric absurdities of Christianity, and wants to write "a poem of the earth." The poetic figure's desolation, in relation to this erratic divinity, is then set in drastic secular contrast by "the police": a juxtaposition broad enough to contain more than a hint of irony. However, most ironies contain a substantial grain of truth, as do "the police," who are here a rather alien force. These watchdogs may refer to the political left who figure prominently in *Owl's Clover* as the keepers of Stevens' conscience. The socialist and divine extremes become the markers of Stevens' newfound responsibility as a poet. Religious and political robes are never wholeheartedly worn by the poet, but Stevens wanted his poetry to provide a manner in its poetics that could address these human needs.

As the title "Anglais Mort à Florence" indicates, Stevens aligns his loss of romantic spiritual autonomy with the death of the English (race, language) in Florence: likely a dig at the exiled quality of English romanticism. Stevens couches his dying romanticism (even Brahms won't do) within a larger decaying Eurocentrism. Stevens' changes at this time were due to external societal pressures, the personal diminishment of a vital romantic response to phenomena, and a different writerly approach to the poetic craft, as Litz also notices: "The years 1934–37 mark a pivotal stage in Stevens' poetic life, the end of his "introspective voyage" and the beginning of a new pattern of poetic development."[7] Near the beginning of *Ideas of Order* we find Stevens "Sailing after Lunch":

> It is the word *pejorative* that hurts.
> My old boat goes round on a crutch
> And doesn't get under way.

> It's the time of the year
> And the time of the day.
>
> Perhaps it's the lunch we had
> or the lunch we should have had.
> But I am, in any case,
> A most inappropriate man
> In a most unpropitious place.
>
> Mon Dieu, hear the poet's prayer.
> The romantic should be here.
> The romantic should be there.
> It ought to be everywhere.
> But the romantic must never remain,
>
> Mon Dieu, and must never again return.   (*CP* 120)

Further mourning romanticism, Stevens italicizes a word heavily used in criticism of his poetry; a word that describes his de-romanticizing project. The poetry "goes round on a crutch" reflexively, performing a nonlinear movement that he deems necessary for contemporaneous reevaluation. God also returns in the form of a French curse, humorously suggesting a priestly role for the poet, who must replenish a deity that diminished alongside romanticism. As J. Hillis Miller has written with help from Nietzsche, romanticism answers to the vacuum created by the death of God.[8] The presence of "God's help" in the previous poem, "Anglais mort à Florence," is doubly ironic in the context of "Sailing after Lunch": "God's help" is another "crutch" for Stevens in face of present romantic decay. Stevens makes this point through the use of French as part of a decaying culture. If we believe the title, "Anglais mort à Florence," then the same goes for the American romance with France, which was once a hotbed of Americana in the roaring twenties. By inserting "Mon Dieu" in the middle of the repeated assertion that "the romantic must never return," Stevens amalgamates the contexts of God and French culture together as elements of a bygone romanticism. While the romantic lunch of the past is inadequate, Stevens finishes the poem by demonstrating that romantic experience still exists: "That slight transcendence to the dirty sail." This soiled past has arisen pejoratively several times, from "wormy metaphors" to "Mon Dieu." However, "the light wind worries the sail" that is the poem Stevens must write for a changing present. First of all, the past's garbage must be trucked away, as we will see in "The Idea of Order at Key West." Stevens explains this necessity:

> It should be said of poetry that it is essentially romantic as if one were recognizing the truth about poetry for the first time. Although the romantic is referred to, most often, in a pejorative sense, this sense attaches, or should attach, not to the romantic but to some phase of the romantic that has become stale. Just as there is always a romantic that is potent, so there is always a romantic that is impotent. (*OP* 183)

"The Idea of Order at Key West" addresses romantic potency by investigating its central source of inspiration, the muse. This famous poem is one of the most critically elusive and contentious in all of Stevens' work. Harold Bloom attempts "to reveal how faithfully [this poem] follows the model of the Wordsworthian crisis poem, in its American Romantic modification. . . ."[9] It is a very romantic poem in its topos—a mysterious female figure singing on the seashore—but the romantic paradigm is questioned from the outset:

> She sang beyond the genius of the sea.
> The water never formed to mind or voice,
> Like a body wholly body, fluttering
> Its empty sleeves . . .   (*CP* 128)

Neither the figure's body nor her voice contains the sea or its representative song. The romantic paradigm of a female body singing for the poet—his muse or instrument—is unquestionably "empty" here, dispossessed. Eleanor Cook argues against Wordsworthian sublimation:

> The woman does not half-perceive and half-create anything; she is the single artificer of her song. She is what the listeners behold—not a woman made into an addressee, listener, younger self, and spirit of place, as Wordsworth made Dorothy. Stevens' woman sings her own song, . . . his sea does not have knowable spirit. It is an inverse ghost—not a spirit shorn of body but a body shorn of a knowable spirit.[10]

Bloom's "model of the Wordsworthian crisis poem" is not the case for Stevens, except insofar as Romantic paradigms are in crisis. John Hollander observes a similar romantic shift in "The Sound of the Music of the Music of Sound":

There is no manifesto about musical figures more powerful or more direct than the beginning of "The Idea of Order at Key West," where the voice of the singing spirit and the "constant cry" of the sea are emphaticaly denied a relation that their forerunners have had throughout the history of our poetry.[11]

While I agree that spirit and sea are logically denied interrelation, this denial is not simple because the poem's music resonates harmoniously:

> The sea was not a mask. No more was she.
> The song and water were not medleyed sound
> Even if what she sang was what she heard,
> Since what she sang was uttered word by word.   (*CP* 128)

The sound of the music has a stronger effect on the reader than the poem's logical denial of mimesis. As the muse echoes "what she heard" "word by word," the poem's cadence and rhyme mimic the logic of mimesis that Stevens is denying. She listens and speaks in the scene and therefore would seem to provide a narrative copy of the seascape, but she is refused the role of symbolic provider. The muse as romantic paradigm is negated while the poem continues to reconstruct a new music that is more powerful than the anti-paradigmatic argument. Stevens' music does not carry the usual symbolic attributes. The active imagery signifies sound and sight but awaits formation. This muse is a figure but not a recognizable trope, or a trope emptied of usual figuration; she is a signifier as yet unsignified, or a signified hollowed of signifiers.

Litz, before Hollander, stated that "Stevens rejects the older romantic notions of the poet expressing the voice of nature."[12] However, there lingers in Litz's analysis the notion that nature is the reference for inspiration: "in Stevens' poem the singer is a maker, building verbal artifice out of the sound of the sea." This view maintains the poem within a two-fold mimetic order, which limits the poem's generative compositional powers to being *about* nature. My point is that while "verbal artifice" is being built, it is not "out of the sound of the sea," or "a response to nature," as Litz also states. Such certainty about a dialogue with nature simplifies the poem's central unanswered question, "Whose spirit is this?"

In order to approach that question, I will return to the undermined dialectic of sea and she that Stevens complicates in the second stanza:

> The sea was not a mask. No more was she.
> The song and water were not medleyed sound

> Even if what she sang was what she heard,
> Since what she sang was uttered word by word.   (*CP* 128)

The first line's caesura divides the identities of she and the sea, neither of which is a mask. We might ask, Masks of whom?: Each other? The observer? Poet? Regardless, Stevens brings them together in the next line, an example of defied romantic logic. Although he argues that "song and water were not medleyed sound," the two entities are called up simultaneously in the poem, and are therefore set in comparative relation so that the negatives fail to deny metaphorical identity.

In the first stanza, she and sea are pushed toward relations of value, mutual exclusion, simile, personification, mimesis, speech, knowledge, and synecdoche. Despite all those relationships, Stevens will not establish a firm metaphor. In fact, she and the sea become anti-metaphorical; "The song and water were not medleyed sound" and not a mask. However, the innovations of grammar and syntax in this line overpower the negative logical argument. The noun "medley" becomes the verb "medleyed" activating "song and water," as well as an adjective describing the singular "medleyed sound" thus unifying "song and water." The word's unusual syntactical usage is itself a medley of sorts, being one word used in three different grammatical ways. This grammatical saturation increases syntactical links, further drawing together she and sea. Even the abundance of spatial relations between she and the sea in the confines of the poem's printed space conglomerates the muses to the extent that the negative "not" hardly denies the medley.

Such a reading seems intricate, but Stevens has yet to complicate the actual argument in the second stanza. The first two lines logically reaffirm each other. The third line, "Even if what she sang was what she heard," introduces a possible condition. Despite the poet's assertion that the two entities do not wear on each other (as masks, medleys), the third line suggests the potential of mimetic reportage by the female subject. Although the condition is left indeterminate, the proposal of musical inspiration teases the reader along with the poem's evolving predicament. The rest of the conditional sentence follows, "Since what she sang was uttered word by word." The speculation about her music is divided into a spoken utterance that breaks down her song. This line's ambling cadence emphasizes the mechanical assembly of the song, whose site is the poem. Perhaps the line's attention to language is the first indication (not couched in the logic of a negation overwhelmed by images, as were the previous lines) that her song is the poet's poem.[13]

To briefly recapitulate, some of Stevens' most effective techniques are at work in these four lines. Indeterminate identity is constituted by several phenomenal elements, all of these existing in many figurative relations. The logic of negation is overpowered by the suggestive capabilities of figures, such as image and sound drawn together by metonymy and metaphor. Often such figuration is not made but merely suggested, so that the reader makes poetry out of suggestion. Words are used innovatively in terms of revamped syntax and grammar, as well as through their placement within the poem's rhythm and meter. Interpretive teasing occurs through various means, such as the possibilities of mimetic definition, metaphor, and the apparent logic of a conditional argument. In the fourth stanza Stevens uses conditional sentence structure more fully to further his inquiry into the causes and effects of composition. Within that framework in general, he usually includes contradiction so as to demonstrate the fallibility of logic, once again. Last of all, reflexive attention to the writing of the poem distracts attention from transparent mimesis. The reader's role as listener of a true story or event is disrupted. The reader becomes involved in configuring the poem's compositional world rather than being told about it.

The question of who originates the lyric is developed in the third stanza:

> Whose spirit is this? we *said,* because we *knew*
> It was the spirit that we *sought* and *knew*
> That we should *ask* this often as she *sang.*   (*CP* 129; my emphasis)

Speaking, knowing, seeking, asking, and singing are all forms of interpretation; a hermeneutical plurality that is rather like a revolving hinge in Stevens' poetry. There is virtually no difference in these forms of knowledge, especially when logic doesn't (literally) hold water in this poem. They belong together indeterminately, but determinedly together. The point is that there is no locatable origin for the spirit. The lack of reference for the spirit and the ocean is the mystery the poet wants to participate in. Although a defined knowledge is well out of reach, there exists between the utterance and knowledge the quest and the song. The quest(ion) operates in dialectical rapport with the mysterious song. Epic striving works in economical exchange with lyricism. By interrogating human creativity, Stevens probes the conditions of existence: "Key West" asks, If we have the song, what sort of exchange is that?—especially when we realize that it is our own, not belonging to a transcendent other.

At this point in the poem, the identity of the singer is questioned together with the content of her song:

> It may be that in all her phrases stirred
> The grinding water and the gasping wind;
> But it was she and not the sea we heard.   (*CP* 129)

Eleanor Cook wonders: "'It may be' that, somehow, 'in' her words (but how, 'in'?) there stirred the 'gasping wind.'" [14] Cook's parenthetical question problematizes the possessive quality of language in the same way Stevens undermines mimetic possession. Stevens is careful to keep her words indeterminate: "But it was she and not the sea we heard." Her "phrases" may compose the wind in an abstract linguistic form, but wind and sea remain uncontainable, just as she is not a mask for the poet. Toward the end of the poem, the questers rather than the questee become questioned. We do not know that the poet and Ramon Fernandez are implied until the end; therefore "we" are indeterminate. The possibility of the reader's involvement strengthens the philosophic urgency of the spiritual quest(ion). [15]

The fourth stanza is to me the most remarkable in terms of "pure poetry." Its lyricism appears and sounds very transformative. Yet this most potent poetry is doubly limited. It is a conditional argument that includes its own counter-argument. Here we have the romantic exorcised:

> If it was only the dark voice of the sea
> That rose, or even colored by many waves;
> If it was only the outer voice of sky
> And cloud, of the sunken coral water-walled,
> However clear, it would have been deep air,
> The heaving speech of air, a summer sound
> Repeated in a summer without end
> And sound alone. But it was more than that,
> More even than her voice, and ours, among
> The meaningless plungings of water and the wind,
> Theatrical distances, bronze shadows heaped
> On high horizons, mountainous atmospheres
> Of sky and sea.   (*CP* 129)

Because this section of the poem has so much in store, I will layer a few readings of it in order to show its many logical defacements. I will begin with a fairly quick reading that provides an overall shape, which will then be retraced in more detail. In many of the poems from *Ideas of Order*, and in "Imagination as Value," Stevens cites the romantic as a denigrating limitation upon imaginative production. The above excerpt of "Key West" begins with romantic considerations of the sea. The conditional argument is "colored" by the metonymic waves, then re-conditioned by a consideration of a sky voice, which is then grounded by the "cloud" metonymy.[16] The quest for originary voice is complicated by basic perceptions. Through perception the poem is composed by showing the "act of the mind" taking precedence over an argument searching for reason and truth: originary still points, such as the sea voice, are shown to be unsensible; they have nothing to do with building this composition. The argument is obfuscated: "If it was only the outer voice of sky / And cloud, of the sunken coral water-walled, / However clear. . . ." The power of the "coral" metonymy as image and sound overtakes, and makes the reader forget, its supposed part of a logical quest for spiritual ownership. Set within a series of images that accumulatively awaken the senses, the coral image acquires an immanence effective within the poem's composition. As part of the ongoing quest(ion), it is a preposterous impediment; a recasting of the lyric point of departure. Stevens shows its dislocation within the argument by continuing with the transition, "However clear," which pretends to function in a logical sequence—one that has been subverted already. It is strange that both the poem's lyrical imagery and its argument share the same sentence syntax, as they work rhetorically against each other: the plodding rhythm and repetition of the "summer sound" lines construct a dull singularity that provide an answer to the argument that is as unsatisfactory as Stevens makes the argument out to be. On top of that irresolution, Stevens heaps "Theatrical distances, bronze shadows" so that the accumulating sensory data overpowers logical formulations.

Let's retrace this part of the poem with more attention to the sound of the music. Stevens conjoins sound with image as one side of a dialectic that plays off the poem's logical debates. Logic depends upon syntax and grammar, which are sometimes altered to lend power to sound and image.[17] Conveniently, this section of the poem can be divided into an argument according to the rhythm and meter of the lines. In answering the previous stanza's question "Whose spirit is this?" the first four lines conditionally propose Nature, that most romantic source. These lines all outgrow pentameter in uneven meters. Their sound sense dominates the meter, cannot be contained by it. The most remarkable case of this is the fourth line, "And cloud, of the sunken cor*al wa*ter-*wall*ed." Here, the caesura precedes an anapest that leads to the onslaught of the underwater image, which is sonically submerged by the alliterative "*awl*" sound. After "sunken," the stress on "walled" picks up the second unstressed syllable of "coral," thereby further submerging the (imagined) physical coral within the water by drowning the hard sharp "cor" stress within the "awl" sounds. (By fitting images of submersion in a romantic landscape, Stevens may be playing with the romantic characteristic of mental submersion.) The claustrophobic sounds press against the barely containing meter, which requires an extra syllable (perhaps a pressure for breath, which may be stifled in the water imagery). Stevens demonstrates a most effective poetic technique that continually arises when poems reach their densest potencies: the sound sense of the poem copies, emphasizes, and mimics physical properties of the image.

This achievement is aided by altering the syntax to cooperate with the innovative play of grammar. As in the poem's earlier use of "medleyed," here again the syntax is made more dynamic by drawing the verb from a noun: "water-walled" performs verbal and adjectival action on "coral," further strengthening the sunken sense by the overloaded use of grammar. What does it mean to have nouns acting as verbs and adjectives simultaneously? Perhaps as adjectives they always modify something else, thereby being interrelative rather than autonomous. As verbs, nouns, once again, can never be autonomous because they are active rather than still; they always participate in a chain of action. This grammatology is part of Stevens' poetics of change.

The next five lines offer a measured distance from the previous immersion. Here we think we read the contemplative poet we can trust (such as the elder Stevens). These lines obey iambic pentameter. "However clear," pretends to function within the poem's logical flow of sentences, which have been already subverted by overpowering images. "However clear" also carries another meaning pertaining to the "air," so that the poet's already precarious argument also engages in a debate about sensory perception: "However clear, it would have been deep air." The measured rhythm and tone, however, gently lead to the only sure appraisal witnessed in the scene, "sound alone," which still perplexes its recipients. Mervyn Nicholson makes this comment:

> To say that it is "sound alone" is to remove from it all abstract meanings, while at the same time allowing the ground of all meanings to emerge. Hearing not only precedes meaning: it makes meaning possible, and hence contains meaning within itself in potential form. In "Key West" the sound of a song changes the sensory experience of the listener. Sound transforms into intensified *color.* . . .[18]

Changing sound into color, like paint into image, is one of the many leaps
Stevens makes between types of figures. Following the caesura that introduces the transition, "But it was more than that," reason again gives way to
sensory perception, and the meter extends past ten syllables (for three lines)
to work in conjunction with the onslaught of images:

> The meaningless plungings of water and the wind,
> Theatrical distances, bronze shadows heaped
> On high horizons, mountainous atmospheres
> Of sky and sea.   (*CP* 129)

The chaotic barrage of "The meaningless plungings of water and the
wind" in a long uneven meter uses similar techniques as the "water-walled"
line, this time making the verb a noun: "plungings" asserts verbal action as
event, thereby giving priority to the sensuality and irrationality of sound
and image.

From that vital imagery's irrational power, Stevens moves in the next
line to a mixture of abstraction and artifice. Although never operating
within parameters of strict mimetic realism, the semblance of a physically
real seascape could be interpreted up to this juncture. With "Theatrical distances," the poem becomes a dramatization of the abstract quest of the
onlookers to understand the spirit of the scene. Those "distances" exist
between "her voice and ours," and between "meaningless plungings" and
"water and the wind," as the continuous sentence links these attributes.
However, that abstract vagueness, which is the mind's interpretive plurality
at work, remains firmly rooted in the physical scene (both the landscape
and the language of the poem as site). "Theatrical distances, bronze shadows heaped / On high horizons" connects the abstract "distances" to seeing the color of the horizons, as in a sunset. While maintaining that
physical reference, "bronze" points to metallic gilding that is materially
crafted, much like the composition of the poem. The plurality of "horizons" amplifies the physical horizon to include the abstract and linguistic
orders in operation. Pushing the abstract linguistic potency, "mountainous
atmospheres / Of sky and sea" stretch the boundaries of mimesis by using
mountains to describe sea and sky. The "mountainous atmospheres" also
work as a metaphor continuing the trope of "distances" within the abstract
mind of the perceiver, as well as being a metaphor of the sheer magnitude
of the seascape.

In lines such as these, Stevens writes abstract linguistic poetry.[19] Charles
Altieri described Stevens within the aesthetics of Abstract Expressionism,

maintaining the model of the mind using abstract allusions, as in Plato's forms. Critics such as Marie Borroff and Glen MacLeod have pointed out that Stevens uses abstraction in the strict etymological sense, as the material condition of language. The formulation "It Must be Abstract" in "Notes Toward a Supreme Fiction" thoroughly proposes the idea that language always carries the weight of a split sign, and that if that split is recognized as a condition of language, it always remains a fictional property. Stevens always inscribes this awareness in his Abstract poetry. The material of language is a requisite, as is the paint of the Abstract Expressionists. I use the term "Abstract linguistic" to differentiate the poetic from the painterly medium, and to register the manner in which the language of the poem becomes a dominant discursive reference. The surface of language is reflexively signified, or made obvious, by altered syntax, which emphasizes imagery ("water-walled," "plungings"). Meanwhile, the words still act as references for externals, but any pretense of accurate mimetic reference is problematized by the arrangement of linguistic images operating in collision on the poem's surface.[20] Stevens manages Abstract Expressionism without losing sight of mimetic orders, however, as witnessed by the way "mountainous atmospheres," still describes a scene. In this style, Stevens is more like Willem deKooning—alluding to signifieds but prioritizing the signifier's compositional commentary—than Jackson Pollock. Dekooning's "Woman and Bicycle," for instance, contains a semblable form of its title, but the canvas is dominated by the Abstract contours of colored paint.

The stanza I've been discussing probably seems too much like liquid to be sensibly contained, but it actually remains part of a simplifiable argument. The first four lines proposed Nature as a limited reference for the spirit. The next five reiterated the poet's ambivalence while asserting sound as one sure thing. The last four built a complex abstract composition without philosophically satisfying the quest(ion). However, the compilation of the whole stanza shows Nature to be an artificially constructed, nonlocatable origin for the spirit.

In his "pejorative" romanticism, Stevens makes poetry a demonstrative craft that shows its "bronze" artifice at work. The indeterminacy of spiritual voice disallows the location of an originary source, or referential power. "More even than her voice and ours," more than the sea, sky, summer wind; all of that traditional romantic Nature music still exists, but as a "body wholly body fluttering / Its empty sleeves." The personified body of Nature is an empty misgiving in the poem's order of things: a signified that lacks vital signifiers in contemporaneous language. Conversely, the new poetic order has become, for Stevens, "meaningless plungings," a sensual

feast without a host. New signifiers compose without a well-worn signified. The poem is now less interested in attributing reason to nature; instead
it concentrates on how the poet perceives and how the poem is written.
"Theatrical distances, bronze shadows [are] heaped" together according to
the poem's composition, with no other discernible laws. By taking idealized orders (the muse) out of poetry's mystique, Stevens materializes old
abstract forms (Nature) into a new syntax of sounds and images that compose logic in their assembly. They are one and the same: the poem's abstractions are compositional.

This stanza stands at the poem's center as a fulcrum upon which much
is determined. Since it is encased in an unfinished conditional argument, it
does not make claims, unlike the rest of the poem. Yet to understand the
poem, we must comprehend its composition. Its lack of a claim, its dissolution into sensory composition is, I believe, the lesson of the poem. To
return to one of Stevens' liveliest readers, Bloom notes its interpretive difficulty as he analyzes the opposition of "Comparison" and "Cause and
Effect." I have been discussing this dialectic in terms of how figural composition undermines logic. Unwilling to allow the stanza to remain conditionally suspended between "Comparison" and "Cause and Effect," Bloom
claims a "crossing" to "Solipsism," which involves a "restitution of Power."
Willing a formal resolution, Bloom reads the stanza within his schematic
poetics, concluding thus: "A voice rises up here, beyond the sea, beyond the
singer, beyond Stevens, for it is more than those voices. What rises up is a
voice neither natural nor human, yet Stevens cannot tell us, or know himself, what such a voice might be."[21] Although Bloom said that the first
stanza "denies mimesis," here he divinely anthropomorphizes the voice.
While Stevens interrogates voices, "it was more than that" does not lead to
a Bloomian transcendental equivalent as much as it directs the reader
through the composition that follows, "among / The meaningless plungings of water and the wind, / Theatrical distances, bronze shadows heaped
/ On high horizons . . ." (*CP* 129). This part of the poem is not a segue
preceding the singer's triumphant singular voice; it assembles an abstract
composition similar to the finale's "Fixing [of] emblazoned zones" (*CP*
130). Bloom's reading nears, then detours from the crux of the poem (the
suspension between *Comparison* and *Cause and Effect*) by falling prey to the
hunt for an answerable source within the logical framework of *Cause and
Effect*:

Our clue must come through the second crossing of the poem, which moves
toward greater expressiveness as opposed to mimesis, moves back partly to a

world of sight and moves also to an internalization of the spirit. Why? Because, though the voice that is great within us cannot be our own, we are under the transgressive necessity of being able to locate it nowhere else.[22]

Bloom tries to ground the question in solipsism by matter of default, or "transgressive necessity." Checking that necessity, we find that "transgressive" means to "infringe, violate, go beyond the bounds of" *(OED)*. This unruly romantic imposition is what the poem works to be rid of from the beginning. I suggest the poem takes the question of origin or spirit and says we can continue to look elsewhere, but that all we have is sensual figuration, the spells of language. The poem's linguistic performances may teasingly move the reader who is trained in the tradition of religious awe as exercised by Romantic poets, but Stevens' images are no longer contained in the tropic baggage of old signified transcendences. The poem's flat abstract compositions do not provide vertical symbolic reference (i.e., God to navel) for the spiritual question. The poem reissues the mystery that likely initiated divine structures in the first place. Stevens shrugs, "God is in me or else is not at all" *(OP* 198).

The "second crossing" Bloom refers to is the impasse that is signified, as in "Of Modern Poetry," by a line break. Its structure says *this is an obvious transition in the poem's development.*

> It was her voice that made
> The sky acutest at its vanishing.
> She measured to the hour its solitude.
> She was the single artificer of the world   *(CP* 129)

These demonstrative lines locate, for Bloom, "an internalization of the spirit." In Romantic poetry (Bloom aligns Stevens with Shelley here) the muse has been just that, although the poem will show us that "the single artificer" is a rhetorical decoy.

> That was her song, for she was the maker. Then we,
> As we beheld her striding there alone,
> Knew that there never was a world for her
> Except the one she sang, and singing made.

The section's confident voice turns out to be ironic within the poem's evolving structure and rhetoric, as her seemingly powerful presence is denied, apart from her part in the poem. "Then we" adds a couple of erratic syllables that remind us that the poet and his friend are viewing this phenomenon, rather than the female figure being the muse incarnate. As their gaze objectifies her, for she is striding vulnerably alone, the next line asserts that the song is the limit of her existence. The poem develops an absolute unification between her, song, and creation, but emphatically not between these and the natural world: "there never was a world for her / Except the one she sang, and singing made."[23]

Bloom recognizes that the poem dissociates itself from the singer, although his reading garnishes romantic wishes here in Stevens' rhetoric:

> [The poem attempts to sublimate] its deepest intentions or desires for utterance, and like all such metaphors it fails. This is not poetical failure so much as it is argumentative or topical failure, for the sublimating metaphor tries to emphasize the resemblance between inner voice and outer ocean, at the expense of dissimilarity.[24]

Bloom is right about the "argumentative or topical failure" that charts automatic mimesis as the poem's equation. But that failure is the poem's topical argument against romantic paradigms that mimetically bond poetry with nature. Similarly, I would describe the authorial intention implied by Bloom in "attempted sublimation" as a rhetorical strategy by Stevens. The poem directly de-sublimates the singer here. Her disappearance from the poem enables the full presence of the masculine poetry addressed to Ramon Fernandez. By transferring the house of order from an externally concocted other to the poem's present party ("Ramon Fernandez, tell me, if you know"), Stevens vivifies spirit within those present rather than those absent sublimations.

This stanza's rhetorical argument simplifies the indeterminacy of the preceding stanza so as to strut the muse out "alone" as Platonic pure idealization, thus isolating her as an essential object of the viewers (poet and reader Ramon). Yet the only definite attribute of this poem's quest so far is the song, whose only legacy is the written lyric. Stevens creates the poem that is indivisible from her song. And the viewers insist that the only world is the one that was sung. It is no accident that once her song is "made" the present turns into past tense and she disappears from the rest of the poem. The poem progresses from the old habit of anthropomorphizing the muse to an abstract poem that posits mystery in composition itself. Remember that "Farewell to Florida" confirms the dissociation occurring here.

The poem's musical configuration changes at the following structural break, after which the poet speaks to Ramon about the tension between order and mystery in a markedly different masculine rhetoric:

> Ramon Fernandez, tell me, if you know,
> Why, when the singing ended and we turned
> Toward the town, tell why the glassy lights,
> The lights in the fishing boats at anchor there,
> As the night descended, tilting in the air,
> Mastered the night and portioned out the sea,
> Fixing emblazoned zones and fiery poles,
> Arranging, deepening, enchanting night.   (*CP* 130)

They, two men together, are without her, and their controlling language shaping their vista seems a paradox in the lyric convention because, as the lights "portioned out the sea," the seascape is divvied up without reference to the mythic muse.[25] If a new myth need be read in this scene, it is of the "rage for order," in Key West or any other perceived place. The myth is of *tilting, mastering, portioning, fixing, arranging, deepening, enchanting*. The italicized verbs emphasize symbolic action: dead nouns are revitalized so that events, compositions are in motion. Aggressive language appears to overcompensate for mysterious bewilderment. Yet the strong language works in a new *dramatic* way that is both straightforward and ironic: ironic because the poem had been searching for spiritual origin, which all of a sudden becomes irrelevant when the idea of an external reference for spirit—transcendence—is discarded; straightforward because the air is cleared of symbols representing an already ordered reality or discourse. This type of poetics creates and resembles acts of perception and thought; readers need not find symbolic referents; composition is literally enacted on the page.

Perhaps this stanza is the first instance in Stevens of a dialogic poetry wherein the poet is cast as Ariel fully presenting the scene to the reader-comrade. It is curious and significant that Stevens' voice is strongest and somehow most modest when assuming full responsibility for poems presented to a formulated reader.[26] Perhaps the dramatic monologue becomes less jesting, less ironic, less oracular when dialogic. By asking "Ramon" (a seemingly arbitrary name)[27] "Why" order takes shape, Stevens invokes the reader's participation in the philosophical quandary composed in the poem's assembly.

Readers may feel that "she" was easily done away with; a convenient female prop for objectification. "The bright shapes a container can contain!" says Theodore Roethke in "I Knew a Woman." Yes. That is the poem's point. The muse is historically made to *answer* for many orders ranging from abstract idealization to mimetic reference. Here, she is made to *question* in her potent but fleeting production. By disallowing her existence apart from her song in the poem, the trope that she is becomes immaterial (and purely material, a figuration). In the last two stanzas the poet and his friend have come no closer in their quest, which actually intensifies at the end (it is not a dejection ode). That is because the feminine figure is no longer objectified as a ghostly foil responsible for the mysteries beheld by the maker.

Through this muse, Stevens charts a fictional life of the immortal beloved. By pointing to the mystery, awe, and violence of her figuration Stevens demystifies the myth as the object of male desire. Instead of procuring a moral polemic in such destruction (is it offensive, or constructive?), the poem concludes by asserting the "rage for order" in language that reaffirms mystery at the source of Creation:

> Oh! Blessed rage for order, pale Ramon,
> The maker's rage to order words of the sea,
> Words of the fragrant portals, dimly-starred,
> And of ourselves and of our origins,
> In ghostlier demarcations, keener sounds.   (CP 130)

Mystery of order evokes musical quests without phantoms but all phantasmagoria.[28]

"The Idea of Order at Key West" exorcises romanticism by bringing the inspirational muse to the surface of the poem and showing her as part and parcel of the masculine "rage for order." In showing us the muse and taking it away (it is not a she, but a figure), Stevens manages to leave the music that muses are known for. The poem still performs a seduction of the senses through musical sounds and images, while arguing that her figuration is an unnecessarily artificial externalization of mythic desire. Stevens' pejorative muse loses her transcendent idealization, her tropic identity (most firmly within the aggressive masculine rhetoric at the end), while the poem still performs a music as seductive as the moving romantic lyrics of the past. This seduction may confound the reader because it belies romantic tradition: Stevens removes the transcendental sign (muse, who doesn't even begin with a name here, only a gender which often becomes neutral) while maintaining the emotional complex surrounding her/it. The reader is left without an object of desire and only with the spell of language. The poem, then, performs, demonstrates, and argues for the supremacy of music over logic.

Beyond that, it shows the romantic to be an organizing principle of thought: a way of understanding the world by linking desires with phenomena in what is known as a body of knowledge, a map. The muse is a compass with which to map Nature. The earth is the object of knowledge: a system that is based on the object and subject split created in the interests of mastery. "Whose spirit is this?" questions the epistemology of this polarization by redirecting attention away from an iconographic imaginary other, and toward a reformulated composition of a present place with unfixed spirit. Stevens shows in this poem's performance that the object is subjective knowledge itself created by musicians. The abstract, then, becomes the literal.

Key West's singer is joined by other muses in the chorus of *Ideas of Order*. The romantic muses of the past become stale "wormy metaphors" that nevertheless burrow through present culture. "Autumn Refrain" is useful here because it clearly illustrates the power of an abstract trope, the nightingale, to create literal experience, even though the linguistic construct lacks a tangible referent. As with the female muse of nature, the nightingale is a romantic supreme fiction that may be false, but still able to voice emotional presence:

> The yellow moon of words about the nightingale
> In measureless measures, not a bird for me
> But the name of a bird and the name of a nameless air
> I have never—shall never hear. And yet beneath
> The stillness of everything gone, and being still,
> Being and sitting still, sometimes resides,
> Some skreaking and skrittering residuum,
> And grates these evasions of the nightingale
> Though I have never—shall never hear that bird.
> And the stillness is in the key, all of it is,
> The stillness is in the key of that desolate sound.   (*CP* 160)

This ode to Keatsian romance brings forward negative capability without hoisting up a capable nightingale to signify the emotion.[29] Another example of "Nothing that is not there and the nothing that is," the nightingale here becomes a feeling that results from fiction, which is a reversal of the Supreme Fiction's "fiction that results from feeling." The strength of longing for the nightingale trope illustrates the power of language to produce emotions through its nominal abilities, rather than its mimetic references to nature. The poem decreates the romantic source, leaving a seemingly raw mysterious emotion at the end in a similar fashion to the end of "The Idea of Order at Key West." By taking away the convenient trope, Stevens creates a new language of desire that seems a little closer to a bare naked self. This de-troped language differs from the pathetic fallacy of romantic Naturalism, which interprets spiritual messages in the landscape rather than in the speaker's emotions. Fewer foils mean fewer fools.

> The truth is that there comes a time
> When we can mourn no more over music
> That is so much motionless sound.
>
> There comes a time when the waltz
> Is no longer a mode of desire, a mode
> Of revealing desire and is empty of shadows.   (*CP* 121)

"Sad Strains of a Gay Waltz" acknowledges that dancing to music with a partner, the way romantic poetry does with its tropes, no longer satisfies the genre of poetry or the spirit of the 1930s:

> Too many waltzes have ended. Yet the shapes
> For which the voices cry, these, too, may be
> Modes of desire, modes of revealing desire.
>
> Too many waltzes—The epic of disbelief
> Blares oftener and soon, will soon be constant.
> Some harmonious skeptic soon in a skeptical music
>
> Will unite these figures of men and their shapes
> Will glisten again with motion, the music
> Will be motion and full of shadows.   (*CP* 122)

The voices are from "these sudden mobs of men / . . . An immense suppression, freed, / These voices crying without knowing for what." In these lines Stevens makes room for the poet of the future, whose responsibility is to represent and inspire the masses. The question remains as to whether Stevens fears or wants to be the "harmonious skeptic." "Mozart, 1935" answers: "Be thou the voice, / Not you. Be thou, be thou / The voice of angry fear, / The voice of this besieging pain" (*CP* 132). Since the Mozart of 1935 is described as the poet, when Stevens writes "Not you," he neglects self-indulgence in favor of his newfound public voice.[30]

The next poem of the volume, "Dance of the Macabre Mice," picks up where "Sad Strains of a Gay Waltz" left off:

> In the land of turkeys in turkey weather
> At the base of the statue, we go round and round.
> What a beautiful history, beautiful surprise!
> Monsieur is on horseback. The horse is covered with mice.
>
> (*CP* 123)

The thanksgiving feast has turned into circular foraging in this poem of the thirties. Still going "round on a crutch," Stevens is now part of a communal enterprise circumnavigating the American legacy. "Monsieur," the forefather of French revolutionary tradition, is later described as "The Founder of the State." Admiring the beauty of the stat(u)e, the subjective mice read the inscription, and dance on the sword that "founded / A state that was free, in the dead of winter, from mice?" The mice-like citizens foraging on the statue were once the prey that fed the nation. The poem quite clearly posits the rodent masses as ironically evil prey up against the patriotic "arm of bronze outstretched against all evil!"

This statue poem is an early instance of Stevens' anti-nationalism, as it is expressed in opposition to a monument representing the fixture of a warring state. The statue is used by Stevens as an artifact impervious to the changing needs of the people, who are therefore dehumanized, here in the form of mice. The fascist state art in this poem, and the disharmony of the romantic waltz of poetry in "Sad Strains" together represent two forces that speak of how far out of touch art has become, and the need for civic revitalization. These exemplary poems provide an ideology similar to the larger project of *Owl's Clover*, which observes the disjunctions of citizen and state due to ineffectual arts and politics. Litz notes that several of the political poems in *Ideas of Order* were written after *Owl's Clover*, or were editions of it: "Stevens began work on *Owl's Clover*, which he once thought of calling *Aphorisms of Society*, in the spring of 1935, and some poems published after that time—such as "Mozart, 1935" and "Dance of the Macabre Mice"—reflect his growing concern with the place of poetry in society."[31] Having sampled these small poems, I will now turn to *Owl's Clover*, in which Stevens meets "the pressure of the contemporaneous" in a poetry composed of contrasting rhetorics.

Chapter 3

Owl's Clover I & II: "How clearly that would be defined!"

S tevens cites "the pressure of the contemporaneous" as the impetus for writing *Owl's Clover*. His deconstruction of romantic poetry and culture in *Ideas of Order* develops into an investigation into the political shape of America in response to the Depression of the 1930s. The primary antagonist in this long poem is the Statue figure, which Stevens calls a "variable symbol." The critic Robert Emmett Monroe calls the symbols of *Owl's Clover* "variously interpretable figural emblems" (*Wallace Stevens Journal* 13:2, 136). While I agree with this label, for the sake of concision I shall call them *tropes,* which I consider to be thematic domains made up of similar figures. This terminological niggling is necessary because Stevens explores the referential capacity of tropes: they are topics of discussion and demonstrative forms in the poetry. In terms of the Statue, this form of inquiry makes sense because the Statue is precisely what Stevens wants to excavate in this long poem.

As a monument, the Statue is a solid, fixed form of representation. It is a rigid masculine art form that is supposed to withstand change. As such, it stands counter to Stevens' poetics of flux. Stevens therefore situates the Statue in contexts that reveal its exclusionary aesthetic. When you look up at a monument, you can't argue with it. In order to unearth the Statue from its solid ground, Stevens deconstructs its imposing authority by mythologizing or rhetorizing its functions as a social art form.

I suggest Stevens questions the creativity of masculine monumentality by exposing the polemics involved in such creations. This polarization between creation and argument is my major focus in this chapter. I see Stevens portraying Statues rhetorically in order to get at the types of persuasion they reveal—psychological, social, political. For example, in the first poem of *Owl's Clover,* "The Old Woman and the Statue," we read about a Statue of glorious horses in a park, which has at its feet a destitute Old Woman. Stevens interweaves representations of the Statue itself, the motivations of the sculptor, and the estrangement of the Old Woman.

In conflating creation and argument, Stevens' rhetorical poetry brings up the issue of the state (Statue) versus the individual, and subsequent concerns about state power as they are solidified in the romance and rhetoric of the Statue. *Owl's Clover* employs the Statue to bring together romance and rhetoric, creativity and argument in a forceful aesthetic that is criticized because it excludes the public from the state artifact. Much of this exclusion, according to Stevens' poetics, is due to how monumental aesthetics alienate viewers from creative process. The next two chapters on *Owl's Clover* will investigate how Stevens deconstructs the monumentality of the Statue trope in order to posit an alternative aesthetic process. Stevens uses the Statue trope because it is civic and monumental. Its supposedly democratic park context is appropriate for Stevens' critique of the Statue's antidemocratic marginalization of the Old Woman.

But first this axis of creation and argument needs further clarification. While it is a polarity that is consistently imploded by Stevens' rhetorical poetry, creation and argument also align with two types of literary criticism. To simplify, twentieth-century critics have tended to analyze literature either formally or polemically. Criticism on Stevens has been dominated by formalists such as Pearce, Riddel, Vendler, and Bloom, who find a great literary and ontological playground in the poetry. Since the poststructuralism of the 1980s, critics have increasingly explored the social contexts of his poetry. Jacqueline Vaught Brogan and Melita Schaum advance the limitless subject of "Stevens and Women" (*Wallace Stevens Journal* 12:2), while James Longenbach and Alan Filreis have written books on "Stevens and Politics" since the fall 1989 *Wallace Stevens Journal* issue of that title.[1]

My argument in this chapter derives from the way in which the poem's performance anticipates, sustains, outlives critical developments from formalism to poststructuralism and recent historical research into Stevens' politics. Socio-historical work tends to produce polemical argument, whereas formalism emphasizes aesthetic creation. This division is the central point of contention in Filreis's argument with Riddel, whom Filreis quotes within:

> But this is just the opposite of what critics have habitually cited as the bad "rhetoric which often resulted when he tried to argue rather than create,"

for in my view, Stevens was trying to "create" here when he should have been arguing.[2]

Filreis, writing with a historical zeal for fact and argument, sees Stevens fall short "*only* when he fails to name or characterize the opposition as belonging to the world of political rhetoric" (*Modernism* 229). In other words, Filreis sees Stevens providing too much aesthetic figuration in lieu of a transparent literal rebuttal. The critical extremes of Riddel and Filreis both want the poetry to do something it refuses to do. I suggest that their opposition of creation and argument, romanticism and rhetoric, is a false division: the point of *Owl's Clover* is to conflate this polarity.[3] This dualism between these critics is a paradigm that I am extrapolating for my argument. As much as I think Filreis overdetermines Stevens' polemics, his scholarship has proven indispensable to me. Filreis makes the point before I do later in this chapter that Stevens and Marxist critic Stanley Burnshaw "propose continual inter-ideological struggle as a model for negotiating opposing positions *that are themselves shifting*" (221). But where Filreis sees political wavering as somewhat of a liability, my point is that Stevens problematizes firm positionhood itself, which Filreis strives to find in Stevens' politics.

Filreis cites Merle Brown, Frank Kermode, and Harold Bloom as three of many critics who describe *Owl's Clover* respectively as a "major betrayal of poetic genius," "an almost total failure," and "incontrovertibly Stevens' poorest performance" (229). In *Poetry, Word-play and Word-war,* Eleanor Cook states: "*Ideas of Order* includes a troubled impulse to speak to and for a society. Stevens is still working this out, and a false path led him to experiment with social satire, here and in *Owl's Clover.* It was a dead end" (119–20). She views *Owl's Clover* as a departure from the literary to the social, which it is, but she sees "social satire" as a cul-de-sac rather than Stevens' increasingly present confrontation with the pressure of contemporary reality. Critical fuel for the rejection of *Owl's Clover* has been supplied by Stevens' act of editing out many satirical passages within a year of its first publication, which cuts away much of its polemic. I suggest that Stevens' retractions were caused by its poor critical reception, which Cook's words encapsulate. However, there are many reasons for these reactions; primary among them is the poem's challenge to critical divisions. While I have named critics of the past 30 years, the resistance was similar in the 1930s, which the poem directly addresses.

While Stevens' conflation of creation and argument in the poem primarily works to criticize the monumentalist aesthetic embodied in the

Statue, I suggest that the aforementioned critical paradigm is harbored in the poem itself, largely as a result of literary culture in the 1930s. It seems as though I'm creating an allegory of the Statue as a monument of criticism. While I don't think this is quite the case, it cannot be accidental that when Stevens criticizes monumental art, he criticizes monolithic criticism. The second section, "Mr. Burnshaw and the Statue," takes on Stanley Burnshaw's Marxist criticism for being a left-wing version of monumentalism (usually associated with the State). Stevens projects Burnshaw's *"To Be Itself"* Marxism as an automatic unyielding aesthetic that is as rigid as the state it aims to destroy. Stevens aims at cracking binary oppositions in criticism and politics. Burnshaw's review of *Ideas of Order* was entitled "Turmoil in Middle Ground," implying the poet's political wavering. But Stevens' middle ground is much more subversive than either side might be: the poet suggests that the whole cultural system, the manner of thinking about ideology, is restricted by the automatic, defaulting, and exclusionary choices made by artists, critics, and politicians who operate according to monumental paradigms.

In addition to the harsh criticism that led Stevens to edit *Owl's Clover,* the changes to the 1937 edition could have been motivated by any number of reasons. In a letter he stated that passages were cut "for the purposes of making it clearer" (*L* 322). But what was opaque about it? I suggest that Stevens was compelled to make it clearer because the poem challenges literary critics to completely rethink their modes of operation. The critics' reservations are due to a divisive taxonomy in the critical tradition that classifies artistic creativity separately from rhetorical argument. *Owl's Clover* presents the critic with a rhetorical poetry that reveals art, especially elite monumental art (signified by the Statue), as a stronghold of power. As we will soon see, Stevens' poetry demonstrates the effects of power, which can be confusing because the poetry's ironic manipulation can be viewed as straightforward persuasion. Most of the transcendences and crystallizations in *Owl's Clover* are used rhetorically to parody the very forms they produce. Each of the poem's five sections create oppositional arguments, which the poem's rhetorical voices show to be interrelated: all forms of persuasion, belief, art, truth are governed by "Impassioned seducers and seduced." The poetry's rhetoric cleaves together oppressive forces and the human degradations that result. The emotional weight of *Owl's Clover* is completely entangled in political forces. All creative representations (in the poem, in the world) serve argumentative, influential, or coercive purposes. By displaying the seductions at work in the state, ideology, religion, poetry, and history, Stevens deconstructs these apparati, showing that their stabilities and fallibilities are a measure of human force, energy in motion, popular momentum. All of these vectors are directed by language, and as such, the poem theorizes language at work, in practice.

The deconstructions Stevens performs in *Owl's Clover* may not sound improbable or alien to readers familiar with Derrida, or with Foucault's theories of historical institutions. But we have to remember that in the thirties, New Critics viewed poems as self-contained organisms. Stevens' readers were especially accustomed to the *pure* poetry of *Harmonium,* a volume in which French stylistics influenced readers to see a Symbolist legacy. The French presences in the poems, their ornamentation, and Stevens' reputation as a dandy projected an image of high art that overpowered the subversions occurring in the poems themselves. For instance, "Thirteen Ways of Looking at a Blackbird" is an Imagist poem that, through its structural flattening of imagined symbolic wholes, argued against a totalizing, autonomous artform. *Ideas of Order* more systematically demystifies much of the organicism that evolved through Symbolisme and the New Critics.[4] But *Ideas of Order* was still measured against the earlier achievement, as Howard Baker's 1935 reading of "Key West" testifies: "This obviously is dipped from the same clear spring from which *Harmonium* came."[5] The contemporary critical culture was not conducive to a poet who "wanted to deal with . . . reality, actuality, the contemporaneous," (*OP* 219) especially when the poetry rhetoricized political, historical, and literary systems all at once.

From Stevens' letters during the time of *Owl's Clover*'s composition and publication we can observe the huge challenge his poetry faced, and forwarded. These letters indicate a fully determined, confident poet who knows he is breaking new but difficult ground: "The book sets a standard. It is easy enough to accept a wellmade book without realizing how much has gone into it" (*L* 312). For instance, the second poem of *Owl's Clover,* "Mr. Burnshaw and the Statue," treads dangerously between leftist politics and aesthetics. Responding to the question of his publisher, Ronald Lane Latimer, who asked "whether there is an essential conflict between Marxism and the sentiment of the marvelous," Stevens writes:

> Marxism may or may not destroy the existing sentiment of the marvelous; if it does, it will create another. It was a very common fear that Socialism would dirty the world; it is an equally common fear that Communism will do the same thing. I think that this is all nonsense. . . . It is an extraordinary experience for myself to deal with a thing like Communism; it is like dealing with the Democratic platform, or the provisions of the Frazier-Lemke

bill. Nevertheless, one has to live and think in the actual world, and no other will do, and that is why MR. BURNSHAW, etc. has taken a good deal of time. (*L* 292)

And although Stevens said "I don't think I shall have any trouble with the other two" poems that follow in *Owl's Clover,* three months later he tells Latimer about toiling over what would become "The Greenest Continent":

> I think I shall have to leave the STATUE IN AFRICA for a bit. I am head over heels in the thing. The specific subject is, I suppose, the white man in Africa. But it may be that no one will ever realize that. What I have been trying to do in the thing is to apply my own poetry to such a subject. (*L* 308)

These poems of *Owl's Clover* are essential to the rest of Stevens' work because they are his most ambitious efforts at fusing the actual world with his poetry. They also provide Stevens' biggest challenges to American culture. *Harmonium* established a poetics, *Ideas of Order* negotiated his poetics within and without the lyric conventions that Stevens wanted to shape for the future, and *Owl's Clover* integrated social politics of the 1930s in a critical developing poetics.

I often use the word "rhetoric" to describe the techniques in *Owl's Clover* that enable the poetry to annul the critical differentiations of *creation* and *argument.* The historical varieties of rhetorical theory are plentiful, yet many theorists of rhetoric speak of the issues Stevens confronts. Gayatri Spivak offers a contemporary view that replicates Stevens' momentous historical accomplishment in *Owl's Clover:* "In the guise of a post-Marxist description of the scene of power, we thus encounter a much older debate: between representation or rhetoric as tropology and as persuasion" (Williams and Chrisman, 71). Paul de Man's theory of "rhetoricity" coalesces Spivak's two rhetorics by showing that (especially modern) literature's tropes often display their contextual manipulations. Similarly, *Owl's Clover* demonstrates how tropes persuade, and how persuasion tropes (how creations are arguments, and how arguments are creative tropes). Stevens' tropes are shown to be argumentative because they are placed in affecting contexts, such as the Statue's marginalization of the Old Woman. By examining how Stevens' rhetorical poetry of the 1930s inscribes difference (in viewpoints, in significations), we can see the importance of integrating literature within its worldly contexts.

Jane Tompkins wrote about literature's necessary rhetorical function in social politics in her 1980 chronicle of literary criticism, *Reader-Response Criticism*. She reminds us, as does Kenneth Burke through Aristotle, of the Greek origins to which poststructuralism returns:

> The insistence that language is constitutive of reality rather than merely reflective of it suggests that contemporary critical theory has come to occupy a position very similar to, if not the same as, that of the Greek rhetoricians for whom mastery of language meant mastery of state. The questions that propose themselves within this critical framework therefore concern, broadly, the relations of discourse and power. (226)

Tompkins finishes her essay by stating that the "perception of language as a form of power . . . so far has been confined almost entirely to the level of theory in contemporary writing, [which] constitutes the real break with formalism and promises the most for criticism's future" (226). With hindsight, we can see how much literature since 1980 has fulfilled that theoretical challenge. American poets such as John Ashbery, A. R. Ammons, and the Language Poets have engaged language theoretically and as a source of power, as has the postmodern fiction of writers such as Maxine Hong Kingston, Michael Ondaatje, Daphne Marlatt, and Jeanette Winterson. Living with this contemporary literature makes a reevaluation of Stevens' rhetorical poetry all the more possible and timely.

Reevaluation has been the order of twentieth-century literary criticism, and so it is not surprising that Stevens and Burke become more comprehensible with poststructuralism. In Michael Beehler's *T. S. Eliot, Wallace Stevens, and the Discourses of Difference,* we can observe how Stevens' rhetorical deconstruction of exclusive categories resonates in Beehler's language of semiotics:

> A sign, therefore, signifies neither presence nor absence—it does not represent something as such—but is rather the residue of this original and sustaining differentiating *force*. A sign is, as "Description without Place" suggests, neither "The thing described, nor false facsimile," but an "artificial thing that exists . . ." (60).

Beehler's language of "sign, presence and absence" can be linked with rhetoric, persuasion and tropology. The sign, like rhetoric, does not carry vertical or divinely sought assumptions of permanence, as would a symbol. The "force" Beehler describes is language in motion, rhetoric's *particular* effect (I find it useful to keep in mind particle physics when thinking of semiotics—theories of signs in motion; I will return to this later). Beehler cites "Description without Place" as a poem that works through/between the dialectic of argument and creation. He is right: that poem from 1947 clearly exemplifies the theory that 1936's *Owl's Clover* sets out as a contemporary subject and metanarrative. I will return to Stevens' later assertion that "The theory of description matters most" in the fifth chapter.

The challenge of this rhetorical theory is that in order to support both *persuasion* and *tropology,* the poetry (and my analysis) must maintain the literal references of persuasion, and the figural tropes (imagination, creativity): real and make-believe. It sounds like a burden, trying to carry actual and imaginary at once, but the trick that Stevens shows us is that you only need one hand. Each "real" thing moves by the power of tropic persuasion. Each "imaginary" thing has "real" persuasive results in action. Part and parcel coexist. Imaginative connotations cannot be disengaged from literal words, just as McLuhan taught us that messages cannot be removed from media.

In art history, creative tropes and actual persuasion have been kept apart because of a belief that time could stand still; that art objects could be monumentalized for eternity; that art had a political neutrality devoid of social power; that there was an official form of representation. The fixity of monumental art preserves itself through time so that art becomes immortal without regard to the social context of its creation or its reception. The artist's power to create, whatever his or her political context, becomes, through immortalization, a free-floating transcendent vision, a divine angel with no ground. Early twentieth-century criticism, with T. S. Eliot at its center, claimed this elite power as universal and objective, thereby ignoring social relations and those excluded. In denying social space, and claiming a monumental time scheme, art was still and omnipresent. The difference that Stevens' rhetorical poetry affords is that every presentation moves and collides with surrounding phenomena. Quantum physics is a good model to keep in mind, as Lisa Steinman has shown in *Made in America: Science, Technology and American Modernist Poets,* as has Dana Wilde in "Wallace Stevens, Modern Physics, and Wholeness."[6] If readers can get out of the trappings of stillness, and instead read words in particular collision—"The world is a force, not a presence" (*OP* 198)— then creation and argument will inseparably be rhetoric in motion.

Turning to "The Old Woman and the Statue," as we read this first poem in *Owl's Clover,* we will look for ways in which the poetry works rhetorically; how contemporaneity is inscribed within its conflation of creation and argument; and how, in this operation, this false opposition is deconstructed.

The first two sections of "The Old Woman and the Statue" present the Statue glorifying its park environment:

> Another evening in another park,
> A group of marble horses rose on wings
> In the midst of a circle of trees, from which the leaves
> Raced with the horses in bright hurricanes.   (*OP* 75)

Notice how the repetitive banality of the first line is contrasted with the upward transcendence of the Statue. Yet the immortal horses compete with the moving leaves, which figuratively outrun the horses by achieving metaphorical transformation "in bright hurricanes." In part ii, Stevens presents a similar aesthetic in the context of the artist:

> So much the sculptor had foreseen: autumn,
> The sky above the plaza widening
> Before the horses, clouds of bronze imposed
> On clouds of gold, and green engulfing bronze,
> The marble leaping in the storms of light.
> So much he had devised: white forelegs taut
> To the muscles' very tip for the vivid plunge . . .   (*OP* 75)

The repetitive awe expressed toward the creation is hyperbolic, and I suggest ironic, because the violence of the Statue's form is contrasted with the vulnerable Old Woman:

> But her he had not foreseen: the bitter mind
> In a flapping cloak.
> . . . .
> The golden clouds that turned to bronze, the sounds
> Descending, did not touch her eye and left
> Her ear unmoved. She was that tortured one,
> So destitute that nothing but herself
> Remained and nothing of herself except
> A fear too naked for her shadow's shape.   (*OP* 76)

The heroic image of the Statue may generate glory in the park as far as the sculptor is concerned, but the Old Woman is "tortured," standing underneath the trampling horse hoofs. "[H]er shadow's shape" is even too much. Since her "fear [is] too naked for her shadow's shape," then that fear is certainly too naked for the gloriously sublime Statue. However, Stevens' depiction of her "naked" resistance to images is itself a form of representation, as we see in section iv:

> The mass of stone collapsed to marble hulk,
> Stood stiffly, as if the black of what she thought
> Conflicting with the moving colors there
> Changed them
> . . . .
> And looking at the place in which she walked,
> As a place in which each thing was motionless
> Except the thing she felt but did not know. (*OP* 76–77)

The dynamic glory of the Statue is overpowered by the poet's witness of the Old Woman's destructive resistance. Although she lacks a creative monument to signify her condition, she willfully requires creative representation. The Statue as a public artifact misrepresents her, forcing her to counter it with a resistance of her own that destroys the hardened marble. Stevens' Old Woman is a figure capable of doing away with ineffectual stately material. In so doing, her condition acts as an argument against the impervious stasis of a monument, and in its destruction we find the beginning of a creative representation for the thirties. Her problem as a character, the reason she is fearfully vulnerable, is that she lacks an objective correlative in her environment to act as a symbol. Even though her represented resistance is precarious, the Old Woman works for Stevens as an emblem of revolt. She is not represented; the park makes her destitute: in this relation we see a depressed citizen of the thirties neglected by the state. Stevens creates a portrait of social force, not pity, and thus begins to question the public climate in America.

In "The Irrational Element in Poetry," Stevens claims that she is representative of both the poet and citizen in contemporaneous society:

> To be specific, I wanted to apply my own sensibility to something perfectly matter-of-fact. The result would be a disclosure of my own sensibility or individuality, as I called it a moment ago, certainly to myself. The poem is called "The Old Woman and the Statue." The Old Woman is a symbol of those who suffered during the depression. . . . (*OP* 226)

The poem's insistence on the absence of objective correlation for the Old Woman in the public sphere is the symbolic order here. The fact that she feels shut out from the Statuesque park, and mentally destroys it, is the poem's symbology. "[T]he thing she felt but did not know" is both the emotion that aesthetically resists the Statue, and it is Stevens' poem. Her representation does not partake in the established symbolic order of the park, and as such she hollows out the park's dominant order. No wonder readers had a hard time with this poem. Stevens was mostly known as a hedonistic dandy, and here his symbolic subject of the thirties is a destitute Old Woman. *Harmonium* established a poetry of bright presence, but here is a poem that undermines presence by showing how presence overrides (false) absence. The Old Woman's unfulfillment is the energy driving the argument of the poem. However, if we interpret the question about "Key West's" muse, "Whose spirit is this?" as a deconstruction of that traditional trope, we can view the Old Woman as a more solid trope that begins to answer the question. This "spirit" was a variable symbol there, as it is here, but the paramour with the "empty sleeves" had been bid farewell until the poet found a "harridan self" for the "maladive" thirties.

The fifth canto presents the Old Woman and the Statue in climactic discord:

> Without her, evening like a budding yew
> Would soon be *brilliant,* as it was, before
> The harridan self and ever-maladive fate
> Went crying their desolate syllables, before
> Their voice and the voice of the tortured wind were one,
> Each voice within the other, seeming one,
> Crying against a need that pressed like cold,
> Deadly and deep. *It* would become a yew
> Grown great and grave beyond imagined trees
>
> > (*OP* 77; my emphasis)

Here the two opposing tropic paradigms are set in strong rhetorical argument. She is the destroyer of lyrical "brillian[ce]," which could make this poem a rhetoric of mourning if words like "harridan" and "desolate syllables" are read spitefully (as you would if you were a brilliant evening). However, "harridan" is a seventeenth-century word for *old horse,* which is likely a joke further juxtaposing the Old Woman stubbornly with the Statue's aggressive horses. And "a budding yew" is a "tree often planted in churchyards," (*OED)* thus possessing a foreboding quality undercutting its brilliance. Also, her self and fate have found some "syllables" that are voiced together with the "tortured wind." In section iii she was the "tortured one," but here she and the weather unite as a mighty force of chaotic flux resisting "brilliant" aesthetic control. They "press back against reality," which is determined by the dominating park symbology.

The strength of the Old Woman and the weather is combated by the sudden introduction of the impersonal pronoun "It," which develops the "brilliant" transcendence that she ruins. The dark park evening acquires an inhuman momentum; "It" gains exclusionary force in this public space, even adorning romantic properties characteristic of Yeatsian apocalypse:

> Branching through heavens heavy with the sheen
> And shadowy hanging of it, thick with stars
> Of a lunar light, dark-belted sorcerers
> Dazzling by simplest beams and soothly still,
> The space beneath it still, a smooth domain,
> Untroubled by suffering, which fate assigns
> To the moment. There the horses would rise again,
> Yet hardly to be seen and again the legs
> Would flash in air, and the muscular bodies thrust
> Hoofs grinding against the stubborn earth, until
> The light wings lifted through the crystal space
> Of night. How clearly that would be defined!   (*OP* 77–8)

The presentation of this glory recuperates the voice of the sculptor, the scene's arranger. Yet this thick problematic triumph has been read by Filreis as representative of Stevens' view or position as being "Untroubled by suffering":

> The final point raised against the Old Woman's argument is based on a bold, basic rhetorical confusion: It is both post-revolutionary and conservative, "Untroubled" at turns because trouble has passed and because the speaker is impervious to "suffering." (Filreis, *Modernism* 225)

But Stevens ironically enacts the poet's stance in a hyperbole of sublime rhetoric in order to denounce the romantic transcendence that neglects her. The gratuitous exclamation of the last line signals romantic victory in a Tennysonian lather that runs against Stevens' whole poetic (which, as one of Stevens' progeny, A. R. Ammons says, never "runs to that easy victory"). That sculpting urge to define demands symbolic totality stubbornly impervious to flux; to the changing human condition of the thirties represented by the Old Woman. If Stevens has to be stationed in the poem, he would side with the Old Woman because of her prominent role as a symbol for the thirties, and because the irony in the above passage parodies the romantic aesthetic that is impervious to "suffering."

Filreis claims that in the last line's definition "the Statue can be reinstated, stronger than ever in making claims on the imagination . . ." (Filreis 227). I argue that the romantic, high-literary verse is hyperbolically undercut with irony. The word "brilliant" is used in a later poem, "Prologues to What is Possible," in the same way, this time to undercut a ship captain's ignorant immanence:

> The boat was built of stones that had lost their weight and being no
>   longer heavy
> Had left in them only a *brilliance,* of unaccustomed origin,
> So that he that stood up in the boat leaning and looking before him
> Did not pass like someone voyaging out of and beyond the familiar.
> He belonged to the far-foreign departure of his vessel and was part
>   of it,
> Part of the speculum of fire on its prow, its symbol, whatever it
>   was. . . .   (*CP* 515–16)

The transcendent "brilliance" carries a muddled grandiosity attributed to the poem's subject, the captain, who symbolically identifies with the synecdochic "speculum of fire on its prow" (*CP* 516). The subject's monumentalism is generated in a head-swelling mash of identities resembling the swirling fatalism closing "The Old Woman and the Statue." However, "The Old Woman" resists the definition that the Statue's apocalyptic vision provides: both poems exhibit artforms that, shutting out the vitality of the poems' subjects, are thus dramatized by Stevens as socially elite, exclusive art.

"Mr. Burnshaw and the Statue" further conflates binary oppositions of stasis and flux, creation and argument, while bringing art and politics to the forefront of its performance. Stanley Burnshaw wrote a review of *Ideas of Order* entitled "Turmoil in the Middle Ground" for the leftist journal *New Masses.* The writing is full of an ideologue's assurance, as in these sentences that represent the gist of the review: "*Ideas of Order* is the record of a man who, having lost his footing, now scrambles to stand up and keep his balance. . . . Will Stevens sweep his contradictory notions into a valid Idea of Order?"[7] The very singlemindedness with which Burnshaw measures Stevens' "contradictory notions" becomes the object of Stevens' rhetorical inquiry in "Mr. Burnshaw and the Statue." To say, however, that Stevens uses the poem chiefly as a retort to Burnshaw would be a mistake. Like "The Old Woman," "Mr. Burnshaw" is a construct for a contemporary predicament. As a political reviewer evaluating poetry, Burnshaw's position is tenuous. The assertion of a firm political stance in relation to art, the notion that politics can somehow address art in a nonaesthetic manner, is the subject addressed and parodied in the poem. A romantic civic monument in "The Old Woman and the Statue," the Statue's symbology is varied in "Burnshaw" to become a Marxist icon. By reversing the Statue from state artifact to subversive icon, Stevens reverses his ideological critique, while parodying the supposition of automatic representability in both instances.

Following the preceding poem's exuberant closure, "How clearly that would be defined!," "Mr. Burnshaw and the Statue" begins:

> The thing is dead . . . Everything is dead
> Except the future. Always everything
> That is is dead except what ought to be.
> All things destroy themselves or are destroyed.   (*OP* 78)

The contrasting tones between this grounded opening and the "brilliant" termination of "The Old Woman" are no accident. All "[t]hat is is dead except what ought to be" does not mourn the past as the only thing worthy of life; "what ought to be" speaks of the ideal future exempt from death because it is becoming. This theory of change is compatible with the Marxism of Mr. Burnshaw. Understandably, Filreis writes that the "voice of section i, belong[s] undoubtedly to the 'Mr. Burnshaw' of the title. . . ." Yet the ideas and rhetoric are characteristically Stevensian. There are no quotation marks, italics, or ironies suggesting an alternative speaker. These four lines represent Stevens' theory of flux, which also applies to his employment of symbols: they are temporary representations that die the moment they attain fixity; once named, they are no longer living in change. Stevens finds middle ground with Burnshaw, the writer of "Turmoil in the Middle Ground," by incorporating a Marxist politic into his poetics of change.

By this I do not mean that the poem is a diplomatic gesture. Instead I suggest that this poem continues to problematize the notion of fixed symbolic identity that was at work in both the Old Woman and the Statue figures. Much of the criticism on "Mr. Burnshaw and the Statue" works to locate variant voices of Stevens and Burnshaw in the poem. Critics as far apart as Hi Simons and Alan Filreis have discussed the whereabouts of the voices of Stevens and Burnshaw according to stanzas. While these station-ings make for good argument and activate the poem within the political history of the 1930s, the idea of autonomous voice within mass social movement is being parodied here. Since Stevens is *responding* to a leftist reviewer, the critical urge is to ground the poem within the actual circumstances that surround it. However, if Stevens wanted merely to argue with Mr. Burnshaw, he would have found a more direct way, such as in one of the many letters Stevens wrote to him. Stevens was stimulated by the predicament posed by the critic. Just as the Old Woman functioned as a symbol of the depression, Mr. Burnshaw's leftist involvement as a poet, editor, and reviewer represented the social implications of poetry's confluence with politics. The poem enacts its predicament, and in so doing uses Burnshaw and the Statue as paradigms for the social critique then required.

The challenge for Stevens is to relocate poetry in this demanding time. He invokes the age-old agents of inspiration, the muses:

> Come, all celestial paramours,
> Whether in-dwelling haughty clouds, frigid
> And crisply musical, or holy caverns temple-toned,
> Entwine your arms and moving to and fro,
> Now like a ballet infantine in awkward steps,
> Chant sibilant requiems for this effigy.   (*OP* 79)

Where "The Idea of Order at Key West" emptied its muse from the newly ordered trope of mysterious spirit, here Stevens saturates the muses, demanding their trope be the thickest of containers for the present. This second section loads reverent ornaments hyperbolically, building irony as the poem continues:

> Bring down from nowhere nothing's wax-like blooms,
> Calling them what you will but loosely-named
> In a mortal lullaby, like porcelain.

Indeed, transcendence is monumentalized here and in the subsequent vision of a perfectly present Platonic apple, until the section's final line quells any doubts about irony: "But this gawky plaster will not be here" (*OP* 79). So the Statue's enduring material representation of transcendent ambitions is denied. However, the poet continues ironically to load the muses as collective bodies of poetic tradition. But before full comment or resolution can be made, before the poem makes definition of the present, section iii moves to the future:

> The stones
> That will replace it [the Statue] shall be carved, *"The Mass*
> *Appoints These Marbles Of Itself To Be*
> *Itself."* No more than that, no subterfuge,
> No memorable muffing, bare and blunt.   (*OP* 80)

This hyperbole of Marxist definition is juxtaposed against the excessive celestial rhetoric of transcendence accorded to the paramours. Stevens answers Burnshaw's request for direct commentary on the real by hoisting up another monument. The ridicule of the inscription is derived from its simple nominalism, the most direct approach of all. Stevens' irony works through the pomp and circumstance of this *"Mass"* appointment, which is itself because it says it is. No genesis, no subjective qualification, no desire in this mass rhetoric, just definition—which Stevens also offered ironically at the visionary end of "The Old Woman and the Statue." In both cases, aesthetic definition of the present hyperbolically reveals the utopias that each aesthetic relies upon, thereby creating parody. While "The Old Woman" faces an apocalyptic romanticism at the foot of the Statue, the Marxist mass inscription itself is utopic, even in its efforts to deny idealistic aesthetics. Stevens is not criticizing communism itself, but the demand for an aesthetic of automatic fixed identity; the demand for mimetic realism.

Continuing the dialectic, section iv is addressed to "Mesdames," and this is where the poetic voice becomes more pensive now that the rhetorical parameters have been drawn. Section iii's Marxist rhetoric that is automatic for the people is contrasted here:

> IV
> Mesdames, one might believe that Shelley lies
> Less in the stars than in their earthy wake,
> Since the radiant disclosures that you make
> Are of an eternal vista, manque and gold
> And brown, an Italy of the mind, a place
> Of fear before the disorder of the strange
> A time in which the poets' politics
> Will rule in a poets' world. . . .   (*OP* 80)

The "Mesdames" trope shakes up the aesthetic stereotypes of the thirties. It is difficult to identify exactly who "Mesdames" are. They're certainly addressees of this poem, in this case a crowd of Shelley enthusiasts, who therefore are familiar with his "Defence of Poetry" credo, "poets are the unacknowledged legislators of the world." Since legislative power is at issue

in this poem, it follows that the Marxists' automatic nominalism is drawn
into this "Mesdames" section following the above quoted lines. Nevertheless, the Shelleyan music opposes the "bare, blunt" rhetoric of *To Be Itself*
Marxism, so that Stevens conflates these apparently disparate aesthetics in
"Mesdames." On November 26, 1935, after writing "Mr. Burnshaw and the
Statue" but still to write the rest of *Owl's Clover,* Stevens explains his musical thinking (likely in reference to "Mesdames") to his publisher, Latimer:

> The music of poetry which creates its own fictions is one of the "sisterhood
> of the living dead" [*CP* 87]. It is a muse: all of the muses are of that sister-
> hood. But then I cannot say, at this distance of time, that I specifically meant
> the muses; this is just an explanation. I don't think that I meant anything def-
> initely except all the things that live in memory and imagination. (*L* 297)

Since the muses are "just an explanation," the critic's task is to see what is
living in the "memory and imagination" of the poem's muses; that is, how
these paramours work as trope. I suggest that the variable "Mesdames"
include muses, Marxists, poets, readers—a veritable carnival. "Mesdames,"
as with the Old Woman and Mr. Burnshaw, is a "variable symbol," as
described in "The Irrational Element in Poetry." However, I find that the
word "symbol" does not account for the fluidity of these tropes, which
"collect in pools," as Stevens says of thought (*OP* 196).

The above letter's refusal to define the poet's muses is counterbalanced
by the more telling remark in a letter to Hi Simons that "Communism is
just a new romanticism" (*L* 351). Section iv synthesizes the Marxist-
romantic dialectic enforced by Burnshaw's review. One side of Stevens'
dialectic categorizes mystic paramours in flowing glorious rhetoric.
Opposing that are the Marxists, hard, "bare and blunt." Contrasting the
masculine mass marble inscription of section iii, the opening rhetoric of
section iv returns to an astral Shelley who is brought down to earth by
"Mesdames." The synthesis parodies both sides, as Shelley is paradoxically
grounded by their "eternal," "radiant disclosures." Stevens shows that an
apparent grounding of an idea can itself be a transcendent, "Italy of the
mind," which is a pejorative romanticism that Stevens otherwise proclaimed dead in "Anglais Mort à Florence." Here it is immediately followed by existential fear: "a place / Of fear before the disorder of the
strange." By conflating the romantic aesthetics of Shelley and Italy with
the naked fear of the thirties, Stevens suggests that any such projected
escapes from fear are romanticizations. Mr. Burnshaw's socialism, then, is
the sublime idealization of the thirties. Stevens goes so far as to say "Marx

has ruined Nature / For the moment" in "Botanist on an Alp (No. 1)."
Just like the Romantic ideal of Nature, the communist dream becomes a
monster trope projecting "A time in which the poets' politics / Will rule
in a poets' world." This sentence sentences Burnshaw and Stevens together
with "Mesdames." In with the muses under the "Mesdames" umbrella are
the Marxists and the poets, who all create politics out of loneliness, fear,
desperation, and idealism.

Stevens further complicates the poet's predicament:

> Yet that will be
> A world impossible for poets, who
> Complain and prophesy, in their complaints,
> And are never of the world in which they live.   (*OP* 80)

Stevens' critique is likely self-referential, and certainly directed at poet-
critic Burnshaw, as this letter attests in its reference to *New Masses,* the
locale of Burnshaw's review:

> MASSES is just one more wailing place and the whole left now-a-days is a
> mob of wailers. I do very much believe in leftism in every direction, even in
> wailing. These people go about it in such a way that nobody listens to them
> except themselves; and that is at least one reason why they get nowhere.
> They have the most magnificent cause in the world. (*L* 287)

As a response to the thirties, Stevens' poem supports the constructive (yet
harsh) criticism of that letter. In the poem's melding of socialism with
romance, progress inadvertently arises irregardless of the literati:

> Disclose the rude and ruddy at their jobs
> And if you weep for peacocks that are gone
> Or dance the death of doves, most sallowly,
> Who knows? The ploughman may not live alone . . .   (*OP* 80)

Despite his parody of Burnshaw's romantic socialism, Stevens optimistically
believes in change, except that he does not propose a plan:

> If ploughmen, peacocks, doves alike
> In vast disorder live in the ruins, free,
> The charts destroyed, even disorder may,
> So seen, have an order of its own, a peace
> Not now to be perceived yet order's own.   (*OP* 80)

Only by destroying the past's "charts," those ideals that navigated disaster, is there hope for a new order. Stevens displays an American anarchism here (still rampant today) that believes in the future (less likely now); a confidence that order will be recast from the ruins. This belief in inevitable change is what makes America so violent and bountifully productive; it is anti-conservative, as the wonderful poetry of section v illustrates:

> At some gigantic, solitary urn,
> A trash can at the end of the world, the dead
> Give up dead things and the living turn away.
> There buzzards pile their sticks among the bones
> Of buzzards and eat the bellies of the rich,
> Fat with a thousand butters, and the crows
> Sip the wild honey of the poor man's life,
> The blood of his bitter brain; and there the sun
> Shines without fire on columns intercrossed,
> White slapped on white, majestic, marble heads,
> Severed and tumbled into seedless grass,
> Motionless, knowing neither dew nor frost.   (*OP* 80–1)

These lines sound with both proletariat and bourgeois overtones, but there is no difference between the parasitism of either class's politics.

Stevens' view of change does not discriminate; it depends upon generations:

> The colorless light in which this wreckage lies
> Has faint, portentous lustres, shades and shapes
> Of rose, or what will once more rise to rose,
> When younger bodies, because they are younger, rise
> And chant the rose-points of their birth, and when
> For a little time, again, rose-breasted birds
> Sing rose-beliefs.   (*OP* 81)

"[R]ise to rose" parodies Christianity by drawing this rose from a "trash can at the end of the world," and so the cycle continues. Flux is signified by the singular vowel change in "rise to rose," which also changes from verb to noun, emphasizing a dynamic grammar (as we observed in "Key West"). The "rose-points of their birth" are similar to Eliot's "stillpoint of the turning world," except Stevens sets his image within moving chanting bodies. Stevens' hope is that the next generation will articulate itself fully, completely, in language and in body. However, within that hope, the repetition of "rose" nears absurdity, especially since it is gleaned from past wreckage. Generational cyclicality, "the pleasures of merely circulating," continually resurfaces in Stevens, and it is debatable whether there is more optimism or fatalism in these successive returns. Inevitablility is the point about change in Stevens' poetry; sometimes the consequences are disastrous, sometimes harmonious. In this case, the dynamic young bodies sound, appear, and are contextualized in harmonious flux. They jibe with Stevens' poetics, rather than force or forge a monumentally fixed aesthetic or situation. Consequently, the often ironic verse gives way to basic, easy moving, cyclical life. When Stevens breaks from irony, he often finishes poems with these optimistic life rhythms.

Stressing the reductive dialectics that this poem works to dispel, section v continues and ends with opposing energies that are transcendently immaterial in face of generational change:

> Above that urn two lights
> Commingle, not like the commingling of sun and moon
> At dawn, nor of summer-light and winter-light
> In an autumn afternoon, but two intense
> Reflections, whirling apart and wide away.   (*OP* 81)

These forces remain distanced "Reflections," and as intentionally vague as they are, their airiness is set against the natural marriages of "sun and moon / At dawn," "summer-light and winter-light" in autumn. These marriages, following the chanting "rose-points" above, receive fuller treatment in "Notes" and work into Stevens' poetics of generational change.

Within this section, the "two lights / Commingle," but not in a cycle of reproductive harmony. However, just as "Key West" proclaimed the sea was not a mask while summoning that mimetic relation, the negative denial represented by these lights is undermined by the positivity of the surrounding similes. I suggest these lights recall the dialectics of section iv, which contrasted, compared, and coalesced romance and socialism (muses and Marxists). As we will see shortly, section vi further corroborates this link with its repeated "whirling." Here in v, Stevens pejoratively contextualizes these contemporary energies as "Reflections, whirling apart and wide away." In doing so, he locates the positions of the poet and critic as "whirling apart." This disparate motion is not a true dialectic, although they "commingle" inadvertently together above the trash that they reflect. The natural generation of sun, moon, summer, and winter takes precedence over the differences of the two lights: they are made arbitrary by their distant abstract motion that fades away while natural cycles continue.

Part vi also addresses "Mesdames," and continues to emphasize change while retracing much of the poem's traveled ground. The recollection and acknowledgment of the political impasse between camps is "renamed a united front against stasis," as Filreis states (234). The "united front" consists of the romantic-socialist, poet-critic dialectic Stevens continues to quash. "Mesdames" face a potential enemy that ends up looking similar to themselves:

> Shall you [Mesdames],
> Then, fear a drastic community evolved
> From the whirling, slowly and by trial; or fear
> Men gathering for a mighty flight of men,
> An abysmal migration into a possible blue?   (*OP* 82)

The "whirling" of the two lights in section v continues here, including on one side the revolutionary "drastic community . . . whirling, slowly and by trial"; the other side of the semicolon presents an elite crew of artists who simultaneously evolve in formation. Burnshaw's review of *Ideas of Order* spoofs that the elites "have all tramped off to some escapist limbo where they are joyously gathering moonshine." Burnshaw's parody is not a criticism of Stevens; rather, he recognizes Stevens' potential to be, but avoidance from being a "cliche . . . of left-wing criticism. . . ."[8] In this sense, Burnshaw's rhetoric parodies stereotypical leftist rhetoric in a way that is similar to Stevens' technique in the poem. Stevens satirizes the cliché of escapism as a flight into the blue, which is his color of pure imagination, here contextualized within a masculine "abysmal migration." Further uniting these tropic communities is the twice mentioned "fear" of "mesdames." As an ironic "intelligence that endures," these muses mystically hover as a collective trope for everybody in the poem. They fear and include both the elite transcendent tradition of poetry as well as the contemporary revolutionaries. So the end of canto vi posits a rhetorically fearful either/or standoff for "mesdames," whose answer must be to fear neither and both.

Canto vii changes the poem's tenor from group synthesis to saturated confrontation. "Mesdames" become grassroots "damsels" circling the Statue in child-like defiance. If we recall the new generation chanting its "rose-points," then a link between youth, language, nature, and revolution would ascribe power to the future of the left. The poet asks the damsels to "cry,"

> This time, like damsels captured by the sky,
> Seized by that possible blue. Be maidens formed
> Of that most evasive hue of a lesser blue,
> Of the least appreciable shade of green
> And despicable shades of red, just seen,
> And vaguely to be seen, a matinal red. . . .   (*OP* 83)

Stevens' symbolism of color engages in a dance parodying its hierarchical representations. Pure "blue" is degraded to an earthy green, and finally "a matinal red," an adjective that the *OED* traces to the Church of England's morning prayer, and, alas, birdsong. As the damsels embody matinal religious innocence "[t]hat enter[s] day from night," red for Stevens is transversely a color of passionate "despicable" irritation. Here, red embodies the folky damsels, the socialist muses defacing state capital:

> Let your golden hands wave fastly and be gay
> And your braids bear brightening of crimson bands,
> Conceive that while you dance the Statue falls,
> The heads are severed, topple, tumble, tip
> In the soil and rest. Conceive that marble men
> Serenely selves, transfigured by the selves
> From which they came, make real the attitudes
> Appointed for them and that the pediment
> Bears words that are the speech of marble men.   (*OP* 83)

As the musical birdies turn into social revolutionaries, Stevens endorses their collective action. After imploding the dichotomy between the blue elites and the red scourges, the poem reissues the dialectically polarized "marble men" following the caesura that marks their very destruction. In this manner, Stevens first kills the fictive Statue trope by pointing to its fallibility, buries it, and, with no mourning, reconstructs its fictional potency. Having then established a potent poetry able to destroy the Statue, the poet quickly regenerates a parallel fulfillment with the "marble men," already subverted. In doing this, Stevens shows how change concurs in different groups, for different purposes: "Conceive that marble men . . . make real the attitudes / *Appointed* for them . . ." (*OP* 83). The italicized verb is repeated from the opposing Marxist inscription of canto iii, and it also dominates here, but in reversed context. Previously the Marxists inscribed *To Be itself* as their motto, whereas the "marble men" have attitudes "Appointed for them" as birthrights. As an enjambed verb, "Appointed" dominates the sentence just as the traditional ("marble men") power appoints a new generation; furthermore, the prosody stresses the alliterative *"ped*iment" bearing their *app*ointed words. In this marble epithet, Stevens displays just how arbitrarily power is monumentalized through inscribed social appointments. Meanwhile, the poetry's syntactical and aural force rhetorically reinforces the content of the language it appoints. Stevens contrasts elite power with the arbitrary revolution inscribed by the earlier Marxist nomination. Both are automatically defined.

In canto vii, the Statue falls at the feet of the dancing damsels while the "marble men" return. In the five lines discussed above, the gentry maintain an artful power that takes the damsels the rest of the canto to claim. There may be some uncertainty regarding the identities of the "you" addressees that close the poem. I suggest that this confusion highlights the implosion of polarized identities. What was previously the "bare and blunt" Marxist inscription, *"To Be Itself,"* "transforms / Itself into the speech of the spirit." "[F]eelings [are] changed to sound," and the revolutionary damsels become "Impassioned seducers and seduced." Since they are "[s]peaking and strutting broadly, fair and bloomed," the address continues to be directed at the feminine crowd present for the poet's oratory. However, this canto constantly stokes the fire that ends it, and all of the personae of "Mr. Burnshaw and the Statue" are thus consumed. The poem's movement—from Marxist Mesdames, to the reflections that commingle yet whirl disparately, to the blues and reds, to the inclusion of the marble men within the updraft of the damsels—consistently implodes forces that depend upon each other for difference and distinction. All of a sudden at the end of the poem, though, their dynamism is consumed in fire. Uniting these forces is the utopic desire for self-expression, unitary identity, and determinate Truth: *To Be Itself.* The credo is a problem because of its automatically assumed nomination that instantly hardens flux into the artistic monument awaiting subsequent destruction. The last lines of the poem present numerous crystallizations that are troubled by automatism: "And are your feelings changed to sound, without / A change . . ." (*OP* 83). Without real change, representational change arises, and because there's glory in representation, art will continue to strut itself into purgation. (To directly continue from the previous quotation):

> [U]ntil the waterish ditherings turn
> To the tense, the maudlin, the true meridian
> That is yourselves, when, at last, you are yourselves,
> Speaking and strutting broadly, fair and bloomed,
> No longer of air but of breathing earth,

> Impassioned seducers and seduced, the pale
> Pitched into swelling bodies, upward, drift
> In a storm blown into glittering shapes, and flames
> Wind-beaten into freshest, brightest fire.   (*OP* 83)

The "change" as a form of representation is encumbered by "waterish ditherings." These precisely sound like nothing because water represents the ongoing flux that washes all supposed changes away; "ditherings," besides also sounding like nothing, are states of tremulous excitement or apprehension *(OED)*, and thereby are associated with doubt and fear, which recalls the Old Woman's nakedness at the foot of the Statue. Etymologically tied up in "ditherings" is "ditheism," or religious dualism, within which this poem vacillates, even if I have yet to call the various utopias religious. The antinomies of the poem find "the true meridian" through "the maudlin," which refers to the debased then repentant Mary Magdalene, as well as the tearful remorse of drunkenness *(OED)*. Stevens traces the movement of uncontained flux into resolute form in a variety of ways here, which are all somewhat cheap and pejorative, as if the formation of ecstasy is too easily acquired. For instance, fear and "tense" desperation, when fleshed out via self-representation, become the strutting peacock of the divinely natural earth. With "Impassioned seducers and seduced," Stevens simplifies the monumental process of those desperately in need succumbing to the proclamation, *To Be Itself.* Such an occasion is couched as a bodily sacrifice wherein the subjects are consumed "into glittering shapes." The aesthetic crystallization acquires the energy of the weather, which for Stevens is the constant change of nature. The poem ends with the violent ecstasy of a beatific vision, which is uncharacteristic of Stevens' poetics. This inevitable fusion manifests apocalypse as the result of the poem's imperative to consolidate disparate groups.

Perhaps Stevens' severing of canto vii admits that his desire to implode polarized groups is as destructive as each community can be. Stevens shows that the search for definition is ultimately an ideal, like any other, that will be destroyed pending its establishment. This burning follows an aesthetic similar to the exact apocalyptic definition that ironically closed "The Old Woman and the Statue." In that poem irony was luxuriously maintained because the sculptor was an easy enemy for the reader to pit against the Old Woman. In "Mr. Burnshaw and the Statue," doom awaits everybody. It is especially destructive because the participants in the apocalypse create the situation that cancels each other out. (This nuclear vision involving Burnshaw and the State coincides with the cold war politics evolving in the

States—the demonization of red communism, such as in Burnshaw's *New Masses,* by true blue patriots.)[9] The forecast's "satire" is not weak, but over-bearing. As disturbing as the poem's denouement is, the destructive Niet-zschean dynamic meshes with Stevens' poetics of change that depend upon generational cyclicality. In this case the "all things must destroy themselves or be destroyed" theory is especially grim because, first, the personae are actual contemporaries, as well as apparent future hopefuls, and, second, Stevens' generational poetics usually depend upon harmonious reproduc-tion. It's not difficult to see why readers objected to this poem and Stevens chopped this canto from the 1937 version of *Owl's Clover.*

Coinciding with idealism's quick destruction is the abrupt style of the poem here. Usually a patient poet of process, Stevens hastily collects his kindling in order to burn it. The final proclamations are cast in a presenta-tive style, but the scene is once removed by the poet's hypothetical stance. It pretends to present or perform in the manner of the Imagist distinction that opts for Presentation over Representation.[10] For example, the poetic voice demands that *"To Be Itself"* be repeated until it "transforms / Itself into the speech of the spirit." We are not witness to the transformation, as we were when the maidens performed a ritual of changing colors, ending with a toppled Statue. Perhaps the forced style of the ending fits with the imposed crystalline aesthetics: both are debased with pretentions toward transcendence. We read a proclaimed poetics (like "Of Modern Poetry") that wants to transform speech to spirit, feeling to sound, and seducers to seduced (and all the vice versas thereof). "Of Modern Poetry" states that poetry *"must* find the speech of the place," and be "of a woman combing, a man skating." But the statement of those imperatives in that instance means that such performances cannot be achieved in that poem. In mak-ing proclamations, Stevens writes "constatively," to use Austin's distinction (which amounts to much the same thing as "representation").[11] Through most of the poem Stevens "performs" romantic seductions while "present-ing" cases in point. He argues that the left operates by romantic performa-tive methods, even though it supposes constative truths. *Owl's Clover* does not fall short in its satire, as Cook says; it dissembles when its satiric irony and parody are forsaken for the sake of a "temple-tone" already knocked. Perhaps the Marxist apocalypse is not a "justification" at all, but a rhetori-cal portrait of a social movement doomed to the same romantic destruc-tive end that closed "The Old Woman and the Statue."

It is not surprising that Stevens cut section vii, as it demonstrates the destruction of a too fast, automatic idealism. Its rhetoric of transcendence gets ensnared between a self-conscious "rhetoricity," and full-blown apocalypse. Ultimately for Stevens' poetics, the power of that depicted *failure* succeeds because it serves as a warning to extreme idealism; an example of what happens when static rigidity is consumed in dynamic process. By ending the revised 1937 edition with section vi, however, the poem hangs on the question put to "you," the variable Mesdames: "Shall you, / Then, fear a drastic community evolved / From the whirling, slowly and by trial; or fear / Men gathering . . . / into a possible blue?" (*OP* 82). This open ending deposits fear for readers to consider amid the dialectic of leftists and patriarchal aesthetes (who are purposefully conflated). This ending evolves performatively in section vi, only asking about an answer, rather than passing down doom as does section vii.

Ending with canto vi is a more typically irresolute Stevens denouement, allowing the Statue to remain intact because the beautifully destructive damsels are no longer in the poem. These cuts effectively tone down Stevens' politically subversive stance, which opposes both Marxist idealism and State dominion by mutually imploding them. Stevens also omits the satiric first line of section v: "A solemn voice, not Mr. Burnshaw's says:" and the section goes from there to present the "trash can at the end of the world" (*OP* 81). This omission censors Stevens' view that Burnshaw's politics are too short-sighted to envision doomful scavenging, and hopeful regeneration. Further contributing to the watered-down revised edition is the complete removal of part iv. This is the crucial section suggesting that "a place / Of fear before the disorder of the strange," such as 30s America, triggers a "poets' politics." Section iv amalgamates Shelley, poets who "Complain and prophesy" (like Burnshaw), and workers, all under the "Mesdames" umbrella, where disorder and uncertainty lead to idealistic projections. However incredible it seems, Burnshaw is completely removed from the poem's content, and it is retitled "The Statue at the World's End."[12]

S. F. Morse writes in his introduction to *Opus Posthumous* that *Owl's Clover* was omitted from *The Collected Poems* on the grounds of being too "rhetorical." Going beyond that apparent criticism of the poetry, what might we say about Stevens' decision to omit polemics, and what does that decision suggest about the cultural climate he wrote within? In the depressed thirties, people scrambled to locate specific truths to help their economic situation. Meanwhile, Stevens writes a long poem about the rhetorical romanticism involved in that human quest for answers. Stevens deconstructed historical process as it was happening. As Stanley Burnshaw explains in a 1961 retrospective about his time at *The New Masses*, the journal was less than discriminating about politics, as it printed work not only by Stevens, but Hemingway, MacLeish, Saroyan, Dos Passos, and Kenneth Burke,

> to list some of the names familiar today. Controversies raged; the world of books had suddenly come alive with excitement. Audiences crowded into theatres and often argued out loud. Literature was reaching sectors of the population that one never regarded as part of the reading public. And better still, they seemed to care.[13]

So much for historical notions of a society of elite artists unable to reach the public, which will take what it can get. The social angst beheld by artists of the thirties had likely more to do with the contemporary pressure to find answers for society. So, many artists turned to Marxist ideology. Burnshaw ironically presents himself in this light in the following third-person chronicle:

> How to speak to such an audience? None of his associates was quite sure . . . they were the blind leading the blind. But tentativeness and humility were unthinkable: the world was separating into two enemy camps and time was running out! One had to act in behalf of mankind, and for anyone with a brain there could be no choice. Like the rest of the intellectual Left, they moved in the serenity of certainty, naive examples of what Mann calls "the automatic tendency to believe that the intellect, by its very nature, takes its position . . . on the 'left,' that it is therefore essentially allied with the ideas of freedom, progress, humanity . . . a prejudice which has often been disproved."[14]

With Burnshaw's "mercy of distance" (Ondaatje) we not only catch a glimpse of the challenge of living in the thirties—so comparable to the 1990s—we can also observe how historically accurate Stevens' conflation of a socialist-romantic aesthetic was in "Mr. Burnshaw and the Statue"; particularly canto iv's "world impossible for poets, who / Complain and prophesy, in their complaints, / And are never of the world in which they live" (*OP* 80). This strong satire (the whole of part iv) was cut from the 1937 edition. A similar editing principle is observable in the change in title, which replaces the particular, local, and satiric bite of "Mr. Burnshaw and the Statue" with the universalized, "The Statue at the World's End," in the 1937 version. By editing "Mr. Burnshaw and the Statue," Stevens negated much of the poem's dialectical critique. "The Statue at the World's End" reduces the previous constructive yet severe criticism that sees doom in the Burnshaw predicament, in favor of a looming glance at utopian-apocalypse. Perhaps the revised poem comments in a more universal and diluted manner on the fearful feeling provoked by the era's economic and political climate. This cautious gesture attempted to appease critics, but it detracts from the rigor of Stevens' social analysis.

Burnshaw speaks of a similar desire to preserve the contemporary left-wing vision for the sake of public followers, regardless of the outcome:

> This startling experience, this sense of direct relationship with one's readers, was not only new in American letters; it could go far to sustain those writers within the Left who were wrestling with their private angels. The reviewer of Stevens, for example. In his darker moments, he would confront his own misgivings about the glory of the life-to-come in the stateless utopia. It would be ushered in, of course, by the Goddess of Industrialization whose handiwork he had already observed in a grim milltown.[15]

It is as though Stevens' poem unpacked this 1961 quotation 26 years earlier. Stevens' "Mesdames-damsels" trope evolved from utopic to apocalyptic thought, just as Burnshaw's "private angels" informed him of doubts that could not be managed by his politics. Burnshaw's third-person bio-history establishes the particular relevance of Stevens' poem to its time. Burnshaw discloses the romantic idealism that Stevens argued was intrinsic to leftism:

> Like Stevens, he had been deeply involved with the Symbolist poets by night and with a business job by day; but unlike Stevens, he quit a remunerative career for the hope of teaching. When his first book appeared, he was writing a thesis on the relationship between poetry and mysticism, at Cornell University, where he had gone to study with F. C. Prescott, author of *Poetry and Myth* and *The Poetic Mind*. Armed with a graduate degree but unable to find a teaching job, he returned to New York (1933) with the notion of living by his pen. Apathy greeted him everywhere except in the office of an impoverished journal, which accepted some of his "proletarian" verse and offered him books for review.[16]

Burnshaw's mystical romantic leanings, and their continuity in leftism, are engaged in Stevens' "Mesdames" trope. Burnshaw's "misgivings about the glory of the life-to-come in the stateless utopia . . . ushered in, of course, by the Goddess of Industrialization" are prophetically allegorized in Stevens' section vii, where "the Statue falls" and the poem ends in "brightest fire." This canto was cut, remember. The end of this canto projects automatic apocalypse, yet its images do not specifically suggest the industrial ravages of Communism. However, either Stevens' fire was (coincidentally?) echoed by Burnshaw, or Stevens knew more about Burnshaw than their loose ties seem to imply. Most likely, Stevens' satiric prophesy for social utopia deduced accurate apocalyptic conclusions.

Whatever the case, it seems Stevens feared both his prophesy and the rhetorical rigor of his dialectical critique. On the surface, canto iv's critique of socialist romanticism, and vii's toppled Statue and explosive finale appear to be part of a developing destructive poetics. What they actually propose is both the inherent destructiveness of the romanticism that Stevens wants to trash, save for its "portentous lustres," and the potential violence of a socialism exercised by a "harmonious skeptic soon in a skeptical music." Historically, Mussolini was in power, and Hitler was on his way. Many of the cut lines prophesize the future, and thus Stevens' following explanation seems inadequate if not untrue: "The poem has been cut a little for the purpose of making it clearer" (*L* 322). Actually he watered down a polemic that clearly argued that socialism is a potentially destructive new romanticism, especially when it functions monumentally, like the stat(u)e it aims to destroy.

Readers of *Owl's Clover* may still think that its polemics vitiate the poetry. This will be the case if the reader holds to either of the traditional binary sets of ideals that the poem deconstructs. On the one side rests aesthetic purity, creativity, tropism; the taxonomic opposite includes political dogmatism, argument, literalism. These dichotomies are accompanied (but not aligned neatly) with elite versus oppressed, seducers versus seduced, traditionalists versus radicals, stale romantics (classicists) versus utopian romantics (socialists), and on and on. Part of the poem's argument presents many of these polar forces as dependent upon each other, as co-parasites that will consume or cancel out each other. That view is not as important in my opinion as the poem's rhetorical suggestion that a monumental art, such as the Statue, oppresses those neglected from the enforced vision, such as the Old Woman. This imbalance demands a polemic to unsettle state complacency. Conversely, polemicists, such as Burnshaw, depend upon the art of rhetoric. When argumentative purists neglect or dismiss poetic seductions, they deny the very rhetorical appeals and tropes that they use for persuasion. Poetry only ruins polemics when polemicists wear fanatical guises that define justice through blindness. Polemics only ruins poetry if the latter is being cherished as a trinket in a glass case that others are barred from. The 1930s demanded a "harmonious skeptic soon in a skeptical music." History shows that the wrong ones—Mussolini, Stalin, Hitler—were chosen.

Chapter 4

Owl's Clover III, IV, V: "The civil fiction, the calico idea"

He turns us into scholars, studying
The masks of music. We perceive each mask
To be the musician's own and, thence, become
An audience to mimics glistening
With meanings, doubled by the closest sound,
Mimics that play on instruments discerned
In the beat of the blood. (OP 97)

Before continuing with *Owl's Clover,* I will provide a narrative outline of its concerns, ambitions, and tropes. "The Old Woman and the Statue" confronts the monument as a cold exclusionary aesthetic, and "Mr. Burnshaw and the Statue" shows that a fixed Marxist polemic partakes in a similar automatism dependent upon opposition through history. These poems critique America's cultural responses in the 1930s. The last three poems of *Owl's Clover* extend to broader contexts. In "The Greenest Continent" the Statue is exported to Africa, suggesting that the Western monument has colonized itself elsewhere. In the poem's narrative, this transplantation precedes a militaristic Christian mission that paradoxically seeks pastoral restoration in the jungle. The imperialism of "The Greenest Continent" is then contrasted with American immigration in "A Duck for Dinner": the poem returns to the public park, but this time immigrants celebrate a kitschy hodgepodge of plasticized culture. Stevens contrasts the immigrants' transplantation of customs to America with a nineteenth-century pioneer figure who turns to Europe once the American frontier is settled. Amid these transmigrations the park is domesticated by a diverse collective, which contrasts with the pioneer's singular quest and the Old Woman's previous subordinate position beneath the Statue. It is in the collective that Stevens wants the poet situated. "Sombre Figuration," the final poem, introduces the "subman" as an "anti-logician" who is an early version of Ariel, the necessary angel of the earth who provides citizens with fresh sight. By making the public his chief concern, the "humdrum" subman figure enables Stevens to reach beyond the ideological contemporary pressure felt so strongly in *Owl's Clover.*

In the narrative, political contexts, tropes, and poetic form of *Owl's Clover,* Stevens urges readers to consider a more chaotic, less rigidly defined reality. In trying to confront chaos, Stevens is just as concerned with order as he was in previous work—even more so, since the poetry takes more disorder to task. But to meet such objectives, ruling orders of the past have to be forsaken, and the Statue is the most monumental, state endorsed, rigid form of stale romanticism in need of dismantling. I suggest that all of the critical targets in *Owl's Clover*—state sculpture, Burnshaw's Marxism, imperialism, Christianity, Eurocentrism—are monumental aesthetics. They forcefully dominate the figures around themselves, and their hegemony is inflexible to the spirit of people. In this manner, these monumental aesthetics are primarily political; they function in order to control rather than to grant expression. I am not suggesting that political art cannot express worthy human concerns, but that a monumental politics serves only the rigid program of its creators, all others be damned. In this sense a *To Be Itself* automatic artifact resists change and becomes an outworn trope much like the muse in "The Idea of Order at Key West." A recent example of this political aesthetic is the Statue of Champlain in Ottawa that had at its feet a servile native Indian, which was promptly removed from the sculpture.

To combat and overturn such structures, Stevens employs a poetry that treats creations as arguments (that appeal to power) and arguments as creations (that are composed); neither has priority. Both display the power of persuasion; the poetry is rhetorical through and through. Because of this rhetoricity, the poetic diction cannot be taken transparently at any given moment: all the words wear masks, and each masked section of text derives much of its meaning from its difference from adjacent passages, and from connections with other similarly troped sections of the poem. Irony, juxtaposition, and hyperbole are stronger here than elsewhere in Stevens' poetry; reverence, sublimity, and revelation are rhetorized in de Manian fashion: these "art emotions" (Eliot) are performed as constructs of powerful persuasion.

This rhetoricity may suggest why the poem was received poorly in critical circles. The previous poetic solaces readers found in *Harmonium* are gone. Most readers of Stevens have agreed that *Harmonium* contains his best poetry; it is the most hedonistic volume to be sure. However, readers have increasingly appreciated the later work because the poet more fully engages with history, culture, and society. I notice Stevens' concern for the problems of his time not only from his poetry, but also from recent criticism on it. Alan Filreis and James Longenbach provide invaluable historical connections. Filreis writes about historical circumstances surrounding *Owl's Clover* in great detail. Perhaps because Stevens' response to his time is Filreis' main project, he sometimes interprets the poetry transparently where I do not. Recall Filreis' complaint that Stevens was "often creating when he should be arguing." Such a criticism suggests Filreis' desire for polemics, which in turn leads to a quest for authorial viewpoints. But these are nearly impossible to locate in *Owl's Clover* because the language is not transparent. The speaker's words are only transparent when they are pedagogical, and in these instances the pedagogue instructs readers not to read transparently:

> He turns us into scholars, studying
> The masks of music. We perceive each mask
> To be the musician's own and, thence, become
> An audience to mimics glistening
> With meanings, doubled by the closest sound,
> Mimics that play on instruments discerned
> In the beat of the blood.   (*OP* 97)

The music of *Owl's Clover* reverberates in the reader's ear in several ways. Chords vary according to their related personae, and so certain characters dramatize coinciding forms of musical persuasion.

Music has been called the ideal artform because it embodies a large range of human emotion; Stevens expressed its capacity early, in 1915's "Peter Quince at the Clavier":

> Music is feeling, then, not sound;
> And thus it is that what I feel,
> Here in this room, desiring you,
>
> Thinking of your blue-shadowed silk,
> Is music. . . .   (*CP* 90)

Despite the poet's early denial of music as sound, sound plays a huge role in Stevens' music, as do emotions and thoughts. In the poetry of *Owl's Clover,* Stevens' music displays its effects and affects through hyperbole. In other words, persuasive music draws attention to itself through excessive styles that display rhetoricity, or unmask the construct of a musical seduction. Such rhetoric, or aural persuasion, appeals emotionally, logically, and to our conscience. Manifesting Aristotle's three appeals—pathos, logos, ethos—for the reader are factors such as hyperbolic language (for emotion), irony (appealing to logic), and exaggerated circumstances (initiating our conscience). If my artificial scenario is more systematic than is the poem, it nevertheless shows that the poem's music forms persuasive tropes that have rhetorical purposes. These masks take on lives of their own in a loose narrative in which authority is lost—fitting with Stevens' view of the 1930s.

As he turns to writing a rhetorical poetry challenging monumental aesthetics, Stevens' use of figural language, his poetics, changes significantly. This change corresponds with what the narrative reveals. The poem progresses from the elite state Statue to the rigid counter tablet of Marxism, to plentiful obelisks and ducks in the park, to the subman listening to citizens' dreams rather than "the agony of a single dreamer." This move from a singular imposition of masculine genius to an anti-cerebral subman who says, "We have grown weary of the man that thinks," has a concurrent development in terms of the poem's literary figuration. "The Old Woman and the Statue" ended with the exclamation of a hyperbolized and ironic reverence for the Statue's definition: its marble horses symbolize the romantic, victorious power of conquest. "Symbol" itself is a figure of conquest because it centrally represents all that it has power over in its referential kingdom.

In "The Greenest Continent" the problem with symbolism is made overt by a wide divergence of geographical and cultural contexts. The Statue in Africa (the early title) demonstrates the ineffectuality of exporting symbols and using them to colonize other domains. "A Duck for Dinner" similarly depicts the pioneer out of time, and out of frontier terrain, so out of purpose. This poem also presents a host of transmigrant symbols, all of which lose some of their signified power because their native contexts are dislocated in America. Yet in this poem the park becomes a diaspora of emblems, each of which loses synecdochic power, yet gains metonymic relations. That is, the park acquires many different attributes, all significant, yet they are aligned in a chain of aggregate representation rather than a synecdochic order with marble horses at center.

"The Greenest Continent" stretches the definition of the Statue from "The Old Woman" and "Mr Burnshaw" by planting it in the African jungle. This image presents the imposition of European imperialism in Africa. The first three cantos of "The Greenest Continent" revel in "the emptiness of heaven and its hymns," as sung by Europe. Within this critique Stevens includes a metaphor of bankruptcy in which Europe is taxed to death. Images of Western, Yeatsian, and/or Greek civilization, a "jagged tower, / A broken wall," are emptied from the libraries of Europe "to people in Maine, / Ontario, Canton" (*OP* 84). The depletion of European idealism is contrasted, in section iv, with "Africa, which had / No heaven, had death without a heaven, death / In a heaven of death" (*OP* 85). In denouncing Christian mythology, Stevens argues once again that heaven is not the mother of beauty. Instead, the poem proposes an African "serpent" image of life-death. Stevens' exoticism implicates the death of the Statue, which "Sleekly the serpent would draw himself across."

In emptying Europe's heaven of its hymns, Stevens repeats a pattern of his poetics that shows no tolerance for outworn signifiers carrying outdated signifieds. "Key West's" "body wholly body, fluttering / Its empty sleeves," and "The Old Woman's" resistance to a nonreflexive "Statue" present disjointed semiologies, as does the concept of a Platonic god in Africa, which the Statue amounts to here. In section iv, as in the "brilliant" canto of definite closure in "The Old Woman," Stevens' criticism is formed by a rhetoric of excess, and thus irony:

> No god rules over Africa, no throne,
> Single, of burly ivory, inched of gold,
> Disposed upon the central of what we see,
> That purges the wrack or makes the jungle shine,
> As brilliant as mystic, as mystic as single . . .
> . . . . . .
> Toward which, in the nights, the glittering serpents climb,
> Dark-skinned and sinuous, winding upwardly. . . .   (*OP* 86)

Many Western traditions are at stake in these lines. The treasure troves of monarchy (common to many civilizations) are linked in a Platonic vision, mystic in its singular divination of a "brilliant" kingdom. As with Stevens' other pejorative uses of "brilliant" ("The Old Woman," "Prologues to What Is Possible"), singular light excludes all darkness around it. However, the serpentine African death spirit works by night, regardless of enlightenment, which "purges the wrack" of night-death. Africa's native symbology is denied for the sake of a squeaky shiny jungle. "Wrack" means damage or wreckage, and also implies "retributive punishment; vengeance" *(OED),* therefore foreshadowing the serpent's reaction. Stevens may draw from Milton's use of the word: "And now all Heav'n Had gone to wrack, with

ruin overspread" (*Paradise Lost,* vi. 670); heaven's lost paradise being crucial
to Stevens' critique. An etymological treasure itself, "wrack" might remind
the reader of Dante, whose Inferno is a place of purging, consisting of a
winding staircase, which, in this poem, Africa's serpents are erratically made
to climb out of context. These serpents are not threatened by Dante's particular brand of Western evil. The serpent, as a metonym of Africa's life-
death god, is "Winding and waving, slowly, waving in air" as it climbs these
fictitious Western stairs: earlier in this canto it had a stranglehold on the
Statue. Every Western monument that intrudes here ends up under siege.
After showing the absurdity of Western godly hierarchy in Africa, the
poem offers the alternative:

> Death, only, sits upon the serpent throne:
> Death, the herdsman of elephants,
> To whom the jaguars cry and lions roar
> Their petty dirges of fallen forest-men,
> Forever hunting or hunted, rushing through
> Endless pursuit or endlessly pursued,
> Until each tree, each evil-blossomed vine,
> Each fretful fern drops down a fear like dew
> And Africa, basking in antiquest sun,
> Contains for its children not a gill of sweet.   (*OP* 86)

The confusions of evil and good in the "evil-blossomed vine," "a fear like
dew," and "not a gill of sweet" take away the false promise of an empty
heaven. Instead, Stevens shows death to be the mother or god of beauty.
The undeniable fact of death conditions secular life—an order of atone-
ment no longer applies—so that each action here and now holds a reciprocal reaction. Here we can see Stevens' philosophy of religion, earlier
established in "Sunday Morning," at work in this African allegory.

   "The Greenest Continent" also reasserts a poetics that was crucial to
"Mr. Burnshaw and the Statue." Like "Impassioned seducers and seduced,"
the characters in this scene are "Forever hunting or hunted, rushing
through / Endless pursuit or endlessly pursued" (*OP* 86). There is no sta-
ble hierarchy here because nothing is entrenched; there are always forces
behind and in front. This concept concurs with the physical motion of particles as they travel according to the conductivity of those around them. In
this framework, death is a meta-monument because it is the only state that
can be imagined as a stillpoint to ground living objects. As such it is a fiction, as much as it is real, because once there, it's gone. Death is, in effect,

a fiction because there's no experience once one is dead. This poem posits the absurdity of any other stillpoint, ground, or fixture. In doing so, Stevens relies on the economy of the natural world, which, as he knows, is near ruin. Perhaps that is why religions and monuments are proposed in the first place: because natural order is not respected; it must be tamed or destroyed because we die in it. Western art has always tried to find a way out of that inevitability.

Stevens makes us aware of Christianity's threat to nature, as canto v portrays an imperial missionary slaughter of African order:

> Forth from their tabernacles once again
> The angels come, armed, gloriously to slay
> The black and ruin his sepulchral throne.
> He quoi! Angels go pricking elephants?
> Wings spread and whirling over jaguar-men?
> Angles tiptoe upon the snowy cones
> Of palmy peaks sighting machine-guns? These,
> Seraphim of Europe? Pouring out of dawn,
> . . . .
> Combatting bushmen for a patch of gourds,
> Loosing black slaves to make black infantry . . .   (*OP* 87)

The absurdity of this violent history is manifested in cartoonish European figures juxtaposed with the African setting. The tragic missionary comedy is then contextualized in book form:

>   This must
> Be merely a masquerade or else a rare
> Tractatus, of military things, with plates,
> Miraculously preserved, full fickle-fine,
> Of an imagination flashed with irony
> And by a hand of certitude to cut
> The heavenly cocks, the bowmen, and the gourds,
> The oracular trumpets round and roundly hooped,
> In Leonardo's way, to magnify
> Concentric bosh.   (*OP* 87)

In using a Latin version of tract, Stevens recalls the historical longevity and formality of this collective enterprise, which could be born out of military treaty, or poetic tract, both of which participate in foreign endeavors. In the *Oxford English Dictionary,* variations of "Tractatus" include "treatise; easily handled person or material; region of indefinite extent"; and "Tractarian: 19th-century English High-Church movement towards an earlier sacramental Catholicism, against liberalism. . . ." Stevens' word-play collects etymological contexts that are parodied by the variant contexts signified in the poem: "This . . . Tractatus" refers to the book embossed with golden plates. The designer of the Tractatus must have had "an imagination flashed with irony" because he must apply his fine artistry to depictions of a violated continent. Assembling this book also reflects Stevens' poetic act that likewise requires "an imagination flashed with irony" in order to construct the foreign imperial scenario of the poem. The cutting circular aesthetics find contextual ground in DaVinci's Renaissance art—the whole bloody enterprise is deemed "Concentric bosh." "Italian painting is based on circles," says Stevens in a letter (*L* 300).

Stevens finishes this section with increased irony, showing the African mission to be a type of pastoral excursion:

> To their tabernacles, then,
> Remoter than Athos, the effulgent hordes
> Return, affecting roseate aureoles,
> To contemplate time's golden paladin[1]
> And purpose, to hear the wild bee drone, to feel
> The ecstacy of sense in sensuous air.   (*OP* 87)

This cartoonish mesh of contexts brings together church missionaries, their sanctuary in Athos, heavenly haloes, a contest for time's champion— all imbued in the sensual retreat of the pastoral. This hyperbolic search for glory is ironic in its ridiculous mysticism. The "Concentric bosh" of the previous passage links images of drinking nectar in heaven, with the retreat of a Yeatsian pastoral that is here imported: "the wild bee drone" being a parody of the "bee-loud glade" in "The Lake Isle of Innisfree."

Section vi confirms the futility of Western monumentality in an Africa that is unresponsive to the Statue here depicted in its Northern cold:

> There it would be of the mode of common dreams,
> A ring of horses rising from memory
> Or rising in the appointments of desire,
> The spirit's natural images, carriers,
> The drafts of gay beginnings and bright ends,
> Majestic bearers or solemn haulers trapped
> In endless elegies.   (*OP* 88)

These lines provide a concise summary of the Statue as it was troped in the first two poems of *Owl's Clover*. Stevens revisits the critique of an automatic artifact, "rising in the appointments of desire," that is supposed to be representative of its people, but which is "trapped / In endless elegies" of Christian idealism now in mourning.

Contrasting with the Statue's Western memorial is the way in which African memory resides in its living beings: "With tongues unclipped and throats so stuffed with thorns, / So clawed, so sopped with sun, that in these things / The message is half-borne" (*OP* 88). Stevens recalls the Greek myth of Cassandra, whose gifted tongue prophesying the fall of Troy was clipped by Apollo. In Stevens' Africa, prophesy has not been eradicated; the singer here still possesses the thorn-like wisdom, as well as the sun-like knowledge, that Cassandra resisted in Apollo, and paid the price for. In African birdsong, the "message is half-borne," which suggests that wisdom is stuck in the bodies that form nature. In this alien Africa, nature is idealized in "the others" that live there and are therefore assumed to be the purveyors of mysterious knowledge. The poem's excess once again ironizes this paradigm of the primitive other (three exaggerated "so's" in a row) and recognizes the limitation of a paradigm in which the message cannot be translated. This "half-borne" message is an early instance of the poetic voice as a half-figure; as an Ariel that requires a reader-compatriot to engage in dialogue (as in "Angel Surrounded by Paysans"). Herein we can see an adumbration of the developing mature poetics of Stevens, which emphasize dialogic interaction. All of the other poems of *Owl's Clover* address issues of civic art, but Stevens had to compose an alternative based on Africa in order to escape the trappings of northwestern monumental paradigms. He had already said "Farewell to Florida," so Africa's exotic nature revitalized Stevens from the symbiotic inertia of right- and left-wing America.

Section vii argues against Western godly anthropomorphism, much like the viewpoint of Stevens' essay "Two or Three Ideas," which argues that the styles of gods, poems, and men are one and must "create a style of bearing themselves in reality" rather than creating totems (*OP* 262). After claiming that "paint[ing] the gods" (*OP* 88) is bourgeois extravagance, Stevens connects that aesthetic privilege to the larger domination at hand in this poem:

> It was a mistake to think of them. They have
> No place in the sense of colonists, no place

> In Africa. The serpent's throne is dust
> At the unbeliever's touch. . . .   (*OP* 89)

"The Greenest Continent" draws together bad measures made in Christian faith and colonization. This destructive partnership is made of a missionary mindset bent on conquering things: part of Stevens' larger argument against definitions, and fixed symbols. Stevens' poetic—as also demonstrated in "The Old Woman and the Statue" and "Mr. Burnshaw and the Statue"—constructs alternative epistemologies for the Old Woman, Marxists, and anti-imperialism.[2] Stevens' recipe for social change depends upon a philosophical, psychological, political, and aesthetic resistance made possible by understanding that oppositional systems rigidly destroy each other. Alternatively, the success of Stevens' politics and poetics depends upon the reader's acceptance of Stevens' semiology; his use of signs that constantly evolve in rhetoric's construction of thought.

Not resting with such pedagogy, canto viii of "The Greenest Continent" quickly proposes a way out of the imperial mess. Stevens calls up Ananke, the god of Necessity and Fate to whom we must pay heed. Ananke embodies an incredible range of experience here. Notably, this god is humanized and simultaneously most superhuman. "Fatal Ananke is the common god" (*OP* 89), an international god whose hymn "Is the exile of the disinherited," thereby taking on a spiritual role suitable for the Old Woman. "[F]or him, a thousand litanies / Are like the perpetual verses in a poet's mind" (*OP* 90). Embodying many of Stevens' ambitions, Ananke is a father of earthly beauty, yet is bleak in his final darkness: he wears a "starless crown," suggesting earthiness, yet as the "Sultan of African sultans" (*OP* 90), Ananke is a meta-god.

As a manifestation of fatal necessity, Ananke is the African alternative to the transposed Western Statue. As such, Ananke encapsulates much of "The Greenest Continent" and therefore stands as a synecdochic symbol. At this point in *Owl's Clover* it is difficult to take an encompassing, definite symbol seriously. Yet death's sure fate is a constant in Stevens' poetics. So the question remains whether Ananke is as full of doom as he appears to be, or whether he's another totalizing symbol, which—because of its ambitious definitiveness—is ironic through excess. Is this necessary, fatal god another monument over-ascribing *To Be Itself*? Perhaps the question of Ananke's plausibility is the point. "The final belief is to believe in a fiction, which you know to be a fiction, there being nothing else. The exquisite truth is to know that it is a fiction, and that you believe in it willingly" (*OP* 189). Besides commenting on faith, this adage carries the double weight of the sign: signifier and signified. Ananke is monstrous because, as an "origin and resplendent end of law," he is a signifier that is made to signify: this being language's fatal necessity. Ananke's grandiosity appears grotesque and artificial, and that monstrosity makes us aware of the god's fictionality, which in turn forces us to think about death—no fiction at all, yet fully fictional as a conception here. As a reader I object to this intrusive exotic demonization, and because this Necessity deliriously confronts me in the poem, it works.[3]

Still, the question of irony remains entangled in the Ananke figure, and this question points us to Ananke's double weight as a sign. Through Ananke we can observe that irony is inscribed into Stevens' fictions; irony is the in-folding law allowing fictionality sustenance, and enabling "signs [to be] taken as wonders," as well as their plastic selves. In *Notes Toward a Supreme Fiction,* the ironic fictionality of heroes more thoroughly instructs readers to play with belief as it informs Abstract heroes. Ananke, while also a markedly constructed figure, is also the "final full, an end without rhetoric." This fatal desire is prescribed a few years later in another imperial poem that is not included in *The Collected Poems,* "Life on a Battleship," to which I return in chapter 5.

Such critical ambition, gloomy forecasting, and political satire may have proven too much to live with all at once, as Helen Vendler observes about Stevens' revised edition of *Owl's Clover:* "Stevens' massive cutting of the original poem is the work of a man embarrassed by his own rhetorical excesses."[4] While I don't think "embarrassment" quite explains Stevens' edits, Vendler is right that Stevens' editing tempered the original's excesses. But the cut passages are the most heavily rhetorical and the most politically critical. Canto vii, with its depiction of European art as bourgeois profanity, "The diplomats of the cafes expound: / Fromage and coffee and cognac and no gods" (*OP* 88), is removed. Omitting this whole canto erases Stevens' argument that decadent materialism fulfills a depleted Western spirit: "Champagne / On a hot night and a long cigar and talk / About the weather and women and the way / Of things, why bother about the back of stars?" (*OP* 89). Stevens' portrayal of the shallow bohemia of Western culture is certainly crucial to the poem. It is a cause of imperial African searchings, which are common to modernist primitivism extant in artists from Gauguin to Bowles. Although imperial expeditions imported primitive aesthetics, Stevens' particular brand of exoticism demonstrates the absurdity of imposing Western mores on Africa. Stevens criticizes the missionary colonization of "The Greenest Continent" in an attempt to compose African paradigms that the West might learn from. "Going native" might be a kind of aesthetic imperialism, but learning from foreign myths is likely more productive and less destructive than is spreading Christianity.

Stevens' explorations, as we saw in canto v's "Tractatus," often make potential linkages between primitivist aesthetics and militant imperialism. Stevens' poem about Africa may allude to the politics of Mussolini, which are mentioned in Stevens' letters of this time. However, the poem does not cite Mussolini or particular aspects of his invasion of Ethiopia, which suggests that Stevens is more interested in the paradigms of imperialism. Mussolini dictated his fascism upon Africa, and the transgressive fatalism of colonization is the "unalterable necessity" dealt with in the poem. In a letter, Stevens displayed a flippant racism common to his time, and now inexcusable. He claimed "The Italians had as much right to take Ethiopia from the coons as the coons had to take it from the boa constrictors" (*L* 290). As racist as that comment is, Stevens uses it for rhetorical effect to mean, in my view, that natural order is based on "Forever hunting or hunted" (*OP* 86). Another letter revised the matter:

> [A]ll of my sympathies are the other way: with the coons and the boa constrictors. . . . A man would have to be very thick-skinned not to be conscious of the pathos of Ethiopia or China, or one of these days, if we are not careful, of this country. But that Mussolini is right, *practically,* has certainly a great deal to be said for it. (*L* 295)

I emphasize *practically* because I think Stevens' point is that Mussolini is right in terms of a Darwinian law of the jungle. The supremacy of "survival of the fittest" takes on huge proportions in this century. In his poems and letters Stevens acknowledges this most crude form of Pragmatism. Stevens deconstructs history's patterns of dominance in an effort to learn from the mistakes, which are often in contemporaneous progress. In "The Greenest Continent," imperialism is shown to be part of an infectious Western "esthetic du mal," which Stevens will develop in that 1944 poem.

In his efforts to rewrite a more acceptable and understood *Aphorisms on Society* (the poem's provisional title), Stevens' editing often betrays his critique's target. Canto ii is cut, with the exception of the first six words. This act sacrifices the precise satire of Europe as a bankrupt wasteland that exports its cultural resources to "people in Maine, / Ontario, Canton" (*OP* 84). These edited lines from *Owl's Clover* comment upon cultural production in the new Western marketplace. Similarly, in the next section, "A Duck for Dinner," the pioneer figure acquires culture through books from Paris and London. These cut sections of poetry were met with resistance in the thirties, but now reveal the cultural contexts binding Stevens in the history that his poetry critiqued. They show the poet at his most rhetorically opinionated, commenting on the political movements of culture in history. Stevens was unlike other modernists in his skeptical demonstrations of American global perspectives from a local viewpoint.

At the beginning of this chapter's analysis, I remarked upon Alan Filreis's preference for the *argument* of *Owl's Clover*, which opposes the majority of the criticism on Stevens that praises *creativity*. My position is that Stevens' development of a rhetorical poetry annuls the polarization of this dialectic. I have illustrated this point by analyzing several passages in which high *creativity* is explicitly performed by Stevens while it is simultaneously the object of rhetorical satire. The next poem's title, "A Duck for Dinner," is ripe with satirical potential. In discussing this poem, I will continue to make use of Filreis' observations, and engage in dialogue with some of his arguments about the poem. I am doing this partly because his historical findings indispensably enrich the poem. Nevertheless, Filreis' historical polemics occasionally overlook how the poem's argument is positioned as a rhetorical dramatization, and not simply as a transparent presentation of an authorial view.

In "A Duck for Dinner," Stevens addresses another situation prescient for American culture: a new civilization largely populated by working-class immigrants. A duck for dinner is a metaphor for the consumer consumption in the park wherein the poem is set, likely a fictional account of Hartford's Elizabeth Park, which Stevens walked almost daily.[5] In this local poem, as in "Mr. Burnshaw and the Statue," Stevens inscribes civic society as the poetic subject:

> The Bulgar said, "After pineapple with fresh mint
> We went to walk in the park; for, after all,
> The workers do not rise, as Venus rose,
> Out of a violet sea. They rise a bit
> On summer Sundays in the park, a duck
> To a million, a duck with apples and without wine."   (*OP* 91)

One of "the sisterhood of the living dead" (*CP* 87), Venus is replaced by immigrant workers as the poem's inspiration, or contemporary subject. The dilemma posed is similar to that of "The Old Woman and the Statue": is the public space and its monument adequately nourishing its citizens? "A Duck for Dinner" specifies the dilemma in a Nietzschean question, "What super-animal dictate our fates?" The answer sides with liberal ideology, although totalitarianism is ominous in its proximity: "As the man the state, not as the state the man . . ." (*OP* 93). Within the balance of these possible ideologies live the people in this park:

> Is each man thinking his separate thoughts or, for once,
> Are all men thinking together as one, thinking
> Each other's thoughts, thinking a singular thought,
> Disclosed in everything, transcended, poised
> For the syllable, poised for the touch? But that
> Apocalypse was not contrived for parks,
> Geranium budgets, pay-roll water-falls,
> The clank of the carousel and, under the trees,
> The sheep-like falling-in of distances,
> Converging on the Statue, white and high.   (*OP* 93)

For the fourth consecutive poem of *Owl's Clover,* the dream of art impelling collective action is shown as a transcendent ideal resulting in "Apocalypse." Clashing with the sculptor's materialized vision are all the other kitschy items of the park, which seem more appropriately part of this culturally plastic place of happy consumption.

The topos of "A Duck for Dinner" is similar to the civic ordering of wilderness Stevens first offered in 1917's "Anecdote of the Jar." Both poems illustrate a formal dominance that is arbitrary and universal (is that jar in Tennessee, Vietnam, or Keats' ode?). In "A Duck for Dinner," a local (though unnamed) park is the site for a conversation about civic responsibility in a new racially diverse, economically and culturally depressed America.

In lines expressing the oppressive ideology and fate that is the poem's concern, the "sheep-like falling-in of distances" present an idea of order imposed by the park's urban plan that herds the public around the monument. The park's designers—architect, sculptor—have immense power upon collective action. Unlike "The Old Woman [with] the Statue," however, this public imports vital culture that will occasionally persevere:

> Then Basilewsky in the band-stand played
> "Concerto for Airplane and Pianoforte,"
> The newest Soviet reclame. Profound
> Abortion, fit for the enchanting of basilisks.   (*OP* 93)

Stevens' humor is not counting on an American melting pot, as these lines follow:

> They chanced to think. Suppose that future fails.
> If platitude and inspiration are alike
> As evils, and if reason, fatuous fire,
> Is only another egoist wearing a mask,
> What man of folk-lore shall rebuild the world. . . ?   (*OP* 93)

Discrediting the present's inheritance of the past, including a personifica-tion of reason that comically masks its sinister fraudulence, Stevens probes the will of the future.

In order to estimate the future, canto ii revisits American history up to the present. Whereas cantos i and iii are voiced by the immigrant Bulgar, section ii's narrative is set in an indirect voice addressing a third person American pioneer:

> O buckskin, O crosser of snowy divides,
> For whom men were to be ends in themselves,
> Are the cities to breed as mountains bred, the streets
> To trundle children like the sea? For you,
> Day came upon the spirit as life comes
> And deep winds flooded you; for these, day comes,
> A penny sun in a tinsel sky, unrhymed . . .   (*OP* 91)

Stevens utilizes the archaic "O" to mourn the passing of the pioneer. Even this device of ironic elegy was tempered to "Buckskins and broad-brims, crossers of divides" for the 1937 edition of the poem. In the poem's rhetorical questioning, Stevens parodically mourns the past's balanced nat-ural order, which literally inspired the pioneer. In contrast, the rest of this verse layers abstract forms, resembling the Cubism of "Key West's" "heaped" composition of "mountainous atmospheres." Here the speaker questions whether "the streets / [Will] trundle children like the sea?" The streets roll children and, likewise, the cities revolve tectonically. Stevens' imagery combines apocalyptic fear, the natural fulfillment of the pioneer, and plastic commerce to ask what kind of sublimity will arise from the future that's being composed here. After the transition to the present at the semicolon, nature is forged into the context of marketed tawdriness that Americans are now accustomed to in public (theme) parks. The conse-quence of spiritual poverty is next expressed in the poem.

In "Key West" I tried to show that the poem's central question, "Whose spirit is this?" was answered by the abstract composition of the poem (and that answer is both *creation* and *argument*). "Whose spirit is this?" continues to be the imperative for *Owl's Clover.* Here the public spirit continues to be sought as something that in 1936 is not represented adequately. Whereas the above lines about the pioneer refer to nineteenth-century naturalistic representations of spirit that Emerson and Whitman expressed before him, Stevens' civic present remains "unrhymed,"

> And the spirit writhes to be wakened, writhes
> To see, once more, this hacked-up world of tools,
> The heart in slattern pinnacles, the clouds,
> Which were their thoughts, squeezed into shapes, the sun
> Streamed white and stoked and engined wrick-a-wrack.
> In your cadaverous Eden, they desire
> The same down-dropping fruit in yellow leaves,
> The same return at heavy evening, love
> Without any horror of the helpless loss.   (*OP* 91–2)

The zeitgeist suffers at the hands of its own nostalgia for the old poetic constructions—here resembling Prufrock, who "squeezed the universe into a ball," which recalls the microcosms of Marvell and Donne. But Stevens presents "this hacked-up world of tools" in a materially haphazard manner that undermines the formal metaphysics suggested by these lines. However, the identity of the subject in "your cadaverous Eden" appears more specific than the general public or the pioneer here. Perhaps it alludes to Geoffrey Grigson, who wrote a nasty review of Stevens, and whom Filreis identifies as the critical speaker behind the Bulgar's mask in canto iii.[6] Whether the subject masks Grigson, Eliot (as the ensuing lines further suggest), or the "buckskin" that is this canto's primary figure, the subject is changed to "their cadaverous Eden" in 1937, thereby replacing the hollow nostalgia on the public's shoulders. The last line makes known Stevens' disgust toward the futile resuscitation of old forms, especially because "the helpless loss" of a "heart in slattern pinnacles" is more powerful than any refabrications such a heart can make.

In Stevens' poetic this apocalypse is less the stuff of doom and gloom than it is of ridicule and frustration. For Stevens a "helpless loss" refers to any event that has already occurred, because monumentalizing it is simply denying death and change. This manner of thinking was uncommon to modernism, and for many readers versed in angst-ridden apocalyptic visions, an Eliot-like doom is exactly what these lines would signify. The tendency to interpret apocalyptic pathos may be the reason why Stevens cut out those last two lines, "The same return . . . the helpless loss." He also removed the references to European cities from the following lines:

The scholar's outline that you had, the print
Of London, the paper of Paris magnified
By poets, the Italian lives preserved
For poverty are gaudy bosh to these.   (*OP* 92)

In cutting the first two lines above from the 1937 edition, the reference to
modernist European tutelage is erased from the poem. In sacrificing that
critique, the poem loses its historical trace of the early-twentieth-century
poetic response to a denaturalized America lacking representation.[7] Perhaps the satire was too strong, too potent, for either readers or the poet to
cope with. Stevens' basic point, which is axed from the 1937 edition, is that
neither a traditional pioneer naturalism nor Eurocentrism feed the contemporary spirit of the new public, paradoxically from Europe:

Their destiny is just as much machine   (*OP* 92)
As death itself, [and never can be changed
By print or paper, the trivial chance foregone,
And only an agony of dreams can help,
Not the agony of a single dreamer, but   [removed
The wide night mused by tell-tale muttering . . .]   in 1937]

It is ironic that by mechanizing death Stevens affirms its natural course. The
Edenic longings and apocalyptic fears inscribed by the "print or paper" of
poets in Europe belong to a long-standing Christian tradition, which is
presented as an anomalous blip in time here. Stevens forecasts "an agony of
dreams" that opposes "the agony of a single dreamer." This vision of necessity turns away from the autonomous artist as visionary savior. The "pressure of the contemporaneous" mass is manifest in "The wide night mused
by tell-tale muttering." This image invokes a collective unconsciousness
"muttering" in an as yet inarticulate language. I suggest that "tell-tale" puns
the tales of the tribe told by single dreamers, while also implying that the
dreaming mass will be the agents exposing the old lies in their collective
night music. It is also the "tell-tale heart" in Poe's story that speaks of the
protagonist's buried conscience.

This indication of the powerful pressure of the collective upon the
poet's consciousness strongly counters modernist individualism, but was
also cut from Stevens' second edition. In keeping with the omitted references to London and Paris, the 1937 edition emphasizes Stevens' reluctance
to provoke open debate with his contemporary modernist exiles. Morse's
decision to put back what was cut allows us to gauge more precisely

Stevens' radical difference from European modernism, and to understand more fully his poetics and motivations. Both editions of the poem include fears of fate that spur Stevens to search for a collectively informed art:

> . . . the sleepless sleepers moved
> By the torture of things that will be realized,
> Will, will, but how and all of them asking how
> And sighing. These lives are not your lives, O free,
> O bold, that rode your horses straight away.   (*OP* 92)

The end of canto ii firmly differentiates the archaic "O free / O bold" pioneer from the mass present. In continuing to draw from the image of horses on the apocalyptic Statue, Stevens amalgamates Biblical myth, the pioneer naturalist, and European visionary modernism as Western tradition whose romance has passed. Anyone who is anxious about changing the ways of their world will recognize the accuracy of "sleepless sleepers," and how such anxieties can influence the daily actions of such people. In willing the will of the future, Stevens is very honest about the uncertainty of "how" change will come. In his reluctance to provide answers, Stevens works by a process of eliminating the poetics, the historical lineages, and the ideologies that serve as monumental cadavers in the present.

Filreis interprets this canto from a different angle, seeing the "Europeanized cultural source-texts [as] the intellectual foundation even of the American roughneck. . . ." And he sees Stevens mourning Eurocentrism, as ruined by "anti-intellectual cultural newcomers." I disagree because Stevens (as does Williams) critiques the exiled modernists' return to classicism, and the point in "A Duck for Dinner" is that nothing in the American heritage will suffice for present concerns. Filreis sees a "reinvented pioneer" to whom Stevens honestly makes an appeal:

> Once this divide-and-conquer strategy has done its work to distinguish foundational pioneer from transgressive immigrant, the speaker urges the reinvented pioneer to see how "These lives are not your lives" and, in nationalist diction—"O free, / O bold"—to mount the heroic Statue *just as it was* and ride "your horses straight away" (*OP* 92).[8]

Filreis switches the verb tense of the pioneer's action from "rode" to "r[i]de your horses straight away," thereby refurbishing him for the present. Filreis goes on to call the poem's polemic, as he interprets it, a "historically preposterous argument," which it would be if it were the one Stevens was making. Stevens never uses "nationalist" or archaic language ("O") without rhetorical gesture. The irony of the Western frontier mentality is lost on Filreis, whose italicized *"just as it was"* speaks of a nostalgia that is reluctant to change, and directly opposes Stevens' poetic.

As much as I differ from Filreis about rhetorical intent, his rigorous historical research links the Bulgar's following critique to Geoffrey Grigson's nasty review of Stevens, "The Stuffed Goldfinch."

> Again the Bulgar said, "There are more things
> Than poodles in Pomerania. This man
> Is all the birds he ever heard and that,
> The admiral of his race and everyman,
> Infected by unreality, rapt round
> By dense unreason, irreproachable force,
> Is cast in pandemonium, filtered, howled
> By harmonies beyond known harmony.   (*OP* 92)

Stevens is likely using the Bulgar to impersonate Grigson's review that makes Stevens the duck for dinner. Here he acknowledges, through the criticism of another, his search for order through irrational music. Stevens' response to another critic demonstrates how badly he wants to meet the challenge of a country devoid of a poetry that meets the people. Though seeing these lines as a self-critique is valid, the potential for a poet's impact looms in the succeeding lines, still in the Bulgar's voice:

> These bands, these swarms, these motions, what of them?
> They keep to the paths of the skeleton architect
> Of the park. They obey the rules of every skeleton.   (*OP* 92)

The mass's will to be herded according to park design goads the poet on. In *Adagia* Stevens writes, "Aristotle is a skeleton" (*OP* 194), suggesting that the rhetorician's designs, like the architect's park, are blueprints for others to follow.

Canto v proclaims, "The Statue is the sculptor not the stone," and in doing so exhibits history as being determined by its designers. This view is the impetus for 1945's "Description without Place," in which the "green queen" determines her age, as do Lenin and Nietzsche. Although Stevens traces the determination of history from ideology, from aesthetics, and from personal psychology, he expresses discomfort about such causation, especially because the few zealots in power destine the rest. Canto v elaborates the sculptor's power in thick irony, set upon a palimpsest of the long Western tradition:

> Exceeding sex, he touched another race,
> Above our race, yet of ourselves transformed,
> Don Juan turned furious divinity,
> Ethereal compounder, pater patriae,
> Great mud-ancestor, oozer and Abraham,
> Progenitor wearing the diamond crown of crowns,
> He from whose beard the future springs, elect.   (*OP* 95)

These images resonate capaciously over time, and could be applied to many historical figures. "Great mud-ancestor" may be the vaguest image; I think this creature belongs to the reptillian "archaic change" oozing in the detritus of "Mr. Burnshaw and the Statue." If Stevens' poetics must have an origin, it is imagined as the earth's "muddy center" from which evolution began. Regardless, the trace of patriarchal power in canto v is suddenly followed by these lines, which lack smooth transition in the poem (as if a line were missing):

> More of ourselves in a world that is more our own,
> For the million perhaps, two ducks instead of one;
> More of ourselves, the mood of life made strong
> As by a juicier season; and more our own
> As against each other, the dead, the phantomesque.   (*OP* 95)

I suppose "More" is the point. The Platonic elite election of the Statue is countered by the democratic consideration of another duck, another park feeding more people.

The last line adds weight and complexity to Stevens' civic hopes. In forwarding multiplicity Stevens foregoes harmony for difference. To have "more our own" we must imagine "As against each other." I suggest that "As" is used causally, metaphorically, and conditionally here. The "mood of life made strong" will occur because of "a juicier season," and that strong life will only be possible if a juicy season is imagined. In addition, the world will be "more our own" if we can exist "As against each other, the dead, the phantomesque," implying that we need to conceptualize our differences as they've been formed by the phantoms of dead generations, which were traced in the previous ironic lines. In utilizing both causal and creative relations, Stevens employs a variation of his conditional simile technique; the "as if" philosophy that Jacqueline Brogan traces in *Stevens and Simile.* This technique allows Stevens to unify *creation* and *argument* into an indivisible rhetoric.

Canto vi immediately shows that Stevens wants his poetics of change, thinking in and about flux, to work with nature:

> If these were theoretical people, like
> Small bees of spring, sniffing the coldest buds
> Of a time to come . . .   (*OP* 95)

Stevens does not proceed to tiptoe through the tulips; he warns us about how easily nature is wrought with sublime fear:

>   —A shade of horror turns
> The bees to scorpions blackly-barbed, a shade
> Of fear changes the scorpions to skins
> Concealed in glittering grass, dank reptile skins.   (*OP* 95)

Here we can observe Stevens' poetry inching toward an "Esthetique du Mal." At this point, however (eight years prior), a comprehensive aesthetic for the sublime is projected as a distant useless abstraction (of the pejorative, rather than the materially effective abstract kind):

> The civil fiction, the calico idea,
> The Johnsonian composition, abstract man,
> All are evasions like a repeated phrase,
> Which, by its repetition, comes to bear
> A meaning without meaning.   (*OP* 95)

While the poet desires the "civil fiction, the calico idea," these ideals remain "evasions." If we recall, "Add This to Rhetoric" makes a choice—"This is the figure and not / An evading metaphor"—which goes against "evasions" and opts for the materially effective rhetorical "figure." "A Duck for Dinner," as with the other poems of *Owl's Clover*, ends without solution because there never can be one, but it slowly edges "inch by inch," like the "Great mud-ancestor" away from past confines toward the hope for better representations.

> How shall we face the edge of time? We walk
> In the park. We regret we have no nightingale.
> We must have the throstle on the gramaphone.
> Where shall we find more than derisive words?
> When shall lush chorals spiral through our fire
> And daunt that old assassin, heart's desire?   (*OP* 96)

This "we" includes the park-goers, for whom Stevens wants to collect and transcribe dreams in his poems.

Filreis praises this "hard-earned we" as a significant move away from the "stock figures" of *"Victorian ideology"* (*L* 289) that Stevens worried about before writing "Mr. Burnshaw."[9] The "we" is earned throughout *Owl's Clover* in many figures that represent the complex contemporaneity of the 1930s. The Old Woman, for instance, is not a realistic figure for an insurance executive/poet to use as his persona, but she best represents the contemporary predicament pressing Stevens' imagination. "The Old Woman and the Statue" materializes as "a disclosure of my own sensibility. . . . The Old Woman is a symbol of those who suffered during the depression." By recalling "The Irrational Element in Poetry," a talk that accompanied Stevens' reading of "The Old Woman and the Statue," we can see that the figures of *Owl's Clover* are far from "stock" concerns:

> . . . I had in mind . . . the effect of the depression on the interest in art. I wanted a confronting of the world as it had been imagined in art and as it was then in fact. If I dropped into a gallery I found that I had no interest in what I saw. . . . To look at pictures there was the same thing as to play the piano in Madrid this afternoon. (*OP* 226)

Mr. Burnshaw and the Old Woman are not "stock figures," but are "a confronting of the world" that approach the "fact" of the 1930s Depression. Stevens' "hard-earned we" began *Owl's Clover* in the challenge of the Old Woman, and it ends "A Duck for Dinner" in the shape of the irrational dreams of a collective public.

The kitschy American park is local and diasporic; its collectivity is composed out of differences constructed in rhetorical relation. The place appears cartoonish and irrational because it lacks traditional symbolic order. The poet composes these "Artificial Populations" in an effort not to define them, but to "let be / The way it came, let be what it may become" (*OP* 100). "Whose spirit is this?" is now an immediate and forward-looking question, whereas in "The Idea of Order" it spoke of a crossroads between archaic and new music.

The final poem in the sequence, "Sombre Figuration," is more recollective and lacks the specific social objectives of *Owl's Clover*'s other poems. Its reformulative distance establishes a more mystical ambience, which makes room for Stevens' "subman," a paradigmatic figure that the rest of Stevens' poetry employs in variations:

> There is a man whom rhapsodies of change,
> Of which he is the cause, have never changed
> And never will, a subman under all
> The rest, to whom in the end the rest return,
> The man below the man below the man,
> Steeped in night's opium, evading day.   (*OP* 96)

This solid beast resides at the poet's core. Making other appearances in poems written in 1919, 1935, and 1942, "Jocundus" enjoys "the gaudium of being" (*OP* 101) rather than the challenge of contemporary social pressure. The "subman" lies dormant and prevents the poet from becoming an ideological chameleon:

> We have grown weary of the man that thinks.
> He thinks and it is not true. The man below
> Imagines and it is true, as if he thought
> By imagining, anti-logician, quick
> With a logic of transforming certitudes.   (*OP* 96)

The "anti-logician" carries the poet's "irrational music," to which we turned in "The Irrational Element in Poetry." Following the above lines, the subman of "Sombre Figuration" differs from the pantheistic Ananke from "The Greenest Continent":

> It is not that he was born in another land,
> Powdered with primitive lights, and lives with us
> In glimpses, on the edge or at the tip,
> Playing a cracked reed, wind-stopped, in bleats.   (*OP* 97)

The subman "was born within us as a second self, / A self of parents who have never died," and as such this figure is part of "the intelligence that endures" from the past through the present. The subman evolves into Ariel, who works dialogically with fellow citizens in 1950's "Angel Surrounded by Paysans."

Canto ii describes as well as anywhere else in Stevens' poetry the tropic functions of this figure, both as a poetic device and spirit in the material world:

> He dwells below, the man below, in less
> Than body and in less than mind, ogre,
> Inhabitant, in less than shape, of shapes

That are dissembled in vague memory
Yet still retain resemblances, remain
Remembrances, a place of a field of lights,
As a church is a bell and people are an eye,
A cry, the pallor of a dress, a touch.   (*OP* 97)

"Whose spirit is this?" from "The Idea of Order at Key West" remains the answering question. The "body wholly body, fluttering / Its empty sleeves" has been transformed into a more intimately present masculine "ogre," who is "less / Than body." The spirit that was an empty signifier, an outline without a core, now has an expansive core yet an elusive amoeba-like shape. The muse or devil is only as external as "vague memory," thus she/he lives among us. Stevens does not limit this figure to a Jungian collective unconscious. Although the subman is core, this figure does not synecdochically stand for the collective; he oozes in it. The possible reading of synecdoche in "As a church is a bell" is dissolved into the metonymic aggregation of "people are an eye / A cry, the pallor of a dress, a touch." Gaudy Jocundus wears, as do Yeats' and Barthes' personae, "a clown's coat" *(Barthes by Barthes)*.[10] The subman is a metonymic agent who aggregates images in a composition:

The man below beholds the portent poised,
An image of his making, beyond the eye,
Poised, but poised as the mind through which a storm
Of other images blows. . . .   (*OP* 99)

Rather like a physical particle in motion, or a bumbling clown, the subman acts as a "catalyst" (Eliot wore a whiter coat) in a narrative that he does not master. The figure of the subman can be as large as "a place of a field of lights," which could be a sightline for the aurora borealis (later coming in "The Auroras of Autumn"). The subman registers "The Irrational Element in Poetry."

Stevens counts Jocundus as a reader, thereby increasing the subman's intimate role in interpretation, while carefully instructing us that he wears an artificial mask, which needs to be read as would any other trope:

He turns us into scholars, studying
The masks of music. We perceive each mask
To be the musician's own and, thence, become
An audience to mimics glistening
With meanings, doubled by the closest sound,

> Mimics that play on instruments discerned
> In the beat of the blood.   (*OP* 97)

Although Stevens says the subman is one of "us," he is so especially as a scholar-reader: he reads the "masks of music" in his writing. His poetry is a readerly trace composing yet another trace for us, but when readers assume the poetic trace "To be the musician's own," then the author is identified as his work. The point is that "The masks of music," not "the musician[s]," are the "mimics." And if music is the mimic, then its echoes produce tropes that are full of rhetorical commentary. The rhetoric of music is "discerned / In the beat of the blood"; that is, in the pulses that are transmitted to the head for processing. In this capacity, the subman functions at apparently subconscious or bodily levels, which escape logical intelligence. This formless matter denies comprehensive interpretation.

I refer you to Stevens' lecture, "The Noble Rider and the Sound of Words," in which he's discussing the losses and gains of twentieth-century poetry:

> I do not know of anything that will appear to have suffered more from the passage of time than the music of poetry and that has suffered less. The deepening need for words to express our thoughts and feelings which, we are sure, are all the truth that we shall ever experience, having no illusions, makes us listen to words when we hear them, loving them and feeling them, makes us search for the sound of them, for a finality, a perfection, an unalterable vibration, which it is only within the power of the acutest poet to give them. . . . [A]bove everything else, poetry is words: and that words, above everything else, are, in poetry, sounds. This being so, my time and yours might have been better spent if I had been less interested in trying to give our possible poet an identity and less interested in trying to appoint him to his place. But unless I had done these things, it might have been thought that I was rhetorical, when I was speaking in the simplest way about things of such importance that nothing is more so. (*NA* 32)

This passage, like all of Stevens' prose, is as interesting for what it hides as what it reveals. "Sombre Figuration" argued against identifying the poet in the poem. Here in "The Noble Rider" lecture, Stevens acknowledges that if he had not identified the poet and provided him with an upstanding role, "it might have been thought that [he] was rhetorical. . . ." This charge had been laid on Stevens a year or so earlier when *Owl's Clover* was published. In that poem Stevens writes a rhetorical poetry that registers potencies that this speech only approximates. The audience wants a concrete answer. Stevens' (anti-)answer lies in the rhetoric of his poetry, a tactic that had been given bad reception, so he avoids it here. Identity and place are nametags that people can hang onto, and Stevens acknowledges their service. But as *Owl's Clover* argues and "Description without Place" will clearly theorize, identity and place are rhetorically constructed, and much of rhetoric's fabric is music. The chords that persuade people need not come from a stereo. They used to come from amphitheatres where leaders roused the public, and now they come from televisions. Music here is a metaphor because the common definition of it too narrowly relies on melody and harmony. However, many dissonances register in our ears, stimulate messages "In the beat of the blood," and move us just the same. So music can be a literal term too, once the metaphor expands its previously narrow definition.

Rhetoric, language that persuades, is not solely made of music. Many other factors, including logic, come into play. Perhaps logic is just the musical narrative. Defining logic is less important than pursuing the relation of music and rhetoric. Rhetoric communicates ideas that we rationalize and intellectualize. Those ideas or contents are wrapped in the music that enters the ear. That packaging may be intricately logical and dry as toast, but the narrative comprehended is made up of sonic nuances. Chances are, the better they sound, the more they'll register. Such is music's role in language. Rhetoric has other provinces than music, such as authoritative command, appeals to fear, and to self-interest (i.e., economic gain). All emotional, logical, and perhaps ethical appeals, I suggest, are bolstered by music: in advertising, poetry, church, and state.

Stevens' alleviation of the "rhetorical" in his talk is nonsense, perhaps ironically so. He leaves out the music of poetry and substitutes mostly an appeal to satisfy his audience's skeptical curiosity. In trying to forego musical rhetoric, Stevens omits his greatest skill. His ability to turn phrases into creative arguments constructs an "irrational" logic that counters our suppositions of logical positivism. Stevens cites "Boileau's remark that Descartes had cut poetry's throat" (*NA* 14), and "The Noble Rider" includes Locke, Hobbes, and the latest enemy, Freud. Without the musical rhetoric that Stevens employs and forwards in a self-reflexive argument of "rhetoricity," Stevens' prose basically plays by the same rules that he opposes. Because of this, the poet has to make up concepts such as "nobility," "imagination and reality" that are both imprecise and rigid (unless you deconstruct them), unlike the fluid manifestations of those labels in the poetry. With prose, Stevens makes concessions to satisfy his audience, or letter addressee. His prose, therefore, is rhetorical in the pejorative sense that it postures in an attempt to be satisfactory, and in those poses Stevens crudely simplifies his poetics. The prosaic masks automate and cover up what the poetry pieces together in composition.[11]

The concern for a vital poetic music in the face of tradition expressed in "The Noble Rider and the Sound of Words" is taken up at the end of "Sombre Figuration." Stevens revisits some "masks of music" already traveled in *Owl's Clover*, discriminating the present as a liquid state in contrast to the solidity of the past:

> The solid was an age, a period
> With appropriate, largely English, furniture,
> Barbers with charts of the only possible modes,
> Cities that would not wash away in the mist,
> Each man in his asylum maundering,
> Policed by the hope of Christmas. . . .   (*OP* 98)

Viewing the past as an English house tropes it in a singular barbarism ("Barbers with charts") suggesting a spreading Christian state. This recasting of the critical imperialism of "The Greenest Continent" is addended by canto iii's vision of the present as it becomes the future: "High up in heaven a sprawling portent moves, / As if it bears all darkness in its bulk." This external ogre is "invisible," seemingly part of a collective consciousness with an unknown fate because poetry has yet to harmonize it: "It is the form / Of a generation that does not know itself, / Still questioning if to crush the soaring stacks, / The churches . . ." (*OP* 98). Echoed here is the critique of industrial apocalypse in "Mr. Burnshaw and the Statue," as is the public willingness to follow the "skeleton" designers in "A Duck for Dinner." The ominous acceleration of *Owl's Clover* converges here into a fearful fascist fate:

> A mass overtaken by the blackest sky,
> Each one as part of the total wrath, obscure
> In slaughter . . .   (*OP* 98)

Mussolini presided in public consciousness at this time, but these lines also prophesize Hitler. As much as Stevens has identified, and predicted the inevitable horror of fascism, the poet is more fearful of it as a revolving phenomenon:

> Which counts for most, the anger borne
> In anger; or the fear that from the death
> Of evil, evil springs . . . ?   (*OP* 99)

The historic repetition of the same legacy is the fear and enemy of Stevens' poetics of change. This brutal depiction of fascism was also cut from the 1937 edition of the poem, another indication that the poet did not want to contend with the monster here created.

Filreis accurately notes "Stevens's deferred anxieties about political reference," and in this instance we concur about "some of Stevens's strongest lines," as Filreis estimates canto iv's "antifascism."[12] But in marking the transition to *Blue Guitar,* Filreis minimizes the significance of *Owl's Clover:* "Gone in a year's time was this powerful suggestion that the prospect of evil, a political catastrophe that 'Can Happen Here,' would exploit 'the form / Of a generation that does not know itself.'" True, but Stevens brings back the prospect of evil with a vengeance in "Esthetique du Mal," written near the end of World War II. And the rhetorical determination of history and the public is strongly developed in "Description without Place," also published in 1947's *Transport to Summer.*

For the time being, however, *Owl's Clover*'s intense ambition to confront the contemporaneous wears the poet out:

> High up in heaven the sprawling portent moves.
> The Statue in a crow's perspective of trees
> Stands brimming white, chiaroscuro scaled
>
> To space. . . .   (*OP* 100)

As delirious as this sounds, it remains consistent with Stevens' view of a future fated by the limitless inscriptions to come. The poem nears its end when "the man below, the subverter, stops / The flight of emblemata through his mind" (*OP* 100). Fatigue actually becomes integral to the evolving poetics of the subman:

> . . . to feel again
> . . . a present time, is that
> The passion, indifferent to the poet's hum,
> That we conceal? A passion to fling the cloak,
> Adorned for the multitude, in a gesture spent
> In the gesture's whim, a passion merely to be
> For the gaudium of being, Jocundus instead

Of the black-blooded scholar, the man of the cloud, to be
The medium man among other medium men . . .   (*OP* 100–1)

This acceptance is unheroic albeit integral to coming to terms with society's reception of poetry. This universal indifferent passion that perseveres *carpe diem* in lieu of urgent socio-political pressures is part of the reservoir constituting "the irrational element of poetry." It set the stage for *The Man with the Blue Guitar,* and the "hum-drum" "medium man" will continually resurface, especially in "Notes Toward a Supreme Fiction."

Stevens rests with a manageable persona. More than that, *Owl's Clover* critically implodes politics and aesthetics through a rhetorical poetry that collapses the dialectic of creation and argument. Stevens does not strive to justify this critical prophesy through the later poetry, or push its potentials; he is not that dogmatic. However, *Owl's Clover* develops a powerful rhetorical language that creates occasion and puts fate in the reader's lap. This ambitious project for poetry revives at maximum potential in poems such as "Esthetique du Mal" and "Description without Place."

Coda: A Defense of *Owl's Clover* by "The Noble Rider"

I have to address some criticisms of *Owl's Clover.* Filreis criticizes the poetry of *Owl's Clover* for not being politically rigorous enough, and somehow not aesthetic enough in comparison, say, to the lauded *The Man with the Blue Guitar.*

> Here again "Owl's Clover" slips into the language for which it is notorious: aphoristic but programmatic, giving the feel of "snippets"—Williams's term for "Like Decorations"—yet long in metrical feet, its rhetoric half-quoting and garbling slogans against which Stevens's speaker-artist is supposed to have been cautioning us, for instance "As the man the state, not as the state the man" (*OP* 93).[13]

Aphoristic programmatic snippets may not appeal to those who favor the sharp form of *Blue Guitar,* or to those who feel Stevens' aesthetic has no place in Marxist territory, but *garbling slogans* are what people remember. Cutting turns of phrase are often quoted; just think of the impact of sound bites, or Shakespeare. Our present-day inundation by rhetorical postures was preempted by Stevens' poetic that is both *creation* and *argument,* as is the forceful poetry in hip-hop music today. So if Williams was right about *snippets,* so was Stevens, although the literary world of 1936 may not have been—

especially if we remember that Stevens' poetry had the high aesthetic reputation, a quality that directly opposes programmatic snippets. How could
criticism contend with a study of sound bites and their fatal implications
in society?

Stevens' meager justification for omitting *Owl's Clover* on the basis of
excessive rhetoric is amplified by the 1942 essay, "The Noble Rider and the
Sound of Words." In preceding discussion I have addressed Stevens' critical
confluence of music and rhetoric in poetry; yet "The Noble Rider" tram-
ples over several lingering queries and accusations that people have regarding this aspect of Stevens. By tracing these conscientious objections I hope
to underline why *Owl's Clover* was cut, criticized, why it is crucial, and why
Stevens' later poetry moved in new but contingent directions.

The essay begins with a citation from Plato's *Phaedrus,* which projects
the soul in the figure of "*a pair of winged horses and a charioteer*" (*NA* 3).
Stevens employs "what Coleridge called Plato's dear, gorgeous nonsense"
to exemplify an imaginative aesthetic that does not bear up on twentieth-
century reality. The essay progresses in an argumentative dialectic between
connotative and denotative art, of which Plato is the connotative dupe. We
readers then have to be careful with Stevens' baggy terms "imagination and
reality," because they're not exact or normal. Plato has no "strength of reality" precisely because "this [soul] figure has lost its [imaginative] vitality"
(*NA* 7). Imagination has to *press back* on reality; neither can be separate.

Not surprisingly, Stevens' pejorative example of denotative art is

> in Washington, in Lafayette Square, which is the square on which the White
> House faces. [A] Statue of Andrew Jackson, rid[es] a horse with one of the
> most beautiful tails in the world. General Jackson is raising his hat in a gay
> gesture, saluting the ladies of his generation. One looks at this work of Clark
> Mills and thinks of the remark of Bertrand Russell that to acquire immu-
> nity to eloquence is the utmost importance to the citizens of a democ-
> racy. . . . This work is a work of fancy. . . . That it is a work of fancy
> precludes it from being a work of the imagination. A glance at it shows it
> to be unreal. The bearing of this is that there can be works, and this
> includes poems, in which neither the imagination nor reality is present.
> (*NA* 10–11)

Stevens' alignment of State and Statue parodies monumentalism here, and
this depiction was similar in "The American Sublime," the title of which
should alert us to the problem.[14] General Jackson strikes the pose because,
as Stevens wonders in the poem: "Shall a man go barefoot / Blinking and
blank?" (*CP* 131). This spiritual poverty is based on bad fanciful art, which

influences Stevens to ground his poetry in America ("Whose spirit is this?"). This reasoning for Stevens' local revitalization is confirmed in his 1948 lecture, "Imagination as Value," read at Columbia University: "It is a commonplace . . . to say that, in this town, no single public object of the imagination exists, while in the Vatican City, say, no public object exists that is not an object of the imagination" (*NA* 140–1). This explains why Stein, H. D., Pound, Eliot, and others exiled themselves in gaudy Europe, while Stevens, Williams, Moore, and others stayed at home to bake the domestic cake.

After charting a history of the linguistic war between connotations and denotations—and referring to "Boileau's remark that Descartes had cut poetry's throat" (*NA* 14)—Stevens gets to the challenge he posed in *Owl's Clover:* to write a poem addressing contemporary pressure while arguing that such social pressure is rhetorical; the product of connotations that think they are denotations (*To Be Itself,* the Marxist insignia being one, the Statue being another). Despite what I see as the success of that difficult composite poem-argument, Stevens could not sustain contemporaneous social or critical pressure, and so this turn:

> A tendency toward the connotative, whether in language or elsewhere, cannot continue against the pressure of reality. If it is the pressure of reality that controls poetry, then the immediacy of various theories of poetry is not what it was. (*NA* 16)

The pressure of reality is not the same as "the pressure of the contemporaneous," the challenge Stevens took up in *Owl's Clover.* The pressure of reality is larger, but I suspect for Stevens contemporary pressure felt like total reality (as his letters and "The Irrational Element of Poetry" suggest). Nevertheless, Stevens had yet to find a satisfactory connotative poetic to contend with the pressure of reality. "The Noble Rider and the Sound of Words" was provoked by an invitation from Henry and Barbara Church to read at Princeton, and it was published in 1942, the same year as "Notes Toward a Supreme Fiction," which begins with a dedication to Henry Church. The dedication reflects Stevens' gratitude to Church for propelling Stevens to theorize the accomplished connotative poetics of "Notes."

Stevens' operative solution is much the same as what was projected in 1939's "The Woman That Had More Babies Than That," which I will soon discuss. Stevens refers in "The Noble Rider" to "Croce's Oxford lecture of 1933," from which we can project the heroes of "Notes" and locate the title of another Stevens essay, "The Whole Man: Perspectives, Horizons."

"If . . . poetry is intuition and expression, the fusion of sound and imagery, what is the material which takes on the form of sound and imagery? It is the whole man: the man who thinks and wills, and loves, and hates; who is strong and weak, sublime and pathetic, good and wicked; man in the exaltation and agony of living; and together with the man, integral with him, it is all nature in its perpetual labor of evolution. . . . Poetic genius chooses a straight path in which passion is calmed and calm is passionate." (*NA* 16)

Next to contemporary pressures, this Wordsworthian "emotion recollected in tranquillity" sounds dilute—for better (capacious scope) or worse (dissolution). In reasoning this retreat, Stevens returns to the romantic, which he'd already overhauled in the thirties. Stevens reasons his return here:

The spirit of negation has been so active, so confident and so intolerant that the commonplaces about the romantic provoke us to wonder if our salvation, if the way out, is not the romantic. All the great things have been denied and we live in an intricacy of new and local mythologies, political, economic, poetic, which are asserted with an ever-enlarging incoherence. This is accompanied by an absence of any authority except force, operative or imminent. (*NA* 17)

Owl's Clover exercised operative forces against imminent ones. The reason why Stevens called Marxism "the most magnificent cause in the world" and "just a new romanticism" is because it operates against imminent force. Stevens, like Marxists, sees imminent force as a huge problem, whether it exists in a lousy Statue, a military state, or an unconscious public prone to fascism. But "Marxism is just a new romanticism" because the leftists of the thirties, for Stevens, claimed an imminence that mirrored their opposition. Which is why *Owl's Clover* feared the revolution would go round and round.

Stevens' treatment of Marxism as romance not only points to Marxism's pretence toward immanence, it also led the poet to further pursue the limits of idealism. Citing Charles Mauron, Stevens takes on a common criticism of his work, asking "how is it possible to condemn escapism?":

The poetic process is psychologically an escapist process. The chatter about escapism is, to my way of thinking, merely common cant. My own remarks about resisting or evading the pressure of reality mean escapism, if analyzed. Escapism has a pejorative sense, which it cannot be supposed that I include in the sense in which I use the word. The pejorative sense applies where the poet is not attached to reality, where the imagination does not adhere to reality, which, for my part, I regard as fundamental. (*NA* 31)

This pejorative escapism would apply to Plato's *Phaedrus*, whereas Stevens cites Wordsworth's "This City now doth, like a garment, wear / The beauty of the morning" passage from *The Prelude* to show "how poets help people to live their lives." Stevens says that Wordsworth's lines evoke "a different and familiar description of the place," perhaps forecasting "Description without Place." The following is a similar forecast of that poem:

> There is, in fact, a world of poetry indistinguishable from the world in which we live, or, I ought to say, no doubt, from the world in which we shall come to live, since what makes the poet the potent figure that he is, or was, or ought to be, is that he creates the world to which we turn incessantly and without knowing it and that he gives to life the supreme fictions without which we are unable to conceive of it. (*NA* 31)

Escapism, then, in Stevens' positive defense of it, is simply a different description of a place that invigorates perception. Escapism is a condition of poetry, and within the parameters of Stevens' positive definition, escapism is a linguistic condition: the signifier *Must Be Abstract*. And this abstraction "creates the world to which we turn incessantly," which could be an escapist retreat. But if the linguistic prophesy adheres to reality, which Stevens "regard[s] as fundamental," then "the world to which we turn" is the future that poetry shapes. "Description without Place" culminates with "what we say of the future must portend," and that "sprawling portent" may seem like witchcraft, as it did to most of the critics of *Owl's Clover*, but Stevens' linguistic spells often foretell conceptions that are only coming to be understood (largely owing to the deconstructive and rhetorical theories forwarded by scholars such as Burke, de Man, Derrida, Austin, Kristeva, and Foucault).

Part of the reason that Stevens' fatalistic "sprawling portent" might sound like ominous hocus-pocus is that *Owl's Clover* presents the synchronic chaos of the 1930s, and thereby leaves fate with the reader. In terms of the future, the reader is threatened by apocalypse as well as being offered hope in a collection of difference narrated by the subman. The contemporaneous picture of *Owl's Clover* sorts through past ideologies, but not historically, only as they corrupt the present. This synchronic approach to history is fundamentally different from, and perhaps diametrically opposed to, the modernist paradigm established by Eliot's *The Waste Land*. Wendy Steiner made me aware of this in "Collage or Miracle: Historicism in a Deconstructed World," which compares *The Waste Land* with Pynchon's *The Crying of Lot 49* (Bercovitch, 323–351). Steiner begins by paraphrasing Paul de Man's notion that "the modernist impulse is paradoxical: at once the breaking free of history through the assertion of a fresh start and the inauguration of history through the initiation of an historical origin" (323). While the fresh start could apply to Pound, Stevens, or Williams more so than Eliot, the school of origins belongs to Eliot and Pound. Steiner discusses Eliot's instruction of readers as pupils who, with enough dogged research, can achieve wisdom: "Eliot's history involved the recovery of determinate knowledge, a sense of culture that only the right immersion in past culture could create" (350). This diachrony is contrasted with Pynchon's quest, which "is not to be imagined as a determinate beginning-middle-end structure, but a continuity of ever enlarging hypothesis and data, punctuated by miracle" (350). This lack of narrative telos, and the sense of a present pregnant with data, is shared by *Owl's Clover,* except "miracle" exists on a smaller, less reverent scale. A miracle, revelation, or epiphany is a sudden realization that in Stevens' poetry occurs with a simple repetition of tropes; incidences in the poem in which the reader's present knowledge accumulates through observing familiar discursive patterns or arguments. *Owl's Clover* synchronizes chaos, whereas *The Waste Land,* while largely in the present, nevertheless reverts back through time. Stevens' chaos slowly and by trial becomes ordered, although much of the "sprawling portent" remains for further generations to sort.

De Man's idea about the paradox of modernist historiography does not apply to Stevens because the poet is not interested in origins, only in contaminants. De Manian paradox, Steiner's "Collage or Miracle" debate, Perloff's "Pound/Stevens: Whose Era?," and the creation/argument polarity are a few examples pointing to the entrenchment of binary oppositions in America. I suggest these dialectics pervade the United States as much as Cartesian Reason plagues all of the West. This problem with the American spirit perseveres because it is a revolutionary dialectic, as Steiner notes:

> The history of America can be written as a sequence of struggles between oppressive officialdom and freedom-seeking undergrounds, with the underground winning and turning into the next oppressor. (345)

I would qualify Steiner's eloquent words by suggesting that "undergrounds" often don't win but continue to struggle nevertheless. As far as modernism goes, Eliot sides with "oppressive officialdom," but where does Stevens fit in this axis? He is not the voice of "the underground," although he resists official modernism. I suggest that Stevens' poetics in *Owl's Clover* remain underground, in a sense, because they have yet to be properly acknowledged. These poetics argue that the dialectic of underground oppressed and oppressive state (i.e., "The Old Woman and the Statue")—the monumental aesthetic of the warring state—derives from stale dead romanticism.

For those who are skeptical about poetics, or supreme fictions necessarily ordering reality, consider some contemporary social prognoses. Consider the willing swarms signing up for fundamental Christianity, and other cults. The problems facing contemporary society dwarf those of Stevens' day, and now there is no central doxa to cohere the fraying fabric of society. Mike Harris became the premier of Ontario for this reason: he sold the public on a "common sense revolution" because most people want badly to believe that common sense exists. Each person has to attempt to keep some sane order of things. Speaking of today's social pathology, Robert Hullot-Kentor's foreboding essay, "Past Tense: Ethics, Aesthetics and the Recovery of the Public World" includes a small example of the larger malaise:

> Individuals are crumbling. The 1994 *Diagnostic and Statistical Manual* of psychiatric illness has concluded that trauma is now so common that it can no longer be defined as an event "outside the range of normal human experience." And whereas anxiety was not so long ago the focus of distress, categories of panic attacks have moved to the forefront. Social phobia—the incapacitating fear of humiliation or embarrassment in social events, often combined with agoraphobia and panic anxiety—has become the single most frequent psychiatric problem.[15]

Hullot-Kentor also factors in that "The unity of the worker as an individual is thus heightened as he or she becomes more helpless by being deprived of union recourse in resisting the demands of production" (*West Coast Line* 152). This specific contemporary problem, triggered by right-wing materialism's ruthless legal dismantling of fair working conditions, was stated in more speculative terms by Stevens 52 years earlier:

> The way we work is a good deal more difficult for the imagination than the highly civilized revolution that is occuring in respect to work indicates. It is, in the main, a revolution for more pay. We have been assured, by every visitor, that the American businessman is absorbed in his business and there is nothing to be gained by disputing it. As for the workers, it is enough to say that the word has grown to be literary. They have become, at their work, in the face of the machines, something approximating an abstraction, an energy. The time must be coming when, as they leave the factories, they will be

passed through an air-chamber or a bar to revive them for riot and reading. (*NA* 19)

Some of this syntax may be misleading. Stevens' primary interest here is in the "way we work," which refers to the abstract implementation of worker energies in subordination to their machinery. Because workers approximate, or have to accede to, the primacy of mechanical production, their spirits and bodies are denied and therefore require revitalization. Today, *progressive* corporations find time to implement aerobics into the work day so that automatons can refresh their brainpower. Stevens was fortunate enough to die just as television was born. He was not aware that, no matter how vital one might feel after corporate exercise, "riot and reading" have become endangered pastimes because corporate television conspires to comatize people until nightmares wake us up.

"Materialism is an old story and an indifferent one," Stevens concludes and moves on to the torrid influx of global events through the 1942 media. Then constructing the figure of "a possible poet," Stevens turns to the words of a Dr. Joad:

> "Every body, every quality of a body resolves itself into an enormous number of vibrations, movements, changes. What is it that vibrates, moves, is changed? There is no answer. Philosophy has long dismissed the notion of substance and modern physics has endorsed that dismissal. . . . How, then, does the world come to appear to us as a collection of solid, static objects extended in space? Because of the intellect, which presents us with a false view of it." (*NA* 25)

Stevens would not dismiss substance in the manner of Dr. Joad. Here we are linking Stevens' poetry, his poetics as linguistic theory, and physics all through what some would consider an escapist process.

Lisa Steinman and recently Dana Wilde compare Stevens' poetics with modern quantum physics. Wilde's primary reference, physicist David Bohm, theorizes an implementation of language that prioritizes verbs, which he calls the "rheomode." Bohm suggests that we currently view the world in terms of stationary and divided objects, and our grammar subsequently treats verbs basically as a way for subjects to master objects. However, if language and grammar revolved around verbs, then flux and interdependency would become our manner of thought, rather than self and other, as Bohm explains:

[T]he ordinary mode of language leads us to fail to give attention to the actual function of the divisive world view that pervades this mode, so that the automatic and habitual operation of our thought and language is then able to project these divisions . . . as if they were actual fragmentary breaks in the nature of 'what is'. (Bohm 46–47)

My point regarding *Owl's Clover*'s critique of ideological divisions in America, and how critics classify Stevens, is that their "world views" exist "as if the[re] were actual fragmentary breaks in the nature of 'what is.'" Rhetoric, although implied by Bohm, Stevens, and Wilde, is the missing ingredient to such theory; it is a concept and force that accounts for movement. Bohm explains that *"rheo* is from a Greek verb, meaning 'to flow'" (31), but he does not get into rhetoric. Bohm realizes the challenge of trying to change English grammar, but sees that as more plausible than theoretical persuasion because "to give a clear expression of a world view contrary to the one implied in the primary structure of language is usually very difficult" (46). Stevens is trying to do this, and he sometimes uses grammatical support as we've seen in his conditional similes, and the present participle verbs in "The Idea of Order at Key West," "Of Modern Poetry," *Owl's Clover,* and we'll see more in "Angel Surrounded by Paysans" in a later chapter.

Stevens says that "the subject-matter of poetry is . . . the life that is lived in the scene that it composes; and so reality is not that external scene but the life that is lived in it" (*NA* 25): "Part of the *res* and not about it." You have likely detected the dramatic discourse here. Drama is another conceptual house in which to view Stevens' show. Maureen Kravec has recently explored the dramatistic aspects of Stevens' poetry. She relies on Kenneth Burke, who uses the "dramatistic" to perform rhetorical theory. As much as Stevens employed dramatic metaphors, he acknowledges: "The poetic drama needs a terrible genius before it is anything more than a literary relic. Besides the theater has forgotten that it could ever be terrible. It is not one of the instruments of fate, decidedly" (*NA* 28). Kravec suggests that Stevens' dramas will not alter fate, but "Esthetique du Mal" is on its way. Physics and rhetoric present effective models of particular motion, compositional and social movement. They are not only models, they are descriptions: "Reality is things as they are" (*NA* 25). This statement is doubly obtuse because it overrides the imaginary gap between imagination and reality; that stride is implied, even though it seems utterly banal: it is immanently banal, though the "as" still intermediates.

After discussing his main point that brings together the music, sounds, and words of poetry, Stevens admits an indirection about his talk:

> This being so, my time and yours might have been better spent if I had been less interested in trying to give our possible poet an identity and less interested in trying to appoint him to his place. But unless I had done these things, it might have been thought that I was rhetorical, when I was speaking in the simplest way about things of such importance that nothing is more so. A poet's words are of things that do not exist without the words. (*NA* 32)

Stevens' lecture describes the poet and his place in an effort to be concrete. If indeed he were "rhetorical," he would be offering poetry—not the desired product. In expressing the limitations of his talk, we can look forward to a statement that Stevens would make in "Description without Place": "it is the theory of description that matters most." If we can develop a better understanding of language's powers, then we might take note of how rhetoric dictates history, as Stevens will do in a public reading of "Description without Place," which follows U. S. diplomat Sumner Welles' postwar expansionist speech.

It is time to turn to these developments of the 1940s. In the next chapter I will suggest that Stevens' poetry is constructed increasingly with metonymy, a figuration that collides with what surrounds it, much like the physical motion of particles, and like a grammar based on verbs. "The Noble Rider and the Sound of Words" ends in such a direction, managing to punctuate the poet's point about the music of poetry in time:

> [W]e turn away from [the past] . . . as something that was noble in its day, a grandeur that was, the rhetorical once. But as a wave is a force and not the water of which it is composed, which is never the same, so nobility is a force and not the manifestations of which it is composed, which are never the same. Perhaps this description of it as a force will do more than anything else I have said about it to reconcile you to it. (*NA* 35–36)

Stevens wants poetry to meet the reader with tidal force. This is why the poems deposit their endings on readers. We construct the narrative from the synchronic chaos of the occasion. Fortunately for readers of Stevens, we have a lot to talk about because the poet asks us to be meta-narrators prescribing fate from poetry.

Chapter 5

The Neglected *Parts of a World* & *Transport to Summer*'s Confrontations

I am thinking about a War, by right or by force, of very unexpected
logic. It is as simple as a musical phrase.

—Rimbaud, *Illuminations*

To legitimize my emphasis on *Owl's Clover* as crucial to understanding Stevens' poetics, I want to demonstrate its continuities in
the poetry that follows. I am not discussing *The Man with the Blue
Guitar*, written during and after *Owl's Clover*, and published in 1937. James
Longenbach and Alan Filreis have done that thoroughly. *Blue Guitar* is
obviously a stylistic departure, with its succinct couplets and jazz rhythms.
It makes for better breathing. Partly because *Blue Guitar*'s aesthetics have
been so lauded, *Owl's Clover*'s rhetorical rigor and political stridency have
been neglected. In a 1954 letter to Alfred Knopf, Stevens excludes *Owl's
Clover*, "Life on a Battleship," and "The Woman That Had More Babies
Than That" from his "idea of a volume of collected poems" (*L* 830). No
reasons are offered. A look at these poems will give us the opportunity to
see what it was that Stevens wanted to abort, and to indicate aspects of
these poems that Stevens develops in two of his strongest poems, "Esthetique du Mal" and "Description without Place." In *The Plain Sense of Things*,
James Longenbach explains the critical dichotomy within which Stevens
oscillates:

> Although Stevens's ideas of ambiguity developed in dialogue with Burke and
> Blackmur, they dovetailed easily with the values of the reconstituted *Partisan
> Review*. Stevens especially admired Philip Rahv (from whom he had learned
> about Stalinism before he wrote "Life on a Battleship"). [He suggested Rahv

to H. Church] for a lecture series at Princeton in 1940 . . . [dogmatic New Critic] Cleanth Brooks was selected instead. . . .

So despite the fact that Stevens was welcomed in the *Partisan Review,* his work remained marginalized in a canon of modern literature conceived in either modernist or Marxist terms. (174)

As a temporarily celebrated poet in left-wing journals of the mid-1930s, Stevens wrote poetry that engaged rhetorically with Marxist ideology, challenging party politics. As an adopted poet who was part of *Partisan Review*'s effort to broaden its literary horizons, Stevens remained outside the circle for the most part, though he maintained correspondences with Burnshaw, Rahv, and Phillips (Cooney 208). Yet the more traditional modern magazines *(Dial, Poetry)* criticized Stevens' left-wing rhetorical poetry as a failure in aesthetics. *The Man with the Blue Guitar* satisfied the critical majority. I am not suggesting *Blue Guitar* is a compromise: its stylistic departure exaggerates a vacillation Stevens maintained throughout his poetry between metrically tight, rhythmic tercets and couplets, and looser stanzas with more prosaic meditations. Both sides of this stylistic polarity were evident in 1935–37, right when the modernist/Marxist dialogue was most active in culture. So although Stevens apparently aborted rhetoric with *Blue Guitar,* and further emphasized that departure with *The Collected Poems'* omissions, these decisions might reveal more about intention and critical pressure than the actual development of Stevens' poetry. "Life on a Battleship" and "The Woman That Had More Babies Than That" are written in 1939, two years after *Blue Guitar* departs from *Owl's Clover*'s rhetoric. These poems, omitted from *The Collected Poems,* continue the rhetorical dialogue with contemporaneous left-wing issues.

"Life on a Battleship" begins with a polemical narrative: "The rape of the bourgeoisie accomplished, the men / Returned on board *The Masculine*" (*OP* 106). Longenbach provides the poem with a historical context by suggesting that *The Masculine* is based on a ship that Stevens wrote to Elsie about in a letter from Key West (173):

> Owing to the disturbed conditions in Cuba there have been warships in port here for a good many months. At the moment, the *Wyoming* is lying at anchor out near the Casa Marina. The men from this great vessel and from others that are in the basin of the Navy Yard come on shore in large numbers and from about four o'clock until all hours of the night they are walking up and down the streets. In Florida they have prohibition under the state laws. The result is that these men flock to ice-cream shops and drug-stores and in general look like a lot of holiday-makers without any definite ideas

of how to amuse themselves. Key West is extremely old-fashioned and primitive. The movie theatres are little bits of things. Well, last night it seemed as if the whole navy stood in the streets under our windows laughing and talking; and that, too, may be a reason why Judge Powell is taking a nap. (*L* 268)

"Life on a Battleship" was written five years after this letter from 1934. In addition to the chronological gap, we see the historical liberties Stevens takes, for one, in changing the ship's name to *The Masculine*. Although the poem does not make firm historical claims, we, however, can gauge Stevens' rhetorical views of an eventual representation thanks to Longenbach's connection.

From the poem alone, we have no idea what the "rape of the bourgeoisie" might be, although the syntax points to some sinister doings by the sailors. With Longenbach's helpfully aligned letter we get a sense of Stevens' joy at juxtaposing the poem's lusty marines causing trouble in town with the actual innocents licking ice cream cones. Quickly though, the poem attends to the issue of class struggle, so prevalent in the thirties, voiced in a soliloquy by the captain:

> "The war between classes is
> A preliminary, a provincial phase,
> Of the war between individuals. In time,
> When earth has become a paradise, it will be
> A paradise full of assassins. . . ."   (*OP* 106)

By framing class revolution within the military intelligence of the captain, Stevens satirizes both sides with a realistic projection of the ironic outcome of these clashing ideologies. Longenbach also informs us that Stevens wrote this poem with Stalin in mind: "Stevens especially admired Philip Rahv (from whom he had learned about Stalinism before he wrote "Life on a Battleship") . . ." (174). Stalin's fascism forced many Americans in favor of Communist ideals to become skeptical. Further in his study, Longenbach surmises that these opening lines "underscor[e] the patriarchal values of the Stalinist left" (226). So in the captain's authoritative rhetoric forecasting the future, Stevens' poetry marries a simple past occasion of American military peacekeeping, an ironic view of a Marxist future, and present political oppression. Without Longenbach's research and Stevens' letters, we would not be able to discern the complex contemporaneous relevance of this poem. However, with these links to historical authenticity, the poetry's engagement with the *actual world* (Filreis) seems paramount. Longenbach and Filreis have provided historical data that demonstrate how Stevens addresses contemporary issues. Poetry that could previously be disregarded as nonsensical and abstract now reveals that abstractions belong to the paradigmatic figures who are referenced in the poetry, whether they are historically accurate or not. Those readers who hunger for factual historical reference points will be disappointed, however, because Stevens is less interested in connecting factual dots than he is in changing the way we view the picture.

The captain in "Life on a Battleship" appears to be "some harmonious skeptic soon in a skeptical music," which "Mozart, 1935" forecasted:

> Suppose I seize
> The ship, make it my own and, bit by bit,
> Seize yards and docks, machinery and men,
> As others have, and then, unlike the others,
> Instead of building ships, in numbers, build
> A single ship, a cloud on the sea, the largest
> Possible machine, a divinity of steel,
> Of which I am captain. Given what I intend,
> The ship would become the centre of the world.   (*OP* 106)

The captain goes on to say, "the world would only have to ring and ft! / It would be done" (*OP* 107). Here again utopia is parodied, as it was in "Mr. Burnshaw's" Marxist inscription, "To Be Itself." Stevens uses identifiable human characteristics, such as greed, to unite politics, aesthetics, and philosophy into encompassing ideology. In the "single ship" Stevens creates a Platonic mystical vision ("a divinity of steel") that is composed of a visionary, monumental aesthetic ("a cloud on the sea, the largest"), which in turn displays political isolation from democratic notions: "unlike the others, / Instead of building ships, in numbers. . . ." This contrast between a singular Platonic vision and a more democratic plurality is familiar from *Owl's Clover,* where the sculptor's exclusionary aesthetic contrasts with the multiethnic park in "A Duck for Dinner." The monumental dictatorship is further emphasized here when the captain urges "that men should wear stone masks." Supposedly this would end "the sorrow of the world, except / As man is natural," the stone masks wouldn't last for long. Including the classical masks may be a dig at modernism's classical revisitation. Regardless, Stevens unites militarism with Marxism, Platonism, and visionary aesthet-

ics through their common aspiration: immortality, or self-preservation in
the face of knowing that the opposite is true.

Canto ii reveals that what I called Platonism is more accurately Cartesian:

> So posed, the captain drafted rules of the world,
> *Regulae Mundi,* as apprentice of
> Descartes:
>> First. The grand simplifications reduce
> Themselves to one.   (*OP* 107)

What follows is a ridiculous philosophical discourse that accumulates symbols of monarchy, and thus resembles the "military tractatus" of "The
Greenest Continent," which united African imperialism with Western
bourgeois art and divinity. Yet the captain's satiric rhetoric culminates with
a question, which for Stevens is likely a solid proposal. The captain asks,

>> "But if
> It is the absolute why must it be
> This immemorial grandiose, why not
> A cockle-shell, a trivial emblem great
> With its final force, a thing invincible
> In more than phrase? There's the true masculine,
> The spirit's ring and seal, the naked heart."
> It was a rabbi's question. Let the rabbis reply.
> It implies a flaw in the battleship, a defeat
> As of make-believe.   (*OP* 108)

To make art of the "naked heart," the captain steps out of character into
the voice of a poet who might say, "The final belief is to believe in a fiction, which you know to be a fiction, there being nothing else. The exquisite truth is to know that it is a fiction and that you believe in it willingly"
(*OP* 189). The poem appears to be arguing that for a symbol of the heart
to endure, one would have to create an emblem that would require a leap
of faith, which is why the captain's question is delegated to rabbis. In the
role of the captain of the battleship, the poet cannot create a poem reli-
giously; "make-believe" betrays "a flaw in the" composition. In turning to
the rabbi at this juncture, Stevens may be conceding the extreme difficulty
of answering to numerous ideological utopic catastrophes. Poetry may
need a priest, but it will never have one. If the rabbi figure indicates a realization of poetry's limitations for Stevens, it also suggests a broadening of

horizons. The rabbi returns in "Notes Toward a Supreme Fiction," a poem marking Stevens' expansiveness, as he addresses World War II while simultaneously striding toward a great poetic system aimed at coping with contemporaneity—always.

The third canto of "Life on a Battleship" continues to illustrate Stevens' increasing breadth of focus. Keeping Descartes in dialogue with the captain, it begins with another Cartesian principle:

> Second. The part
> Is equal of the whole.
>   The captain said,
> "The ephebi say that there is only the whole,
> The race, the nation, the state. But society
> Is a phase. We approach a society
> Without a society, the politicians
> Gone, as in Calypso's isle or in Citare,
> Where I or one or the part is the equal of
> The whole. . . ."   (*OP* 108)

Like the Old Woman and Mr. Burnshaw, the captain is a variable persona as his voice increasingly sounds like the poet in this poem's progression. References to *The Odyssey* align him with Ulysses, that wily captain of narrative poetry. Introduced among the Descartes/captain dialogue are "ephebi," who become the model audience of "Notes," and the dialogic other of the later poetry. Here, however, the young audience resembles more closely the "Mesdames" of *Owl's Clover,* made up of the destitute Old Woman, parlor ladies, poets, Burnshaw, and the proletariat. The battleship "ephebi" are more specifically left-wing intellectuals concerned with the "race, the nation, the state." The poet-captain's perspective broadens with "But society / Is a phase." The macro-systemic view here overarches the statesman-poet's detailed issues expressed in *Owl's Clover,* but is no escape. Using *The Odyssey's* narrative involvement in plot, specifically how Odysseus gets lost "in Calypso's isle" and has trouble charting his geographical and narrative courses, Stevens connects this traveler with the lost politician unable to see the forest for the trees. The close proximity of politicians to their politics enacts this loss in objectivity, wherein the politician, like Odysseus, does not know how to proceed because he is too subjectively embedded in the story. In such situations, personal desire overrides a responsibility for others, and subjectivity is realized in the shape of the state: "Where I or one or the part is the equal of / The whole." This synecdochic megalomania fits with the poem's Cartesian context: "I think, therefore I am" prioritizes individual reason to the exclusion of all else. Stevens brings to the fore a ridicule of Descartes in the contexts of Odysseus and the American navy: "Given what I intend / The ship would become the centre of the world."

From there the poem carries "a dozen orchestras" of instrumental disturbances, all denied by the captain's philosophy, "the part is equal of the whole." That is, "Unless society is a mystical mass" (*OP* 108), which reintroduces the notion from "Sombre Figuration" of fate being determined by a collective irrational momentum. Forwarding the macro-systemic view that lacks conceptual order, the captain continues:

> This is a thing to twang a philosopher's sleep,
> A vacuum for the dozen orchestras
> To fill, the grindstone of antiquest time,
> Breakfast in Paris, music and madness and mud,
> The perspective squirming as it tries to take
> A shape, the vista twisted and burning, a thing
> Kicked through the roof, caressed by the river-side.   (*OP* 108)

The ancient problem of relentless violence is given a pressing momentum here that is concurrent with the time the poem was written, two months before the Russian-German alliance precipitating World War II. In these compressed lines we find tropes that exist in several poems surrounding this one: the "twang" of *Blue Guitar* and "Of Modern Poetry," the skeptic's music in face of the mass house wreckers in "Mozart, 1935," "The Greenest Continent's" collision of antique muddy Africa with bourgeois Europe, and the oncoming questionably sublime breakfast in Naples in "Esthetique du Mal." Stevens aims the twanging artillery at an apparent "mystical mass." And what is the target of this shooting?

> "On *The Masculine* one asserts and fires the guns.
> But one lives to think of this growing, this pushing life,
> The vine, at the roots, this vine of Key West, splurging,
> Covered one morning with blue, one morning with white,
> Coming from the East, forcing itself to the West,
> The jungle of the tropical part and tropical whole."   (*OP* 108)

Since this is the captain speaking, the guns are fired on his ship. Yet "on" remains ambiguous because when guns fire "on" something, this usually means that that something is a target. "On" might also imply that the sniper shoots when "On *The Masculine*," suggesting that this gendered domain is responsible for the firing. The next line, beginning with "But," juxtaposes the *Masculine* warring logic with "this growing, pushing life"—a feminine wisdom that is "caressed by the river-side." Generation is then tied up in this "vine of Key West," that resembles the African vine encircling the Western Statue in "The Greenest Contininent," which is "Coming from the East, forcing itself to the West, / The jungle of tropical part and tropical whole.'" What Stevens once located in an antique Africa (the serpent carrying death-in-life) now moves West. This recontextualization is colored blue then white, which were the colors of the elite in "Mr. Burnshaw and the Statue," and will be the colors of the monk-assassin in "Esthetique du Mal." The American colonization of an Eastern natural chaos is transplanted to Key West. In terms of Stevens' letter to Elsie, Key West nears the shores of Cuba where eastern Communism takes root in new tropics; and where the battleship *Wyoming* parks the sailors protecting American shores while they lick ice cream cones like emperors.

This complex of contexts illustrates the quickfire spillout of inferences from Stevens' rhetoric. This style anticipates "Add This to Rhetoric," the *Parts of a World* poem discussed in my introduction that concludes with "Add this. It is to add" (*CP* 199). In this simple credo we can incorporate the "More" that was requested in the subman's park, and again find that Stevens' rhetorical method is metonymic, "This is the figure and not / An evading metaphor." And yet in the heavily rhetorical poems of the 1930s, Stevens plays with referentiality by asking readers to add rhetorical relevances that are triggered by the poems. Even in the studio composure of "Add This to Rhetoric," the poem begins, "It is posed and it is posed." Stevens' rhetoric makes us aware of postures through dramatically posed figures that embody traditional systems of thought: "So posed, the captain drafted rules of the world" (*OP* 107). The battleship captain's megalomania is part of a Western paradigm that unites Odysseus, Descartes, and the U.S. navy, which we come to understand from the individual sensibility of the captain. We then can apply this new knowledge in perceiving our world.

Stevens' lessons differ from other modernists such as Eliot and Pound. While their figures strike telling historical poses, their objective personae are not accompanied by reflexive expression about their roles in composition. For the sake of historical immediacy, Eliot and Pound direct readers toward specific poetic contexts, whereas Stevens brings the scenario into present mind. This distinction can be framed by aligning Stevens' poetry with the deconstructions of de Man and Derrida. De Man's "rhetoricity," to recapitulate, refers to literature that has a persuasive function while also displaying awareness that rhetoric works as trope, as a constructed paradigm. De Man's rhetoricity, like Stevens' fictions, takes into account "the recurrent confusion of sign and substance" (*Blindness and Insight* 136). Stevens' poetry registers by tracing historical thought processes (epistemes) as they evolve and affect the present.

The fourth and final canto of "Life on a Battleship" serves as a Hegelian, and Koreshian, synthesis:

> The first and second rules are reconciled
> In a third: The whole cannot exist without
> The parts. Thus: out of the number of his thoughts
> The thinker knows. The gunman of the commune
> Kills the commune.   (*OP* 109)

Although these rules are attributed to Descartes, we can also observe the poem's speaker tracing an aesthetic evolution. Number one, "The grand simplifications reduce / Themselves to one," is divine and symbolic because the reductions serve a dominant master; the second, "The part is equal of the whole," is synecdochic; and the third approximates metonymy, a figure that requires other attributes in composition—"it is to add." When the gunman kills the communal parts, Stevens shows the destructiveness of symbolic and synecdochic hierarchy. The gunman cannot differentiate between dictatorship and democracy: a dictator is ruled by his symbolic power, whereas a democrat understands the metonymic composition of his commune that is based on "It is to add."

Addressing the captain, Stevens then introduces the "sceptre" of fate, which we know from *Owl's Clover.* Twice in the final lines Stevens repeats "Our fate is our own," but then the poet calls for "the hand of one"

> that seizes our strength, will seize it to be
> Merely the sceptre over long desire,
> Merely the centre of a circle, spread
> To the final full, an end without rhetoric.   (*OP* 109)

While taking fate into our hands encourages me, the poem ends by repeating the synecdochic power of one part for the whole. Disappointingly, the conclusion rings rhapsodic rather than ironic. If I am right in reading a crescendo here, then the updraft demonstrates Stevens' unresolved search for a hero, as Longenbach suggests. Up to this juncture

Stevens has proposed medium-man Jocundus, and Ananke as possibilities. While the subman is meant to stand for others, especially for irrational interests that have yet to be represented, "Life on a Battleship's" search for "some harmonious skeptic soon in a skeptical music" remains too susceptible to the battleship gunman, even after rigorously examining his destructiveness. "Notes" soon provides extension with abstract comic heroes.

The other possible interpretation of this ending is that it is a grand irony. While the poem contains comparatively little irony, the "final full . . . end without rhetoric" is yet another apocalyptic, impossible desire. Perhaps Stevens displays a longing for "an end without rhetoric" insofar as the poet craves a clear direct speech not engaged in dialectics. As much as Stevens' study of rhetoric has taught him, scholarly wisdom will not placate the desires of the "naked heart," "the true masculine." As written in *Adagia:* "There are two opposites: the poetry of rhetoric and the poetry of experience" (*OP* 187). The "poetry of rhetoric" involves Stevens' future concerns, his efforts at change for "the intelligence that endures" belonging to the Sister of the Minotaur. The "poetry of experience" comes from "the naked heart," which is masculine. "Sombre Figuration" said "we grow weary of the man that thinks." Stevens is caught in a double-bind that he cannot escape because it would entail sacrificing either his rhetorical investment in the future or his humanness. As with *Owl's Clover,* Stevens exposes a lot of social and epistemological contradictions in an apparent progress, but lacks resolutions. Longenbach similarly notes, ". . . Stevens's politics often appear divided on precisely this fulcrum: wanting to preserve the integrity of every part of the world, he nevertheless fears the anarchic energy those parts set free" (217). And I would add, Stevens desires (yet ironically) the force of a singular leader, which Longenbach describes as the captain's "totalizing voice." The dilemma of the last two verses of "Life on a Battleship" is that the captain's voice increasingly sounds like the poet, and the poet's refrain to the captain echoes the captain. Stevens arranges this paradox by using the Ulysses paradigm to bridge this captain-poet opposition. Stevens' critique of *Masculine* order intensifies with his susceptibility to the power he so fears. The poet has moved closer to the problem, but solutions are elusive. We must look forward again to the Necessary Angel as a consummate figure.

"The Woman That Had More Babies Than That" lacks the sharp rhetorical challenge of "Life on a Battleship," although it provides an alternative to the *Masculine* by enlarging the scope of the spirit. These two poems, which were published as a pair in "both the *Partisan Review* and the first edition of *Parts of a World*" (Longenbach 226) indicate Stevens' transition from the thirties to the forties, wherein Stevens moves from diagnostic to curative poetry.[1] They bridge the masculine aesthetics that Stevens challenged and his ambitions for a world embodying feminine attributes of generativity and nonviolence. This is not to say that Stevens simply chooses a feminine poetry; in confronting the "man-locked set" (as described in the later "Angel Surrounded by Paysans"), the poet engages with World War II and many late poems address Ulysses. Future masculine heroes develop from battles of sexual archetypes, confrontations that increasingly turn into marriages.

The poem begins with "An acrobat on the border of the sea" (*OP* 104). I take this figure to be an autobiographical persona of the poet, because he observes change in the repetition of the waves, which are generated by The Woman That Had More Babies Than That. The sea is a feminine storehouse of music, enunciated in the "Berceuse, transatlantic" cradle-song. The sea is collective loosely shaped memory, and as such it resembles the dreams of the citizens in "Sombre Figuration." The woman that is more generative than the sea is Stevens' Gaia. She is a feminine version of the medium man that Stevens searches for in 1939; she holds fate:

> She is not the mother of landscapes but of those
> That question the repetition of the shore,
> Listening to the whole sea for a sound
> Of more or less, ascetically sated
> By amical tones.
> > The acrobat observed
> The universal machine. There he perceived
> The need for a thesis, a music constant to move.   (*OP* 105)

As a persona for the poet, the acrobat attempts to fill the role of the "harmonious skeptic soon in a skeptical music," but remains merely a circus performer, small in relation to Gaia.

Longenbach suggests that "Stevens diminishes the power of childbirth as nothing but mere repetition," and that "true creativity consists not in childbirth but in the masculine rage to order" (226). I grant there is a rage for order here, but I suggest it is moreover a reverence for disorder. And to further challenge Longenbach's claim: if childbirth is "nothing but mere repetition," that nothing is existence itself; and "repetition" speaks not only of the generation trope that Stevens always returns to, but "repetition" also challenges the poet to improve life cycles. As earth mother, Gaia houses the repetitive data of history. As a storehouse, she reminds the poet of historic brutality, as well as posing the ideal of natural regeneration. Stevens grants her with a collective wisdom that I think is similar to the "Mesdames" trope from *Owl's Clover:* "Mesdames" became a community of various factions of poets and ideologues, all of whom believed in their causes. Under the rubric of "Mesdames," these civilians were cast as Stevens' muses. "More Babies Than That" amplifies this collective circumstance. Rather than diminishing childbirth, Stevens diminishes the rage for order as a derivative desire that men concoct in response to the fading echoes of motherly wisdom:

> Berceuse, transatlantic. The children are men, old men,
> Who, when they think and speak of the central man,
> Of the humming of the central man, the whole sound
> Of the sea, the central humming of the sea,
> Are old men breathed on by a maternal voice,
> Children and old men and philosophers,
> Bald heads with their mother's voice still in their ears. (*OP* 105)

The repetition of words such as "central" and "men" display the urgency with which these fellows vainly and tentatively try to tap into the earthly maternal power that resounds in their ringing heads that are bald for the second time. Stevens parodies his own poetic effort, that of medium-man, but is comfortable knowing that his words pale in comparison to the lost original lullaby.

> The self is a cloister full of remembered sounds
> And of sounds so far forgotten, like her voice,
> That they return unrecognized. The self
> Detects the sound of a voice that doubles its own,
> In the images of desire, the forms that speak,
> The ideas that come to it with a sense of speech.   (*OP* 105)

As an abstract double, "mon semblable, mon [m]ere!" this cradle-voice is known as the Interior Paramour. While she's certainly maternal here, this other modifies a lot in Stevens' career. He began writing verses for Elsie; in the 1930s the other became contemporary pressure (whether in the shape of the old romantic muse, or Stanley Burnshaw); in this poem Gaia extends Stevens' conception of the other from the confines of "Battleship" polemics to a reconsideration of the irrational sea that spurns his writing; in "Notes" the "voice that doubles as its own" becomes the reader and the

soldier. The later poetry increasingly seeks dialogic interaction with readers in efforts to write for common purposes that reach public audiences.

To reach such goals, Stevens continues to reject cold monumental aesthetics, and accepts the civic composition:

> If her head
> Stood on a plain of marble, high and cold;
> If her eyes were chinks in which the sparrows built;
> If she was deaf with falling grass in her ears—
> But there is more than a marble, massive head.
> They find her in the crackling summer night,
> In the *Duft* of towns, beside a window, beside
> A lamp, in a day of the week, the time before spring,
> A manner of walking, yellow fruit, a house,
> A street. She has a supernatural head.
> On her lips familiar words become the words
> Of an elevation, an elixir of the whole.   (*OP* 106)

In proposing the conditions of a classical Medusa in terms resembling the
statue aesthetic criticized in *Owl's Clover,* the poet arrives at what the icon
arrives at, a failing impasse, signaled by the dash ending line four. By giving her "a supernatural" rather than a marble head, Stevens creates a spirit
living "of the whole." Interestingly, the *Duft* ("dufter") is a town register,
a record of all the babies, or business office *(OED),* suggesting that this
muse does accompany the poet at Hartford Indemnity & Insurance Co.,
rather than being partitioned off in another world at home or in the park.
As a *Spiritus Mundi* she supplants the *Regulae Mundi* ruling "Life on a
Battleship."

In "The Woman That Had More Babies Than That," the maternal muse
perseveres. This tropic paramour went under the "Mesdames" umbrella in
Owl's Clover, which was composed of Marxists, sculptors, and poets. Now
the poet, as "An acrobat on the border of the sea," listens to the larger "irrational element in poetry." As in "The Irrational Element" essay, in this
poem Stevens extends the treatment of the muse (from *Owl's Clover*)
beyond the differential polemics of social ideology and romantic statues.
The poet's movement toward irrational or even supernatural concerns
could be interpreted as an escape from contemporary pressure. 1942's "The
Noble Rider and the Sound of Words" answered that charge by stating that
while poetry is an escapist process, pejorative escapism would entail
defaulting from contemporaneity. The subman's interest in public dreams,
and the civic locales of the last two *Owl's Clover* poems as well as the end-

ing of "More Babies Than That" situate Stevens more intimately with his environment. I suggest that in "Life on a Battleship" and "More Babies Than That" Stevens was conditioning himself in order to confront larger evils at hand.

> *The ultimate self-effacement is not*
> *the pretense of the minimal,*
> *but the jocular considerations of the maximal*
> *in the manner of Wallace Stevens.*
> —Mark Strand, *The Sargentville Notebook*

"Esthetique du Mal" and "Notes" take on malady and war as subject matter, and respond to thinking about pain by generating pleasure. Stevens can only achieve a *Spiritus Mundi* by showing that the *Regulae Mundi* of the thirties—stale romantic legacies, monumentalism, automated polemics, imperialism, militarism—are inadequate rhetoric. We'll soon see that "Esthetique du Mal" works through the problem of sublimity gone awry, and asserts "the gaiety of language is our seigneur." "Description without Place" constructs a coherent fate through a theoretical language that attends to rhetorical power.

The polemics, historicity, epistemology, rhetoricity, and creative portraiture mixed together in "Esthetique du Mal" make for some turgid verse in the minds of some critics, such as Helen Vendler. But I argue that the form of this heavily ambitious poetry, which changes according to verse sections, fully supports its capacious argumentative inquiry into human evil. The topic requires an amalgamation of various discourses. As with *Owl's Clover*'s "pressure of the contemporaneous," Stevens' writing of evil aesthetics has to be more than political and more than aesthetic: rhetoric has a capacious allowance that the criticism of modern poetry had not adequately accounted for up to here; that is, with the exception of an uncharacteristically tentative suggestion from Pound in 1936, writing in *Guide to Kulchur* that modern poetry's "transition may have been from literary to rhetorical" (293).

Stevens explores rhetoric's role in harmful aesthetics (esthetique du mal) by focusing on the sublime. The sublime is associated with feelings of power, whether generated from the subject or interpreted as if nature's (traditionally divine) presence effects sublimity. "Esthetique du Mal" shows how rhetorical power informs the sublime. The poem entangles sublime rhetoric with political rhetoric, thereby developing a "politics of emotions." Rhetoric teases ego with political emotions such as power, greed, control, and fear. These emotions are projected in the historically anecdotal personae of "Esthetique du Mal," which resemble the character scenarios of *Owl's Clover,* "Life on a Battleship," and the upcoming "Description without Place."

These poems all show that "what we say of the future must portend." And in Stevens' frame of reference, portent is not truth championed; rather, it is a rhetorically persuasive, or adherent language. The better the rhetoric, the greater the contextual adherences. As much as Stevens credits rhetorical force as a historical determinant, he also deconstructs traditional rhetoric by studying "the recurrent confusion of sign and substance" (de Man) in the perceptions of his characters. The language of "Esthetique du Mal" points to the substance of referential signifieds (phenomena, volcanoes) consistently to draw attention to their rhetoricity, their action as signs, both in the external and literary worlds. Rhetoricity enables poetry to awaken, unearth, decreate, recreate, activate, and create new thoughts in new applications. A "gaiety of language" more powerfully vivifies people than catalogues of knowledge about the world, because learning occurs at the poem's surface; from the language's enigmatic suggestions we think of signified phenomena and how they are recontextualized in the poem and the world. The poem's language unmasks established constructs of the world. As I argued last chapter, Stevens' rhetorical poetry explicitly marries *creativity* with *argument:* the two categories that criticism has often kept from each other:

> Natives of poverty, children of malheur,
> The gaiety of language is our seigneur.   *(CP 322)*

I have outlined what "Esthetique du Mal" aims to accomplish in my terms, but the poem was provoked by a World War II soldier's request. This context is provided by Filreis, and it lends to the poem's theoretical nature (though it is arguing for a physically responsive language) an intimate objective. Filreis gives more evidence of Stevens' involvement in his time. The poem was written in response to

> a scolding given *Kenyon Review* in a recent issue. It was a letter to the editor from a soldier, which Ransom quoted as part of his editorial comment for the Spring 1944 issue. The soldier found "the poetry in *Kenyon Review* lamentable in many ways *because it is cut off from pain*" .... First of all, the soldier made an *exception* of "poets of charming distemper *like Wallace Stevens*

(for whom we all developed considerable passion)." Yet he called upon Ransom to support poems of "muscle and nerve," and hoped to see more poetry of reality. (Filreis's emphasis; *Wallace Stevens and the Actual World* 134)

"Esthetique du Mal" is a curative poem, which builds from the diagnostic process familiar from *Owl's Clover* in an effort to reason with our insanity. As the poet explains in section v, this new reach for human sympathy is only beginning to look "Within the actual" (*CP* 317), which is where the poet finds "muscle and nerve." All the past's stale hells occurred "Before we were wholly human and knew ourselves." Of the past Stevens writes, "The death of Satan was a tragedy / For the imagination" (*CP* 319), because we no longer possessed an inverse divinity into which we could compartmentalize sin.

I think Stevens exaggerates the fait accompli, "wholly human and knew ourselves," in order to demonstrate how far we have to go, suggesting that this path has barely been trod, thus necessitating much future travel. I will return to the hope of section v, but now cite the opening verse's diagnostic "Esthetique du Mal":

> He was at Naples writing letters home
> And, between his letters, reading paragraphs
> On the sublime. Vesuvius had groaned
> For a month. It was pleasant to be sitting there,
> While the sultriest fulgurations, flickering,
> Cast corners in the glass. He could describe
> The terror of the sound because the sound
> Was ancient. He tried to remember the phrases: pain
> Audible at noon, pain torturing itself,
> Pain killing pain on the very point of pain.
> The volcano trembled in another ether,
> As the body trembles at the end of life.   (*CP* 313, 314)

Here we have ephebe—the 1944 soldier on leave next to the eruptive volcano, the bourgeois romantic artist, Hugh Selwyn Mauberley, or Ernest Hemingway: does it matter? The American Exile In Europe is not only a bourgeois romantic, but his archeology of sublime presences portrays him as a classicist as well. He is bored by the boiling volcano groaning the sublime. His wisdom—searching for the proper references—has saturated his knowledge of pain to the extent that the audible volcano exists "in another ether," another plane of reality close to death. Despite all this, the figure is happy in the bourgeois order of his occasion:

It was almost time for lunch. Pain is human.
There were roses in the cool cafe. His book
Made sure of the most correct catastrophe.
Except for us, Vesuvius might consume
In solid fire the utmost earth and know
No pain (ignoring the cocks that crow us up
To die). This is a part of the sublime
From which we shrink. And yet, except for us,
The total past felt nothing when destroyed.   (*CP* 314)

The narrative presents the aesthete's justified self, whose indirect reportage suggests that "Vesuvius might" become all-consuming. As such, the volcano becomes a variable and elastic symbol, like we saw in the Statue, the Old Woman, the brilliant yew, Burnshaw, "Mesdames," and all in *Owl's Clover*. As it groans, it becomes coolly indifferent to the foreboding cocks foretelling inevitable death. The lessons of history crowed by cocks are little more than anthropomorphic pathetic fallacies. So "a part of the sublime / From which we shrink" suggests that we know pain from the past and from nature but do not confront it, no matter how close or ominous, and conversely, that nature's power is indifferent to us. Ephebe reads paragraphs on the sublime under the volcano from which he shrinks. The sublime, Stevens suggests, involves its own sublimation.

The poem's beginning and end present the contemporary sublime, whereas the middle sections (to which I'll return) theoretically provide alternatives to the surrounding problem. Therefore, I am jumping ahead to canto xiii. At this point in the poem, with Satan gone, the tragic flaw is "This force of nature in action" (*CP* 324). This line describes "the unalterable necessity" of the son's repetition of the father's "necessity of being / Himself," which echoes Joyce in *Ulysses:* "History, Stephen said, is a nightmare from which I am trying to awake" (Joyce 28). While this tragic force is our heritage, we also shrink from volcanic "nature in action" time after time. Stevens identifies this hapless sublime condition—the same one that generates religions and demons—as the "destiny unperplexed, / The happiest enemy."

Continuing to demystify the "Esthetique du Mal," the poem proposes the very personification of virtue, a monk, as a carrier of the evil we have to confront:

        And it may be
That in his Mediterranean cloister a man,

> Reclining, eased of desire, establishes
> The visible, a zone of blue and orange
> Versicolorings, establishes a time
> To watch the fire-feinting sea and calls it good,
> The ultimate good, sure of a reality
> Of the longest meditation, the maximum,
> The assassin's scene. Evil in evil is
> Comparative. The assassin discloses himself,
> The force that destroys us is disclosed, within
> This maximum, an adventure to be endured
> With the politest helplessness. Ay-mi!
> One feels its action moving in the blood.   (*CP* 324)

This persona is no simple demonization; danger lurks in the best of us. In the monk's colorful painting of divine assurance, the "force that destroys us is disclosed." The "fire-feinting sea" implies that nature's godly high jinks are composed of "sham attack, deception, pretence." The *OED* informs us that *feint* has military, commercial, and inscriptive etymologies. This word concocts similar contexts as "tractatus" does in "The Greenest Continent." In both poems Stevens forwards aesthetic havens (the cloistered Mediterranean, Europe's Africa) in order to betray hegemonic enterprises involving religion, commerce, militarism—all are forms of aesthetic mastery that "murder to dissect" (Wordsworth). Yes, it seems a severe judgment on art, but the "rage for order" is the sublime killer here, as the monk's "ultimate good" becomes the "assassin's scene," "Ay-mi!"

Canto xiv delves further into this conundrum in a political context:

> Victor Serge said, "I followed his argument
> With the blank uneasiness which one might feel
> In the presence of a logical lunatic."
> He said it of Konstantinov. Revolution
> Is the affair of logical lunatics.
> The politics of emotion must appear
> To be an intellectual structure.   (*CP* 324)

The movement of "Esthetique du Mal" here resembles *Owl's Clover*. Victor Serge, like Stanley Burnshaw, initiates the verse as a discussion. Serge's comment refers to Konstantinov, thus amplifying the resonance of the poem's discussion into comparative historical environs. With help from Filreis and Pinkerton, we find that Serge's words are lifted "verbatim from

Dwight MacDonald's *Politics*" (*Actual World* 142). As with the historical ground Longenbach provided for "Life on a Battleship," Stevens' discourse is localized within history. Filreis's footnote informs us that

> Konstantinov told Serge of treachery that had undone Lenin's Central Committee, its source being unnamed "powerful capitalists" in the United States. Knowing that repelling this plot would require "an inquisitorial genius," Konstantinov went to the committee with evidence of the plot; he was deported to Siberia in the early thirties. (321)

The "politics of emotion" Stevens suggests is shown by Filreis to have an historically documented context, rather than appearing merely as an abstract theory. Dwight MacDonald presents Konstantinov as a conspiracy theorist exposing corrupt Soviet-American politics. Konstantinov deconstructed the system by rendering the rules of the political game, and for that he is considered a "logical lunatic," and sent to Siberia. For Stevens, Konstantinov serves as anecdotal evidence showing that the structure of politics is fed by emotional power, itself sublime. History, like poetry, exercises rhetoric in combat: each discourse marshals its own exiles. "Esthetique du Mal" theorizes rhetoric while taking stock of its eventual ramifications, which were not so good for Konstantinov. "The politics of emotion must appear / To be an intellectual structure." Because Konstantinov overturned the political "intellectual structure" of Russia, "His extreme of logic would be illogical" (*CP* 325). Konstantinov heroically exposed hypocrisy, which made him disposable to the state.

Stevens makes more of the narrow bounds of logic—and sublimity, as they work together in the esthetique du mal—by comparing lakes and oceans in canto xiii. I suspect that Stevens is especially interested in narrow reason because his poem attempts to enlarge rationality by including a politics of the emotions, for which he was already banished once, after *Owl's Clover*. In the following lines, Stevens unites revolution, logical lunacy, history, ideas of order, and the politics of emotion through personal anecdote:

> One wants to be able to walk
> By the lake at Geneva and consider logic:
> To think of the logicians in their graves
> And of the worlds of logic in their great tombs.
> Lakes are more reasonable than oceans. Hence,
>
> . . . .

> One might meet Konstantinov, who would interrupt
> With his lunacy. He would not be aware of the lake.
> . . . .
> His extreme of logic would be illogical.   (*CP* 325)

In casting the subject of the poem somewhere between "I" and "we," and within the desire of an international politician's privilege, Stevens again parodies the folly of history's expert logic locked "in their great tombs." Whereas the monk faced the endless sea, this lakeside stroller searches for order by Lake Geneva. The problem is that the lake is easier to map than the sea, but our acrobatic poet speaks of irrational elements at the sea's edge. In aid of this challenge, Stevens draws the reader into a congenial landscape by using the pronoun "One." While the poet wants us to imaginatively arrive in such spots, he does not want mere exercise or inhabited make-believe. Our involvement is always displaced in "the next to, la cote de" (Barthes) layer of rhetorical comparison ("it is to add"). "Hence, . . . // One might meet Konstantinov, who would interrupt / With his lunacy." The revolutionary is inserted in Geneva's peacemaking context to show his delusionary exclusion from this context. Konstantinov is presented as a lunatic, much like the navy captain of the *Masculine*. Stevens displays the inadequacy of thinking in terms of total systems (i.e., lakes), which bar us from perceiving larger surrounding contexts.

The final canto, xv, diagnoses this tragic flaw in repression, a manner often found in zealots:

> The greatest poverty is not to live
> In a physical world, to feel that one's desire
> Is too difficult to tell from despair.   (*CP* 325)

Vendler states of this that "Stevens describes his own paralysis" (*On Extended Wings,* 211). I disagree with Vendler's reading of this verse as confessional for several reasons. The whole poem is a response to a soldier's pain, perhaps a universal soldier through time, but not the poet's self-indulgence. Stevens here copes with the "politics of emotion" in history and the history of thought in literature and philosophy, of which he is part, but surely the poem's vectors direct our attention outward. The poem focuses on Konstantinov's macro-logical thinking, which we can contrast with the monk, Dante, Nietzsche, and the volcanic ephebe. Then verse xv explicitly opposes "non-physical" despair against the poet's full sensuality:

> Perhaps,
> After death, the non-physical people, in paradise,
> Itself non-physical, may, by chance, observe
> The green corn gleaming and experience
> The minor of what we feel. The adventurer
> In humanity has not conceived of a race
> Completely physical in a physical world.   (*CP* 325)

Recalling the scholar "reading paragraphs on the sublime" in the shadow of Vesuvius, likewise "the non-physical people, in paradise" exist in "another ether" with the vain promise of a cornfield that they may not see even if they fall in it. This parody complements "Sunday Morning," in which heaven also appears to mute and mutate human experience into a diminished minor music. Always urging the "adventurer / In humanity," Stevens reiterates the innovative physical promise of "the great poem of the earth" here. This muscular physicality is not just wishful thinking; it already exists in the poetry's flexible capacity. "Esthetique du Mal's" rhetorical poetry is able to stride through many discourses because the language draws attention to its physical effectiveness:

> Natives of poverty, children of malheur,
> The gaiety of language is our seigneur.   (*CP 322*)

In the "gaiety of language," vivification replaces knowledge. The "rage for order" that kills experience through classification is supplanted by cohering the physical and cerebral:

> The green corn gleams and the metaphysicals
> Lie sprawling in majors of the August heat,
> The rotund emotions, paradise unknown.
> This is the thesis scrivened in delight,
> The reverberating psalm, the right chorale.   (*CP* 325, 326)

Music forms knowledge. Since it is made of metaphysical chords, paradise is unknown, not lost or found or even grasped; the concept is empty though it may be fulfilled. Even the poet's pronounced "thesis" is emotionally intoned.

This poetry realizes some of Stevens' ambitions announced in "The Noble Rider and the Sound of Words," written two years previous. As I discussed in the coda of my last chapter, music stimulates the nerves of readers, as does this rhetorical poetry, which relies on sounds. In musical, rhetorical, neurological, and physical conduction, the presence of logic would be rather like a toll-booth delaying progress, or cholesterol clogging the bloodstream: logic, though we can't write without it, is a form of censure. My chief contention is our assumption that it can somehow supersede, control, master, take precedence over the music of rhetoric.[2]

Fred Hoerner's essay, "Gratification and its Discontents: The Politics of Stevens' Chastening Aesthetics," cites Kristeva's theoretical prioritization of *significance*—poetry's disjunctive mode that attends to the process of producing claims—over transcendental *signification*. In "Esthetique du Mal," the argument posits "non-physical people" "reading paragraphs on the sublime" as those for whom *significance* has been lost to *signification*. Hoerner employs critics who emphasize *significance*, for example:

> Beehler outlines Kant's sublime with a particular interest in "subreption," the fiction, Kant says, that lets us write *as if* poetry were a journey beyond itself. The problem that subreption shares with transference occurs when the desire for language that transcends itself is so strong that it elides the "*as if*" that capacitates speech—that places in metaphor the delusion that marks fanaticism. (Hoerner 87)

"Subreption," then, identifies language's nontransparent mediary role. In poetry that claims to be objective, or in realistic prose, writers "elide the 'as if' that capacitates speech." Stevens dramatizes this automatic aesthetic in the ephebe who literalizes the sublime but cannot feel it; conversely, the battleship captain is ruled by his greedy ego, which is an example of "the delusion that marks fanaticism." In order to alleviate the twin evils of fanatic domination and spiritual inertia, Stevens' poetry insists upon *as if* in utterance and representation. "As" inscribes metaphorical linkage, conscious comparison, and thought, rather than transcendently assumed knowledge; "if" necessitates our conditions, the contexts of physical existence. As Hoerner argues,

> Readers face the paradox that poetry manifests divine presence *and* the historical process that constructs that presence. As Jacqueline Brogan helpfully argues, these contrary trajectories in Stevens' poetry result from the interaction of unitive and fragmentary poles of language simultaneously. (*Wallace Stevens Journal* '94, 81)

Hoerner's "divine presence" is the "reverberating psalm, the right chorale," the music of poetry. Music functions as a "unitive pole," to borrow Brogan's term; it is the intonation whereas the "as if" reflexive nature of Stevens' language points to the poem's fabricated sounds. De Man's "rhetoricity" accounts for both poles—tropic and deconstructive. In addition, I suggest that Stevens' rhetorical method factors together creation and argument; his poetry consistently displays the mutual complicity involved in statements that pretend to be either "pole." Stevens' poetry attracts quite a crowd of theorists intent on cracking Descartes' dichotomous leap of faith. A Robin Blaser poem, "Nomad," sets it straight: "I am, therefore I think," an epigram that I suspect many Cartesian objectors have thought of.

To return to "Esthetique du Mal's" final juncture, we find a poetry to lead us out of the darkness, yet it hits an impasse as far as evil presence goes.

> Speech found the ear, for all the evil sound,
> But the dark italics it could not propound.
> And out of what one sees and hears and out
> Of what one feels, who could have thought to make
> So many selves, so many sensuous worlds
> As if the air, the mid-day air, was swarming
> With the metaphysical changes that occur,
> Merely in living as and where we live.   (*CP* 326)

Although Stevens provides an "Esthetique du Mal," he does not offer a shield for malady. This may seem disappointing; as this denouement deflates it comes to rest. Perhaps my interpretation of possible failure at this point is part of the problem; we desire victory because we're so accustomed. Yet if Stevens offered a cure for evil we would rightly be suspicious, as that would be another dialectical demon, another satanic trope with which to measure our virtue. Instead, even traditional figures of virtue such as the monk, the scholar, and the diplomat possess sinister leanings. Stevens' alternative is brought forward "in a physical world" experienced with a vivid language that never loses its physicality to a quest for mastered knowledge. This canto's utopia is complemented by the "wholly human" portrait of "true sympathizers" in section v.

The critical history of "Esthetique du Mal" betrays a plethora of value judgments that vary according to the poem's sections. Most critics, with the exception of Vendler, who treats it as a rehashing of other poems, say that it approximates Stevens' best verse (Brogan, Longenbach, Weinfield). Yet critics differ markedly about which bits are best. These judgments lead me to believe that merit is a matter of taste. Henry Weinfield's fine critical piece, "Wallace Stevens' 'Esthetique du Mal' and the Evils of Aestheticism," rigorously confronts how Stevens' aesthetics criticize the sublime while they redo the very genre. I agree with Weinfield's thesis, although I would add that Stevens reissues the sublime excessively, so as to ridicule its studiously entrenched tradition, as I hope that my analysis has shown. Weinfield often credits the best verse where I find letdowns. He calls the "final ten lines of [the poem] the greatest . . ." (36). His reasoning is that the verse resembles Wordsworth's "Prospectus" to *The Recluse* in powerfully rendering the "sublime in humanistic terms," and that the final lines "enable him at last to regain his balance." Weinfield senses balance between ethics and aesthetics; and between attacking Satan (with aplomb) and projecting sentiment (disgracefully). When Stevens ends poems walking the tightrope it means we readers can close the book knowing the master acrobat has not fallen. However, Stevens is a radical poet taking risks, so we must expect him to fall and get back up again, over and over again. And because he's so durable, I find the risks more interesting, whether they achieve balance or not. Often I dislike balance because it runs "to that easy victory," as A. R. Ammons says. Balance is a criterion that critics feel comfortable with. Weinfield's judgment echoes Burnshaw's critique that said, "*Owl's Clover* is the record of a man who, having lost his footing, scrambles to regain his balance." In the case of the conclusion of "Esthetique du Mal," Weinfield's judgment does not appear accurate if we take into account a letter from Stevens that throws balance into question:

> The last poem ought to end with an interrogation mark, I suppose, but I have punctuated it in such a way as to indicate an abandonment of the question, because I cannot bring myself to end the thing with an interrogation mark. (*L* 469)

To me, the last seven lines of "Esthetique du Mal" provide a happy way home, but lack the directive found in the beginning of verse xv, which indicted a lethargic paradise. "Merely in living as and where we live[?]" is a tepid denouement, which in my opinion is effective only insofar as the stanza "could not propound" "the evil sound" or "the dark italics" (*CP* 326). The poem's risky inquiry failed to find a demon source, and so we go on living with that threat, and a project for the "children of malheur" in "the gaiety of language."

The projected secular warmth of sections v and vii, deemed sentimental by Weinfield and Vendler, show more poetic risk. Section vii, the anthologized war poem, "How red the rose that is the soldier's wound" (*CP* 318, 319), is an effort to recreate "What is Possible" for the contemporary soldier. For Stevens, "sentimentality is a failure of feeling" (*OP* 189), so either he fails miserably here or these critics do. Fortunately, I have as arbiters Mr. Filreis, soldiers (the dictees of the poem), and anthologizer Oscar Williams. In its time "The Soldier's Wound" was given high praise by Williams in the *War Poets* anthology, and it was chosen by Commander Richard Eberhart and Master Sergeant Rodman in *War and the Poet: An Anthology of Poetry Expressing Man's Attitudes to War from Ancient Times to the Present* (*Actual World* 137). The poem satisfied three types of wartime people: soldiers, military literati, and even some stateside literati.[3]

Let's look more closely at canto vii to see if it is a sentimental failure. The soldier's red rose-wound gains redness in time reaching back to the crucifixion. As history's symbolization grows, so grows "time's red soldier deathless on his bed." Isn't that excessive symbolic regress into diluted oblivion heightened (over-determined, saturated) by the exclamation, "How red the rose that is the soldier's wound"? This line evokes powerful pity, while I suggest at the same time that the voice's pathos is cheap because it sounds *as if* it were coming from "Mesdames'" poet laureate. It resounds like a common pathetic exclamation, yet the image's redness works; in that combination we find a perverse marriage: hyperbolic pathos sickeningly accumulates the blood of many soldiers, who symbolically have become "The soldier of time grown deathless in great size."

Against this immortalization the poem returns to a circle of comrades surrounding the soldier in summer. This way, life ends at its peak season.

> No part of him was ever part of death.
> A woman smoothes her forehead with her hand
> And the soldier of time lies calm beneath that stroke.   (*CP* 318)

The nursely gesture enacts "the actual, the warm, the near" (v) final action. Rather than belittling or sentimentalizing or immortalizing the soldier, this active and final death takes away immortal glory from the war poem, leaving the soldier to die in peace and affection. The end of the poem gives us a singular "soldier of time" whose death is not part of a collective symbolic bloodbath. We might compare this encounter with Sartre's "The Wall," where the victim on death row dreams about fun in the sun with his loved one. In the throes of the big sublime, Sartre's characters need not "read paragraphs on the sublime," as they are purely physical people (to the gruesome extent that their bodies overtake their minds). Sartre prioritizes bodily existence and rejects essentializing mortality in the habit of traditional philosophy. Similarly, the end of Stevens' elegy does not belittle war (as

Weinfield and Vendler say) in the statement, "In which his wound was good because life was." That is not the easy way out, rather,

> In the yes of the realist spoken because he must
> Say yes, spoken because under every no
> Lay a passion for yes that had never been broken.   (*CP* 320)

Neither God or poetry can fulfill immortal promise, yet verse can make the final "no" a "yes" up until the final "no." Stevens clearly acknowledges death: "The mortal no / Has its emptiness and tragic expirations."

Living in this Nietzschean world means that the soldier's request for a poetry of "muscle and nerve" continues to be answered in a poetry of physical action, in which a "woman smoothes her forehead," and people are "combing, skating, and dancing" as forecasted in "Of Modern Poetry." This may at first sound tritely existential, but Stevens does not stop with physical generativity. Canto v's "true sympathizers come" "Within the actual, the warm, the near," which "Ties us to those we love" (*CP* 317). We as scholarly readers may be a bit disgusted with such apparent sentiment, but is that not because we have been critically trained in schools of skepticism that betray certain ethical practices, such as love, for the sake of hardheaded wisdom? It is much easier to see the faults of fraternity and liberty than it is to practice successful ethical ideals.

Stevens develops a poetry of "muscle and nerve" that is able to face violence through verse that gestures past the confines of the poem in search of others. It is an innovatively ethical poetry that is more than aesthetic. In order to accomplish this, Stevens takes an anti-intellectual stance against the past's aesthetic ordering of masculine figures, and the poet's personae live in domestic surroundings. This pacifism occurs through the poet's acceptance of feminine power, and it projects the speaker among citizens, rather than studiously apart. Cantos v and vii demonstrate these ethics in action, but canto x explains this mellowed sublime.

Canto x recreates the poet's attraction to muses, calling them the "nostalgias," which makes sense if we recall the singer of Key West. After tracing maternal, Jungian, sexual, Freudian, exotic, and mythical muses, the poem rests with

> The softest woman,
> Because she is as she was, reality,
> The gross, the fecund, proved him against the touch

> Of impersonal pain. Reality explained.
> It was the last nostalgia: that he
> Should understand. That he might suffer or that
> He might die was the innocence of living, if life
> Itself was innocent. To say that it was
> Disentangled him from sleek ensolacings.   (*CP* 322)

The "softest woman" shields the poet from the esthetique du mal, which is a studied "impersonal pain." As in "More Babies Than That," the poet becomes a child to Gaia, which simply means he respects the earth. In doing so, the sublime, which had previously been a source of terror and destruction, here is cast as part of "the innocence of living." This reversal of original sin makes "innocence" a nearly arbitrary demarcation that is only meant to point out that death outpowers people. The polarization of good and evil is reversed and nearly eradicated, save for the poet's insistence that we must say "yes" and accept the big "no." This restatement of "death is the mother of beauty" reaffirms the poet's refusal of immortal and monumental aesthetics. The masculine rage for order is subsumed by love. In this quieted situation the poet's persona is a merger of masculine and feminine types.[4]

This is not to say that Stevens' poetry proceeds in a balanced fashion. In order to implode binary oppositions and achieve sexual equanimity, the hyperbolic demands of genders must be expressed. This surplus aesthetic, which attracts contacts and contexts into thinking bodies, is what Marx had in mind in "The Method for German Philosophy," as Fred Hoerner explains in relation to Stevens' volcano image: "a form that exceeds itself. That self-excess, Eagleton argues, defines Marx's 'poetry of the future,' which occurs as production exceeds ideologically imposed measures that would convert production to the interests of a particular moment . . ." (89). Hoerner's words on Eagleton on Marx describe Stevens' project. In "Esthetique du Mal" and further in "Description without Place," Stevens writes a "poetry of the future," wherein productive processes do exceed the "ideologically imposed measures" of his era—and in the case of "Description without Place" the poem far exceeds the imposed context of Sumner Welles' speech on American globalization, which Stevens' read the poem "next to" at Harvard. Thus, these poems "convert production to the interests of" broader occasions (contexts/readers), as Michael Davidson too argues, rather than to "the interests of a particular moment." Here we have lyrics excessively catapulted from the confines of moment and place into cultural dialogue.[5]

The ideas that I have developed in this chapter inform "Description without Place." To briefly recapitulate, *Parts of a World* and *Transport to Summer* largely pit synecdoche against metonymy in the production of compositions, contexts. Stevens' project in the late 30s and 40s is similar to a statement Gertrude Stein made in an interview in 1946: "Each part is as important as the whole. . . ." In "Life on a Battleship," the "it is to add" of metonymy was swept up in the "part as the whole" of synecdoche. In narrative terms, the captain accumulated self-interested properties into his *Regulae Mundi* enforced world vision. "The Woman That Had More Babies Than That" retraced the poet to the position of "An acrobat on the border of the sea" who listened to "the irrational element of poetry." Stevens again realized the magnitude of the earthly scope within which the poet sees. That aperture required the acrobat to step back from "the pressure of the contemporaneous" *Regulae Mundi* and delve into the *Spiritus Mundi*.

In "Esthetique du Mal," Stevens addresses our inherited reversion to sublime thought in face of "mal" (pain, suffering, evil). The poem proposes that "mal," what was known as evil and now is more simply violence and suffering, can be attributed to how we aestheticize experience (Christian paradigms serve as large examples). Arguing beyond the demands of malice, Stevens suggests that the human esthetique du mal informs everyday thinking because—like the cloistered Mediterranean monk composing his blue zoned "versicolorings"—partial ideas engrave whole desires that border on fanaticism. Sublimity is a condition of living on earth—being a part in awe of the whole—and that condition leads to a desire for a synecdochic *Regulae Mundi* because that law affirms a concentric self, a whole and total identity. As an alternative to a securely enclosed notion of identity, "Esthetique du Mal" administers figures who reach outward *(Spiritus Mundi)* while realizing they are parts in an ever-changing whole. Such figures foresee their metonymic role, "it is to add." "Description without Place" develops further the "as if" condition of adding things. "As" infers various tropes posed within language and communication, and "if" makes each demarcation a proposal set within contextual conditions. Every step involves forward projection yet is a hypothesis to consider.[6]

"Description without Place" began as a section of "Notes Toward a Supreme Fiction." Longenbach cites the latter as "crucial for Stevens" because "he needed to recognize his beliefs as constructions at the same time that he recognized their efficacy—the actual power of the phrase 'as if.'" However, Longenbach uses Freud's *The Future of an Illusion* to point out a problem with the philosophy of "as if." Through Freud, Longenbach says "the theory of fictionality collapses in practice" (287). I suggest that fictions become realized in practice.

Language is assembled for the audience to consider simultaneously with the staged production. In "Description without Place" the "green queen" is a costume and an act. Drama is an effective metaphor for "seeing" the poetic techniques at work in canto i's performance.[7] The poem dresses up as it goes out; it composes as it projects:

> It is possible that to seem—it is to be,
> As the sún is sómething séeming and it ís.
>
> The sun is an example. What it seems
> It is and in such seeming all things are.   (*CP* 339)

The language proposes the sun as a representation, something that comes to be. The sun is presented as "materia poetica," and its example implies that all matter is hypothesized this way. The syntax is framed within argument, yet metaphorically plays with logic and resemblance. The first couplet's play is emphasized by the prosody in the second line, in which two anapests enclose two trochees. The second line, as the consummate part of the analogy, has metrical balance at either end of the line, which perfectly contains the strong double trochee, "something seeming." The only syllable I have left out is "is," the verb that equates the sun to its seeming and its being. Using simple language and alliteration to register the rhythm, Stevens' syntax strongly enunciates the composition of the scene. The proposition, "It is possible," is realized in an alchemy of logic, syntax, sound, rhythm, semiosis, grammar, and ontology.

Then this case that completely states itself is set as "an example," a performative part, not of a whole now, but of "all things" (linguistically contained and mimetically referential) that work similarly but independently. The poetry is rhetorical and metonymy is its primary figure: "It is to add" in the manner of "as if."

Stevens wrote "Description without Place" with specific purposes in mind; the poem's pedagogy was intended for a particular occasion, as the poet tells Henry Church on April 4, 1945:

> ... I am going to read a poem before the Phi Beta Kappa at Harvard next June.
> I am about to settle down my subject: DESCRIPTION WITHOUT PLACE. . . .

It seems to me an interesting idea: that is to say, the idea that we live in the description of a place and not in the place itself, and in every vital sense we do. This ought to be a good subject for such an occasion. I suppose there is nothing more helpful to reading a poem than to have someone to read it to, and that particular audience ought to be a good audience. (*L* 494)

Stevens read "Description without Place" at Harvard's June 1945 convocation next to Sumner Welles' "The Vision of a World at Peace."[8] The performance of Stevens' oratory collided with a speech that composed world events. Viewing the two speeches together, we can see that Sumner Welles' "seemings are the actual ones" (*CP* 339), especially since he's espousing the role of American global policy in the United Nations' determination of the world. Welles represents the *Regulae Mundi* and Stevens the *Spiritus Mundi*. Welles' seemings are regularized into world rules; his words construct metaphors that become definitions; America is the captain's ship that "would become the centre of the world" (*OP* 106). The *Spiritus Mundi* that Stevens juxtaposes with Welles is more complex, and difficult to define. The poem is read metonymically next to Welles' speech; it is an attribute of the convocation event. As such, the poem's descriptive role adds excessive contexts to the place of Welles' rhetoric. Entitled "Description without Place," Stevens' poem is marginal, out of place, yet it is read in an indisputable location. But the title also infers that Welles' speech is "Description without Place"—a metaphor describing the content of American foreign policy.

In addition to my interpretation of Stevens' reading as a symbolic act within a specific historical context, I will observe this same pattern of layering rhetorical difference next to established contexts in the poem itself. Descriptions of "Nietzsche in Basel" and "Lenin by a Lake" prop up and pose these historical figures so as to reconstruct their contextual importance. As such, they resemble the examples of Mr. Burnshaw and Konstantinov. Yet the poetry's formal treatment of these "real life" characters hardly differs from constructs such as the Old Woman, the captain, the monk-assassin, green queen, or, I would argue, Sumner Welles. The similar referential treatment between real and abstract figures is contingent upon Stevens' poetics of rhetorical commentary. Language fully orchestrates our conceptions of personages—real or imaginary—and Stevens takes this liberty with the utmost seriousness. *Ideas of Order* examined the romantic legacies in poetry and culture that Stevens necessarily worked through by sorting through stale tropes in order to freshen life with new ones. "Description without Place" announces in its title and theoretical unfolding that language determines fate according to whichever rhetoric holds power, and consequently the poet offers a counter-rhetoric "because what we say of the future must portend" (*CP* 346). Stevens' poem is a counter-rhetoric because it deconstructs and rhetorizes the process of description. Welles speaks in the tradition of rhetorical oratory, which intends to appeal to the audience, but refuses to acknowledge its manipulative operation. "Description without Place" makes rhetorical manipulation reflexive; the poem explores rhetoric's effect on history by proposing that the rhetorician prescribes history by linguistically seducing people.

The power of language depends upon how fully an utterance registers in the mind of the listener. "Description without Place" immediately displays language's control of socio-political contexts, as dominant figures linguistically color their eras. The poem shows that authority can be attained through the rhetorical power of language, as well as through social status. These two avenues often work in tandem in Stevens' poetry, as he explores the potentials of rhetorical power by various means. Powerful figures are presented as dangerous, while poetic insurrections that draw attention to the rhetoric of power are optimistically encouraged. The poetry of "Description without Place" fully attends to the role of *significance* in forming rhetoric.

As shown in my opening discussion of "Description without Place," Stevens stresses language's ability to manufacture concepts through subtle entanglements of sound and rhythm, which work together to wrap content into a seductive package for the reader. Meaning is continually assembled, such as at the end of canto ii when the poet, referring to the by now multi-colored queen, asks:

> What subtlety would apparition have?
>
> In flat appearance we should be and be,
> Except for delicate clinkings not explained.
>
> These are the actual seemings that we see,
> Hear, feel and know. We feel and know them so.   (*CP* 340)

By often reversing expectations of presence and absence, Stevens recreates images and apparent beings out of nothing but language. The "subtlety" of "apparition" refers to the coloring of the queen in the previous lines, which "apparition" then decreases. "In flat appearance" projects beings that lack description, save for the "delicate clinkings" of sound; the onomatopoeia overpowers literal reference so that the reader hears the effect of language. Sound overtakes sight at this point, and with that dominance the reader lacks a foreseeable ground based on mimetic realism. This unsettling sense, as often in Stevens, is then echoed in the syntax: "not explained." Yet the rapid movement of the poem never rests, and somehow remains casual. The affirmation of "These are" counterbalances the previous uncertainty, as the poem's narrative refers to "seemings that we see," which revitalize the earlier colors. And again typical of Stevens' compositions, the previous queen trope that was questioned in a decreation is sensually recreated with denser compositional textures. The "apparent" changing colors are apparitions, "the actual seemings that we see." The ghostly oxymoron is manifested by our new awareness that "seemings" are processed. Yet we also "Hear, feel and know" them, as the poem convinces us by temporarily removing sight, and entrusting our senses to musical affect. By activating several senses, and making other forms of knowledge such as logic and ideas relative, something as seemingly innocuous as intuition ("We feel and know them so") is granted a composite power. The "delicate clinkings" pervade the poem's logic: long "e" assonance unites "be and be," "These," "seemings," "see," "Hear," and "feel;" while the internal rhyme of the last line tells us we "know" "so." Stevens explains "delicate clinkings" as we hear "clinkings" register in ear and mind.

Canto iv's case studies of Nietzsche and Lenin dramatize how these figures alter history through their affected ideologies. History is usually charted in space and time, but here is composed of tropes and motion, tropes in motions controlled by the minds of Nietzsche and Lenin. The historical axis of space and time is unsettled by tropes that overpower their localized contexts. Pathology's domination of space and time does not traditionally constitute historical texts. But here Stevens portrays narratives of affect that determine history. The poem's presented occasions depict decision-making processes that appear delirious because they are sensual, yet each figure's thought process is rhetorically convincing, if not accurately critical of his ideas. We read Nietzsche and Lenin each struggling for representation; engaging in wars between metaphor and metonymy, and synchronic and diachronic narratives, as the captain did in "Life on a Battleship" written six years earlier.

Nietzsche's tropes take dominion over their limited space—a pool—without regard for time:

> Nietzsche in Basel studied the deep pool
> Of these discolorations, mastering

> The moving and the moving of their forms
> In the much-mottled motion of blank time.
>
> His revery was the deepness of the pool,
> The very pool, his thoughts the colored forms,
>
> The eccentric souvenirs of human shapes,
> Wrapped in their seemings, crowd on curious crowd,
>
> In a kind of total affluence, all first,
> All final, colors subjected in revery
>
> To an innate grandiose, an innate light,
> The sun of Nietzsche gildering the pool,
>
> Yes: gildering the swarm-like manias
> In perpetual revolution, round and round . . .   (*CP* 342)

Narcissus stirs the historical soup. Transfixed in revery, Nietzsche's "total affluence" is the rich historical knowledge and power wielded in his image. His "first" and "final" subjection is an exaggerated scenario of the "first idea" of the sun imagined by ephebe in "Notes." Nietzsche's "innate grandiose" ego belongs to the power of an established being whose every thought reflects his "total affluence," which becomes philosophy. In describing Nietzsche as "grandiose," yet using "grandiose" as a noun rather than an adjective, Stevens demonstrates how descriptions, adjectival qualities are affectations that become identities. This offshoot of "Notes" is a song of rhetorical power, as the "swarm-like" "curious crowds" are conversely nouns that "Wrapped in their seemings" become adjectives in Nietzsche's pool: the masses are de-scribed in Nietzsche's formal reverie; they're his adjectives. The fact that the "human shapes" are "souvenirs" means that their stasis is savored only by Nietzsche's "gildering."

In terms of time and space, the "forms" are confined within the pool of Nietzsche's thought, which bears no relation to anything other than the tropes that may exist there. Nietzsche's vision is a transcendental reverie that denies time, and likewise the composed people are taken out of context into his tropical pool. This sort of dislocated representative domain has mistakenly been attributed to Stevens the poet, rather than seen as an objective of his poetry's diagnosis: the dangerous psychological void that articulates history. With the aid of the letters, biographical material, and historical digging by Filreis and Longenbach, such a case for a Stevensian abstract reverie cannot be sustained. Stevens certainly does abstract history, which history cannot avoid no matter who writes it, but the poet's tropes now have increasingly discernible references, which make the abstractions all the more rhetorically poignant.

In the case of this portrait of Nietzsche, Stevens had been reading "Jakob Burckhardt (who was a friend of Nietzsche's at Basel)," who influenced Nietzsche to see poetry "as an aspect of history"(*L* 452–53). Henry Church encouraged Stevens to pursue an anecdotal image of Nietzsche in Basel, partly because, as Filreis claims, Church admired Nietzsche, but Stevens had put "down *The Genealogy of Morals* before reading far enough into it" (*Actual World,* 157). Likewise, Stevens' depiction of Lenin was influenced by Edmund Wilson's *To the Finland Station,* of which Stevens says: "People are reaching a point where they are very much interested in the personalities of the Marxians, early and late. That is about as far as I myself go" (*L* 381, *Actual World* 159). As usual, Stevens' levity reduces the substantial gleanings we take from the poetry; nevertheless, we can derive that Stevens read Nietzsche and Lenin as figures whose personalities fascinate history as a case of "Description without Place."

As "Description without Place" demonstrates, language is composed by and composes many other ways of knowing. The senses undermine reason and constitute epistemology in ways that are hard to measure. Time and space are no longer firm x-y axis points that grid knowledge. The issue of time and space becomes evident when the portraits of Lenin and Nietzsche are contrasted:

> Lenin on a bench beside a lake disturbed
> The swans. He was not the man for swans.
>
> The slouch of his body and his look were not
> In suavest keeping. The shoes, the clothes, the hat
>
> Suited the decadence of those silences,
> In which he sat. All chariots were drowned. The swans
>
> Moved on the buried water where they lay.
> Lenin took bread from his pocket, scattered it—
>
> The swans fled outward to remoter reaches,
> As if they knew of distant beaches; and were

> Dissolved. The distances of space and time
> Were one and swans far off were swans to come.
>
> The eye of Lenin kept the far-off shapes.
> His mind raised up, down-drowned, the chariots.
>
> And reaches, beaches, tomorrow's regions became
> One thinking of apocalyptic legions.   (*CP* 343)

Where Nietzsche maniacally plumbs the depths of his reflective consciousness, Lenin destroys present "space and time" for a revolutionary tomorrow. Where Nietzsche is immersed in a deep pool in which all space is saturated with meaning and time is nullified, Lenin negates his surroundings but looks far ahead in his narrative. Nietzsche's deep thought is metaphorical because all is insular comparison, and Lenin metonymically searches for the next utopia, hoping for an allegory. Lenin scatters the present swans (poets like Nietzsche who fly vertically) with his bread, denying the depth of "the buried water where they lay."

As birds of poetry, the swans are an ideal bunch who subscribe to the "As if" conditional similes of Stevens' poetics. As with Nietzsche, however, "distances of space and time" are dissolved so that swan-poets participate in an ongoing soulful exploration ("swans far off were swans to come"). In this regard the swans are a less satirical version of "Mesdames" from *Owl's Clover*. Also corresponding to that long poem is the similarity between Lenin and Burnshaw as communists. But where Burnshaw's utopic vision defined his present, "The eye of Lenin kept the far-off shapes." Both communists conclude "thinking of apocalyptic legions."

In the portrait of Lenin and ensuing movement toward the close of "Description without Place," representations become increasingly registered in a language that cleaves to materiality:

> The slouch of his body and his look were not
> In suavest keeping. The shoes, the clothes, the hat
>
> Suited the decadence of those silences,
> In which he sat. All chariots were drowned. . . .   (*CP* 343)

"The style of poetry, men, and gods are one," Stevens states in "Two or Three Ideas." Materiality is often used by Stevens as a way to unite material fabric with the bodies that clothes dress and their fabricated spirits.

These linguistic adherences are increasingly allegorical in the later poetry. Canto v presents "a summer's day" as a "column in the desert." We read material language that dresses and dramatizes itself, while it also presents an arbitrary picture language divorced from realism. It is material in that there are no transcendent references, and the poetry is abstract because signifiers create signifieds of their own invention; representations do not correspond with accepted reality. So we might ask, as Stevens does, "If seeming is description without place," then what is seamed? Description without place is not description as we know it; it is not mimetic representation, but is new found allegory, as we see in canto v:

> If seeming is description without place,
> The spirit's universe, then a summer's day,
>
> Even the seeming of a summer's day,
> Is description without place. It is a sense
>
> To which we refer experience, a knowledge
> Incognito, the column in the desert,
>
> On which the dove alights. Description is
> Composed of a sight indifferent to the eye.   (*CP* 343)

The poetics of "The Idea of Order at Key West" and "Esthetique du Mal" advance here. "Whose spirit is this?" continues to be answered in the abstractly composed "seeming"; some people (such as Harold Bloom) might say this seeming belongs to the poet and it is therefore solipsistic spirit, but I disagree, because the "spirit's universe" is located in the words of the poem, which belong to every listener. We are in the midst of a *Transport to Summer;* that season is the spiritual goal; it's also the name of this volume, and the poems within flesh out the goal. "Esthetique du Mal" ended with the human adventurer conceiving a physical race "in a physical world" (*CP* 325). Yet such conception derived from "the metaphysicals [that] / Lie sprawling in majors of the August heat, / The rotund emotions, paradise unknown." Although transport to full summer was in process, both the means to get there and the prize remained metaphysical. The "sprawling" forms too closely resemble the futurist paintings of Miro and Kandinsky, in which abstract forms float in space. And although the spirit will have a hard time achieving physicality, in "Description without Place" Stevens more completely describes the summer's day as linguistic material. In "Esthetique du Mal" the summer day appeared to be a goal rooted in realism, even though it meant to signify the metaphysical spirit, and even though the "As if" relation inscribed that poem too. But in "Description" the poet is explicit: "Even the seeming of a summer's day / Is description without place." Rather than sprawling metaphysicals, we get this spiritual summer day described as "a sense / To which we refer experience," which posits this linguistic trope as a sensual, mediated, and experientially based construct. Language may simply describe a summer's day, but it remains "a knowledge / Incognito," dressed in the material disguise of language, which reveals more about the speaker's contexts than it does a summer day ("Shall I compare thee to . . .").

The poem alerts us to epistemological limits through the sudden metaphor of "the column in the desert." This monument appears disparate and arbitrary when compared to the summer day in "Esthetique du Mal," which came to encompass several human faculties. Its automatic erratic arrival in the poem call up pejorative expectations from this reader—owing to Stevens' treatment of monuments throughout the thirties—but the poet signals a major change in his poetic with this column "on which the dove alights." At the end of World War II people need this bird of peace, and it is interesting to recall that Stevens read these lines adjacent to Sumner Welles' American imperial "peace" talk. Stevens' doved column does not contradict Welles; it can, however, work as a metaphor describing the tropical allure of Welles' rhetoric: "A Vision of the World at Peace" is a column in the desert, an American monument in the barren wastelands of elsewhere. Welles' vision, and the suddenly imposed column, are object(ive)s of peace that, if successful, doves and students will flock to without questioning the imposition (creative and argumentative) a monument makes. Why do monumental rhetorics and statues work? They are presences in absences; present significations that fill uncertain or barren absences.

The statues of the thirties imposed defined agendas, whether automated by state establishment or leftist radicals. The poet here has carefully constructed this column from a theory of language in which representation is far removed from the reign of definite knowledge. The monument Stevens comes up with is, like the others, excessively arbitrary. The poet acknowledges that people need something solid to flock to, like the park in "A Duck for Dinner," and that such a monument (even if it's a fixed linguistic trope) cannot fully represent everybody. The problem with the Old Woman at the foot of the Statue was that the monument's cultural elitism enforced her social marginality. Stevens elides that problem here by making the desert column necessarily abstract. Sure we can see it, but its arbitrariness in the poem makes it a displaced metaphor of the sunny spirit, a metaphor that looks like a symbol but lacks an easy symbolic equivalent. Of the awkward metaphor's search for allegory, or search for supreme fictionality, the poem reads: "Description is / Composed of a sight indifferent to the eye" (*CP* 343).

After this semiotic shift, the rest of canto v seems easy:

> It is an expectation, a desire,
> A palm that rises up beyond the sea,
>
> A little different from reality:
> The difference that we make in what we see
>
> And our memorials of that difference,
> Sprinklings of bright particulars from the sky.
>
> The future is description without place,
> The categorical predicate, the arc.
>
> It is a wizened starlight growing young,
> In which old stars are planets of morning, fresh
>
> In the brilliantest descriptions of new day,
> Before it comes, the just anticipation
>
> Of the appropriate creatures, jubilant,
> The forms that are attentive in thin air.   (*CP* 344)

Maybe too easy, because once realism is dismissed, and representation becomes a nexus of possibility, we might wonder where the actual has gone. Before attending to that danger, I want to recapitulate the way in which Stevens wants poetry to precede the coming day. Kristin Ross interprets Rimbaud's poetry as *avant la lettre:* a forewarning of the future that serves as a critical representation of the present. Stevens likewise projects "appropriate creatures," whose abstract appropriations are apropos a portentous future. These figures include the heroes of "Notes," but in "Description without Place" language is more explicitly the hopeful vehicle, thereby ridding the leap of faith upon which heroes depend. Without the necessity of having to look to a supreme being, even if abstract, we as readers can more directly look to and use language as the vehicle for change. Belief is made a conscious issue that depends on the success of its rhetorical com-position. Conversely, failure of descriptive rhetoric, or failure of *significance* (a term I prefer), is built into this linguistic poetic. Readers can decide when language loses *significance* and becomes *insignificant,* such as when the predominant objective of *signification* conveys a blunt, limited, forceful, hasty, or unthoughtful message. In a successful rhetoric or poetry of *signif-icance* the automatism of a leap of faith toward an abstract entity is averted. We can certainly still be suckered, since that is what language's seductions do, but a language of *significance* inscribes the rhetorical seduction:

> Description is revelation. It is not
> The thing described, nor false facsimile.
>
> It is an artificial thing that exists,
> In its own seeming, plainly visible . . .   (*CP* 344)

Canto vii addresses risking the actual as a challenge for language. Stevens seems optimistic in thinking that the most persuasive and responsible lan-guage wins. We have to rely on the poet's virtue. Such ground trembles, but to my mind it is sensible because it means if the poet fails us, or we reject his authority, then we are responsible for it all.

> Thus the theory of description matters most.
> It is the theory of the word for those
>
> For whom the word is the making of the world,
> The buzzing world and lisping firmament.
>
> It is a world of words to the end of it,
> In which nothing solid is its solid self.

This prophesy of postmodernism depends upon reflexively composed rhetoric for success.

Stevens returns to "the speech of the place," and even if description is only utterance, it is what makes people:

> As, men make themselves their speech: the hard hidalgo
> Lives in the mountainous character of his speech;
>
> And in the mountainous mirror Spain acquires
> The knowledge of Spain and of the hidalgo's hat—   (*CP* 345)

The hidalgo's characterized speech abstractly mirrors Spain as "an artificial thing that exists," just as the "mountainous atmospheres" compose Key West, and Lenin's clothes suit his decadent dissolution. The hidalgo's speech is the garment by which he is known; Stevens makes it "mountainous" by descriptive metaphor. The written characters composing this speech then reflect ("mirror"-like) Spain's characteristics, through which Spain learns of itself.

Fred Hoerner, drawing from Marx and Engels in *The German Ideology*, describes this as a "poetry of the future" that exceeds ideological boundaries. The question here is whether Stevens' excessive attention to descriptive power trivializes Spanish actuality. William Carlos Williams thought this section of the poem did. Trying to determine Stevens' political stance is always precarious because our taxonomies for such judgments are exactly the definitions that the poetry undermines. In writing about the rhetorical power of description, Stevens takes poetry's focus away from "what" is presented and draws attention to "how" presentation creates representation. Stevens undermines what is presented through linguistic subversions that reflexively inscribe, make obvious, rhetorical seductions. The final lines of the poem display an excess of language, abstract coloring, and portend poetry's importance.

> It matters, because everything we say
> Of the past is description without place, a cast
>
> Of the imagination, made in sound;
> And because what we say of the future must portend,
>
> Be alive with its own seemings, seeming to be
> Like rubies reddened by rubies reddening.   (*CP* 346)

Inscribing that linguistic primacy in the later poetry allows Stevens not only authority, but also intimacy with his readers.

As mentioned earlier, I have transcribed sections of "A Vision of a World at Peace" and juxtaposed them with passages from "Description without Place" so that we can have a closer look at the rhetorical contingencies between Welles and Stevens. I suggest that Stevens is offering a "theory of description [that] matters most," and that the poem prescribes a practice that can be implemented next to any rhetoric. Welles' speech is encased in the language of "Vision," and I suggest that Stevens makes much out of Welles' vision because its description portends future world order. Stevens wrote this poem explicitly for the Harvard Phi Beta Kappa occasion. In comparison to PBK poems of years previous to 1945, "Description without Place" functions anti-generically, undercutting Welles—whom Stevens would likely have known about since the diplomat had been delivering much the same message across America for a while.[9] The following excerpts are manipulatively collided together so that you, the reader, can approximate the young Harvard audience of June 1945.

WELLES OPENS: "Those words, a world at peace, represent the craving of hundreds of millions of people in every quarter of the globe. They constitute the ideal towards which the democracies have been groping for many generations. That is the goal towards which the men and women and the governments of the United Nations are striving today." (*Virginia Quarterly Review* 481)

STEVENS: An age is a manner collected from a queen
           An age is green or red. An age believes

           Or it denies. An age is solitude
           Or a barricade against the singular man

           By the incalculably plural. . . .   (*CP* 340)

WELLES: "It is only in the Western Hemisphere that an ordered civilization remains intact. . . . [T]he regional system which the American Republics had in recent years been gradually building up stood them in good stead at the moment of the world crisis. The international machinery which they had constructed for common defense, as well as for common progress, worked when the need arose. Today, in this time of great uncertainty, that mechanism still functions not only for the benefit of the Western Hemisphere, but for the benefit of all mankind. . . . It is almost impossible for the human mind to grasp the magnitude of the staggering problems with which the people of the United Nations are faced today as they commence to undertake the task of partial reconstruction" (483).

STEVENS: There might be, too, a change immenser than
           A poet's metaphors in which being would

           Come true, a point in the fire of music where
           Dazzle yields to clarity and we observe,

           And observing is completing and we are content,
           In a world that shrinks to an immediate whole,

> That we do not need to understand, complete
> Without secret arrangements of it in the mind.   (*CP* 341)

WELLES: "There is no alternative between our full participation in the United Nations Organization and world anarchy. The immediate and primary obligation of the people of the United States must, therefore, be to bend every effort towards making the Organization work—work in the interest of world peace and thereby work in their own interest.

It would be wholly illusory also not to recognize that the Charter of any International Organization . . . must inevitably result in compromises, many of which will fall far short of the ideal which the peoples of various countries may individually uphold." (484, 485)

> STEVENS: Things are as they seemed to Calvin or to Anne
> Of England, to Pablo Neruda in Ceylon,
>
> To Nietzsche in Basel, to Lenin by a lake.
> But the integrations of the past are like
>
> A *Museo Olimpico,* so much
> So little, our affair, which is the affair
>
> Of the possible: seemings that are to be,
> Seemings that it is possible may be.   (*CP* 341–2)

WELLES: "It may be that the traditions of generations of isolationism are still working subconsciously in our minds. It may be that public opinion itself does not yet comprehend that out military, material, and moral influence in the world of today is not yet being exercised to the due advantage of the people of the United States. But this truth, I think, cannot be questioned." (494)

> STEVENS: The future is description without place,
> The categorical predicate, the great arc.
>
> It is a wizened starlight growing young,
> In which old stars are planets of morning, fresh
>
> In the brilliantest descriptions of new day,
> Before it comes, the just anticipation
>
> Of the appropriate creatures, jubilant,
> The forms that are attentive in thin air.   (*CP* 344)

WELLES: "To us of this generation is given the power to help to shape the future of mankind. No student of the world's history can fail to be conscious that the destinies of the human race in the coming years will be determined by the decisions which the American people now reach." (496)

A letter written in April 1945 cited by Longenbach (282) indicates that, while writing the poem, Stevens was preoccupied with thoughts of Barbara Church's parents living near "the area of fighting" in Europe. Stevens realized that people, whether in Europe or the United States, lived according to descriptions of places, and that these maps were under constant revision, destruction.

More amazing to me was that Stevens wrote this poem so saturated with the potential of language as the war was ending, and that such potency transposed perfectly to deconstruct the fully loaded, self-righteous diplomacy of Sumner Welles. The poetry's familiar technique of extrapolating ideas into larger metaphors excessively repeats the growth pattern of meager seeming to dominant being. By theorizing the rhetorical dimensions of Welles' world vision, "Description without Place" de-scribes the dawning of a new era as yet another of history's fanatic fantasies. Unfortunately this American imperial dream won. And I'm sure that much of Stevens' portent diffused into that day's air. However, revisionary hindsight allows us to see the poem succeed in a rhetorical deconstruction of society's undertakings. Amalgamating various contexts and constructs under the rubric of historical determination makes the basic point of the poem: that language has unbelievable power to stimulate action, regardless of truth value. Consequently, we should be aware of the production of historical *signification* by attending to *significance*.

My next chapter will further examine Stevens' deconstructions of dominance. Previous chapters have suggested that Stevens' poetry has investigated and reconstructed romantic order, contemporaneous social politics of the 1930s, and rhetorical dominances in and about World War II. These issues are continued and integrated in Stevens' theoretical reworkings of the 1950s—reaching back to Homer, far into the future, to home in Connecticut, all the while calling upon readers to see change through.

Chapter 6

Lyrical Dialogues with Epic Narratives

The poetry of the 1950s, *The Auroras of Autumn* and "The Rock," delves further into traditional sources of authoritative and rigid language—namely epic teleology. Stevens opens up monolithic linguistic structures, exposing "narrative secrets," as Bonnie Costello says.[1] The poetry operates in dialogue with epic forms, interrogating narratives, often by asking readers their opinion on these matters. Readers are sometimes presented in the scene of a poem, and sometimes the poetic voice directly addresses the listener. These strategies construct coproductive social occasions that undermine epic totalities, and question the cultural definitions taking shape in America in the fifties.

The modernist literary forays of Joyce, Eliot and Pound had already revitalized Homer's *Odyssey* before Stevens made it the focus of much of his later poetry. Stevens' subversion of the epic form is more extreme, however, because his poems refuse to accept the authority of linear narratives. Stevens undermines epic narrative teleology by resisting destinies, even as they are minutely ushered in by the definitive finalities of words. Instead, he recontextualizes words (and narratives; *as* narratives) as palimpsests, never taking lightly past etymological contexts but nevertheless suggesting they be overhauled for the sake of a less destructive present and future. As early as 1942's "The Motive for Metaphor," Stevens opens up the lyric as a negotiable medium that requires readerly cooperation. As opposed to the celebration of a supposed moment in time, the lyric becomes a dramatic textual occasion in which poetry's rhetoric displays the enigmatic materiality of language. The poetry of the fifties especially realizes its site as a ritual, and forwards the poet's persona as a "half-figure," thereby presenting a dialogic model in which the reader completes the poem.

Modernist poetry's epics share certain "family resemblances," which are described by M. A. Bernstein in *The Tale of the Tribe: Ezra Pound and the Modern Verse Epic*. Besides Pound, Bernstein details the epics of William Carlos Williams and Charles Olson via four characteristics common to epic verse:

> (a) . . . a narrative of its audience's own cultural, historical, or mythic heritage . . . (b) The dominant voice narrating the poem will, therefore, not bear the trace of a single sensibility; instead, it will function as a spokesman for values generally . . . communal . . . (c) Consequently, the proper audience of an epic is not the *individual* . . . but the *citizen* as participant in a collective linguistic and social nexus. . . . (d) The element of instruction [is] deliberately foregrounded in an epic. . . . (14)

Although Stevens may share some of these goals, none of his poems are epics that claim a representative perspective of a communal heritage. Stevens rarely assumes the role of communal spokesman, nor does he instruct the collective. Importantly recognizing the poet's role as a visitor, Stevens acknowledges that linguistic wizardry is confined to the poem, yet suggests that poetic patterns of rhetorical influence carry on in the actual world. Stevens' lyrics condition their occasion with reflexive signifiers that provoke new contexts (in the poem, then out of the poem). The poetry presents an ethical interaction in which the lyric is no longer possessed by its author. Stevens' poetry urges the reader to participate, rather than admire a monument, or follow a program.

Michael Davidson's essay "Notes Beyond the *Notes:* Wallace Stevens and Contemporary Poetics" observes Stevens' influence

> as occupying three general areas: the use of the long poem in producing a destructive or decreative poetics; the operational or performative use of language to create a philosophical poetry; and the transformation, by these means, of a poetry of *place* into a poetry of *occasions.* (Gelpi 144)

Davidson traces the manner in which these influences decreate Romantic poetic ideals (Truth, Beauty, Joy) and inform the long poems of many contemporary poets. Davidson postulates a poetry in which the narrative is not concerned with plotting a destination. Pursuing Davidson's third area, I suggest that each Stevens poem progresses as an occasion in which the reader recognizes the narrative as a composition. Recognizing its compositionality, readers may still follow a story, but since fictionality is always dramatized in the poem, readers are involved in configuring meaning rather than being told a story about the world.

In this sense, the very *occasion* is performed linguistically. Because the words on the page compose subject matter, Stevens disrupts the suppositions of linguistic mimesis, which aims to represent time and *place* in the world. The epic is the most capacious genre in making these representative claims in culture (Bernstein 14). While modernist literature revitalized the epic, I suggest that Stevens investigated and problematized the epic's manipulation of language and culture (in a similar manner to the way in which Davidson argues that Stevens decreated Romanticism). Stevens questions language's capability to tell linear narratives, especially as they mean to represent culture. Stevens' critical approach to epic containment in poetry is similar to Joyce's deconstructions in *Ulysses,* which Kenneth Burke called "the Anti-Odyssey."[2]

Ever aware of the claims of representation, Stevens (like Joyce) brings the epic down to a quest(ion) of language. Conversely, Homer's Odysseus conquered land, and achieved heroic identity. Stevens makes each signification epic. The play between signifier and signified is one of issue and return. Each utterance is a disembarking cry that comes home possessing meaning. "The poem is the cry of its occasion" ("An Ordinary Evening in New Haven"); a "chome" registering in the listener's ear. As much as Stevens recognizes the power of incantations, his poetry problematizes the possession and definition of the occasion's meaning. Stevens shows definitive symbolizations to be stories of mastery, epics. Countering dominant and inflexible styles of language, Stevens demonstrates the impermanence and malleability of the lyric, so that poetry meets the challenge of representing mutability without monumentalizing it.

In "The Motive for Metaphor," the poem's narrative speaks of a quest for, and evasion of, signified identity. The title informs us of a search for figurative language, and the poem's opening lines introduce a figure in nature. Although the narrative seems typically romantic in its portrayal of such a subject, the scene is situated within a context of personified speech.

> You like it under the trees in autumn,
> Because everything is half dead.
> The wind moves like a cripple among the leaves
> And repeats words without meaning.   (*CP* 288)

Between each line lies an implicit comparison; if these implications can be figured out, then we might approach the motive for metaphor in this poem. "You like it" implies motivated desire in the subject; the verb "like" suggests attraction and simile, furthering the subject's position in the process of motivating metaphor. The "half dead" "autumn" resembles the subject who "like[s]" the season, while the "wind" is personified by the simile "like a cripple." The wind is even more human since it "repeats words without meaning." As usual in Stevens' poetry, the subject and surrounding phenomena bear upon each other while not quite being metaphorical reciprocals. They remain separate and distinct as much as they cohabitate. Reflexive language ("repeats words") powerfully signifies the simulacra being conjured. All of the scene's parts correlate among motivated desires that are dramatically enacted in (and by) the poem's language: "You like it," "half dead," "like a cripple," and "repeats words without meaning" are all half-meanings teasing the reader and desiring consummation. They are unfulfilled metaphors that get us thinking because they are potent and evolving.

The poem dramatizes figuration—a subject in nature within language—as an adventure that accumulates suspense for a heroic and meaningful return, thereby resembling epic teleology. But instead of telling the reader what happens next, Stevens' next stanza provides another metaphor with which to compare the first stanza: "In the same way, you were happy in spring, / With the half colors of quarter-things" (*CP* 288). Instead of attending to the subject's unresolved inarticulate autumnal desire, the second stanza offers an analogy; yet another metaphor to build upon the comparisons provided in each line. The poem resists being about an easily locatable topic; it is not primarily about autumn, wind, leaves, spring, or the bird and moon that follow. These are the metaphorical referents of the past.[3] About the *motive* for metaphor, the poem's stanzas build tropes through the repetition of half-ness, partial-ness, the genesis of expression. Why does Stevens continue to use natural symbols here? Tradition? Well, maybe in spite of it, Stevens points to them as half-entities; things that captivate us because they die and return (like language).

> Desiring the exhilarations of changes:
> The motive for metaphor, shrinking from
> The weight of primary noon,
> The A B C of being. . . .

Death presides over this desire for change (it "is the mother of beauty," after all). The subject is "shrinking from / The weight of primary noon" because the moment is fully present without shadows or simulacra. Resisting the sublimity of that moment is an acknowledgment of its sublime temporality: the "weight of primary noon" contrasts with its fleeting diminishment at the hands of time. Noon's full presence makes the moment sublimely dominant, such that there is no occasion for metaphor. While the shadowless noon dominates, the passive subject receives primary sensual data, and thereby becomes an agent of metaphor—to such an extent that the subject disappears from the poem while remaining the implied subject. Fully present noon is tied to a loose metaphor of identity constituted by language: "The A B C of being" suggests primary building blocks; the beginning of the alphabet is like the beginning of a day's shadow following "primary noon" (A also being Alpha, the first star in the universe). Then quickly "of being" calls up identity or ontology. We are left wondering whether "A B C" begins to write the subject's being, whether these primary letters characterize elemental form, or whether this poem's decreative subject might bring all sensual matter together in metaphor.

As with the other transitions between stanzas, indeterminacy is appended by more layers of suggestion. In the final stanza, sensory images accumulate rapidly, making logic increasingly difficult, which causes the motive for metaphor to be stronger. Stevens dramatizes the sublime as a moment that makes expression nearly impossible, and that challenge is cause for poetic occasion. The reverence Stevens lends to these occasions makes each signification of epic proportion, yet lyrically tenuous. Stevens wants epic grandeur in each utterance while maintaining poetry as impermanent song. The last stanza presents the challenge of articulating primary sensual experience in a series of concocting images, sounds, and responses:

> The ruddy temper, the hammer
> Of red and blue, the hard sound—
> Steel against intimation—the sharp flash,
> The vital, arrogant, fatal, dominant X.

Characteristic of Stevens, these sensations are strongest when most logically undeveloped. Gone are the natural referents. Instead we get "Steel against intimation." "Steel" does not belong to a mimetic picture created by the poem. Here language becomes a suggestive half-measure that only invokes more possibilities and less certainties. "Steel" follows from "the hammer / Of red and blue," a metaphor implying colliding colors. "Steel" also follows "the hard sound—" of what? Colors? The hammer? Signification? The latter is often the lurking referent in Stevens. But then, "Steel against intimation" introduces the contrast of cold metal against human emotions, thus reminding readers of the frail protagonist afraid of self-expression. Also lurking in Stevens is Nietzsche, whose "The Hammer Speaks" is a parable of steely creation in face of pliant, yielding timidity. In Nietzsche's parable, "the diamond" chastises his brother, the "kitchen coal," for "self-denial" and a lack of creative "destiny." Consequently, the diamond blesses the coal with a "new tablet," which reads *"become hard!"*[4] "The Motive for Metaphor" also shows a process of organic crystallization, in which "the hammer" of senses becomes articulated "X." Stevens and Nietzsche both play epic surmountings together with the lyrical utterance. Stevens' poem ends with "X," the variable signification that is "arrogant, fatal" because once signified, it does not change, and fatal because it no longer lives in the poetic genesis that lead up to it. "X" marks the spot, which Stevens' subject does not want fixed. "X" is also "vital," as the sign beginning communication, or the expressive signature that the poem's subject avoids.[5] Stevens is careful to leave the identity protectively undiscovered.

Being a lyric that begins by suggesting romantic desire, the identity of "X" is curiously provocative. "X" is ungendered, some might say the arbitrary chromosome, which might lead to psychological interpretations of Stevens' Interior Paramour.[6] Many of Stevens' romantic lyrics are directed to (of/from?) this paramour, whose source of identity can range from his mother, to his wife, to his anima, to the muse of your choice. However, signifying an identity from Stevens' arbitrary marker would betray its role in the poem; the never fully born, never dead "X" remains cloaked as a mysterious symbol, much like the traditional muse. The poem also has a love lyric's opening address, and Stevens' romance with the linguistic paramour happens to follow the lyrics he stopped writing to his wife Elsie.[7] Although poetic tradition and Stevens' biography direct the motive for "X" to feminine sources, the last stanza hammers out an aggressive language worthy of Lacan's masculine signifier. Although the motive for Stevens' metaphor remains elusive, the fluid and dynamic language of the first three stanzas opposes the monumental rigidity of tradition's "man-locked set" (*CP* 496). The last stanza's adjectives describing "X"—"fatal, dominant, arrogant"—are early indicators of Stevens' further excavations of deathly stasis, possession, dominance, and authority, which the poet increasingly associates with epic language in the late poems soon to be discussed: "The World as Meditation," "Prologues to What Is Possible," and "The Sail of Ulysses." Stevens' poetry often posits masculine power in traditional representations of culture. His many statues, for example, stand as state artifacts, which are challenged in his poems of the thirties. Stevens also expresses language's contexts through the poetry's etymological palimpsests; its manipulation of word lineages that the poet was known to dig up in dictionaries. For instance, in "The Figure of the Youth as Virile Poet," Stevens re-contextualizes the Minotaur myth in order to develop an evolving mythos for the future.

Jacqueline Vaught Brogan's important essay, "'Sister of the Minotaur': Sexism and Stevens," employs a title taken from "The Figure of the Youth as Virile Poet," in which Stevens observes gender traits in language's history:

> The centuries have a way of being male. . . . In effect, what we are remembering is the rather haggard background of the incredible, the imagination without intelligence, from which a younger figure is emerging, stepping forward in the company of a muse of its own, *still half-beast and somehow more than human, a kind of sister of the Minotaur.* The younger figure is the intelligence that endures. It is the imagination of the son still bearing the antique imagination of the father (*NA* 52–53; Brogan's italics).[8]

Brogan criticizes Stevens' convenient (Jungian) use of feminine typecasting as a means to "fragrant portals" of masculine discovery. Again in this language we can detect the masculine quest/feminine mystery, epic/lyric dialectics that contibute to language's inescapable traditions of gender stereotypes. I think Brogan nears Stevens' motive for metaphor when she points to the search for the "healing-point in the sickness of the mind" in "Artificial Populations" (*OP* 138). In this poem Stevens searches for a "music that lasts long and lives the more." Its endurance depends upon sexual balance, and here we can see masculine descriptions in conjunction with feminine characteristics: "The rosy men and the women of the rose." It would be a mistake, or at least a terrible reduction, to read Stevens' curative poetry biographically, as Brogan noted as well. In "The Figure of the Youth" essay's next intertext, we can see that the myth is part of a developing ethos: "*No longer do I believe that there is a mystic muse, sister of the Minotaur. This is another of the monsters I had for nurse, whom I have wasted. I am myself a part of what is real . . .*" (*NA* 60). Stevens is not divulging secrets here, though perhaps he employs a rhetorically intimate strategy for hooking the reader into his fluctuating myth. By using a revelatory language, Stevens makes irony out of his former mythic pronouncement, and also mocks several tropic personae by denouncing them, and aggrandizing his full emergent presence (as if it could exist freely and autonomously). Brogan neglects quoting the last intertextual reference that concludes "The Figure of the Youth as Virile Poet":

> *Inexplicable sister of the Minotaur, enigma and mask, although I am part of what is real, hear me and recognize me as part of the unreal. I am the truth but the truth of*

*that imagination of life in which with unfamiliar motion and manner you guide me
in those exchanges of speech in which your words are mine, mine yours. (NA 67)*

Stevens closes his speech by placing his mask within a dialogue that continues for "the intelligence that endures" (*NA* 52), rather than some mythic privation held close to the poet's breast. As the intelligence that endures, this sister is not bound to epic Greece; rather, she departs from contextual place (even if mythic), becoming present and future "occasion." If there is a muse here, it is projected as a future reincarnation of mythology's neglected sibling. As in "The Motive for Metaphor," Stevens' discourse refers to "words" that are constructed between *"what is real . . . and unreal,"* thereby requesting inventive dialogue to be continued by listeners. Stevens turns to siblings, generations, and marriages in his poetry as models for an always unsatisfied but emerging poetic language. As we will see in Stevens' later poetry, the halfness from which Stevens increasingly speaks requires that the reader "coproduce" the text, as Davidson says. I suggest the reader's doubling is key to opening up poetry's epic mastery as participatory lyric occasion. The dialectically gendered poetry becomes a dialogic process attempting to reach people by asking for authority rather than delivering it.

The manner in which Stevens' poetry counters discourses that monumentalize worldly events can be put into the context of postmodernism's challenges to discursive dominances of the past. Julia Kristeva's *Revolution of Poetic Language* theorizes avant-garde writing as social change. Her essay "From Symbol to Sign" succinctly shows the breakdown of language's mimetic authority.[9] Paul Bove's *Destructive Poetics* cites Stevens within this linguistic historical shift, but Bove traces a deconstruction of Western metaphysics back to Heidegger, or perhaps as early as Whitman: "Demystified literary history and literary interpretation is marked by an awareness that all genuine uses of language are destructive, that is, that they stand oriented towards the future in a discontinuous, nonimitative relation to the verbal events of the past" (xiii). "The Motive for Metaphor" resists fixture and represents figures in flux, genesis, gestation. The evolutionary poetics of Stevens, and Kristeva's poststructuralism largely derive from Mallarme, whose Symbolist poetry sometimes employs metaphors of pregnancy to ascribe creativity, as does Joyce. Generative metaphors have been employed by Derrida as well: "Here there is a kind of question, let us still call it historical, whose *conception, formation, gestation, and labor* we are only catching a glimpse of today." "Structure, sign and play in the discourse of the human sciences" was originally delivered as a paper at Johns Hopkins in 1966. I suggest that Stevens pre-dated Derrida's historical question in his poetic search of the motives for metaphor. All of these writers share an avant-garde belief in the power of language to revolutionize cultural thought. Stevens' theoretical poetry suggests that if a healthy culture is to survive, language has to incorporate change and regeneration within its articulation.

The halfness "that would never be quite expressed" in "The Motive for Metaphor" finds its entelechy in Stevens' constructed readers. "Notes Toward a Supreme Fiction" addresses an ideal reader, "ephebe," thereby positing the poetic voice as existing for the listener. The half trope is familiar to us from "The Motive for Metaphor," as the state of becoming fulfilled through language's marker, "X." In "Notes," the poet invites "ephebe" to color in the poem's linguistic landscape through the "begin again" of decreation and subsequent recreation. Stevens then proposes fallible heroes, such as Mac-Cullough, who, like Bloom in *Ulysses,* welcome readers by virtue of their anti-heroic modesty. These early "half-figures" are versions of the "Angel Surrounded by Paysans," the poet's necessary persona that relies upon the countrymen for whom he enables clearer sight.

Before employing its personae, "Notes Toward a Supreme Fiction" suggests an epic narrative structure while subverting the very form that encases it. The poem's title announces a quest, and immediately the prologue fulfills it:

> And for what, except for you, do I feel love?
> Do I press the extremest book of the wisest man
> Close to me, hidden in me day and night?
> In the uncertain light of single, certain truth,
> Equal in living changingness to the light
> In which I meet you, in which we sit and rest,
> For a moment in the central of our being,
> The vivid transparence that you bring is peace.   (*CP* 380)

The epic's typically male conquest is quelled by the exchanged gift of brotherly love: "The vivid transparence that you bring is peace" stresses a gift in the last syllable, "peace." The lyric moment is not transcendent, it is transparently shared without monumental consequence. Although Stevens' poetry is written in a far from transparent language, the transparency achieved here is equated with peace: a marriage occasioned through the artifice of language. The prologue's address to Henry Church sets a tone requesting peace with the reader, "ephebe," from whom the listener is accepting the gift of knowledge: the poem.

The ease of the transparent gift between Stevens and Henry Church as fellow aesthetes perhaps serves as a catalyst for the rest of the poem's search for a poetic ontology in time of war. The poem's heroes can be viewed as a series of projections in an effort to reach the wartime needs of the reader. Beginning with Church, Stevens moves to the ideal "ephebe"; to the "latent double," "Beau linguist," and "major man" MacCullough; the many marriages of *It Must Change; Canon Aspirin;* and the "Fat girl, terrestrial." While these heroes are modest in their dependence on abstract conception, the final hero of the epilogue, the soldier, is set apart by his wartime reality. The soldier is displaced from the abstract process of Stevens' poetics. The reciprocity Stevens desires between poet and soldier in the epilogue was, at the time, an immanent need for the poet. In terms of the poet's developing style, "Notes" includes readers in an effort to "face the men of the time and to meet / The women of the time" (*CP* 240),[10] as the poet projected in "Of Modern Poetry."

By 1950's "Angel Surrounded by Paysans," the poet, in the guise of an angel, demonstrates a more confident public voice, asking *one of the countrymen:* "Am I not, / Myself, only half of a figure of a sort . . .?" A "half-figure," the poet as "the necessary angel of the earth" allows the paysans to "see the earth again, / Cleared of its stiff and stubborn, man-locked set" (*CP* 496). This figure allows Stevens to move between the epic/lyric dialectic. By neither telling stories nor singing songs, but by clearing away static resistances, the poet coalesces attributes of earlier heroes in order to reach readers. Like "The Man on the Dump," the necessary angel engages in what Bove calls destructive poetics. But as Bove points out, standing on the trash heap of history enables the poet to sift through history's language as it lives in the present, thereby recreating it for the future. The poems are decreative so that the figures and tropes of the past can be reconfigured again, anew, as the sun is in "Notes." For instance, the decreated figure of the comic vagabond in "Notes" is a mock-hero wearing "sagging pantaloons." The visual imagery of his baggy clothes, complemented by the spacious aural imagery of "pantaloons," creates open spaces that the reader can fulfill. He is a comic masculine version of the "body wholly body fluttering / Its empty sleeves" from "The Idea of Order at Key West": Stevens opens up cluttered symbols of poetic tradition, such as the sea and muse, so that they can be recreated by the poet and his solicited reader (Ramon). In "Paysans," however, the angel-poet becomes the empty hero requiring flesh to fill his clothes. Language is treated as a flexible material made of sounds and images that are fulfilled by the reader's response to the poem and poet-angel.

The reader, then, is asked to embody the poem. In "Final Soliloquy of the Interior Paramour," the reader is asked to "Light the first light of evening, *as* in a room." In "Debris of Life and Mind," the protagonist envisions a dream-woman, only for her to disappear, causing an abrupt personal request in the last line that seems to jump out of the poem's enclosure: "Stay here. Speak of familiar things awhile." We are invited conditionally (the condition is language) to fulfill the poems as negotiated texts.[11]

These "half-figures" embody poetic signification at work because they are signs demanding cooperation. Such figures could also appear futile in their dependency, but Stevens is creating a modest ideal that undermines authority by requesting a co-habitated poetic world. In order for poetry to be vital, the lyric must move beyond univocal musing to enacting its place as occasion. Stevens' poems force the reader to make meaning by using language as the site of production: a living space. In "Paysans," the angel speaks to the people of his fleeting role, which demands reciprocity, while finally suggesting that readers are responsible for their outlook beyond the confines of poetic discourse:

> And, in my hearing, you hear its tragic drone
>
> Rise liquidly in liquid lingerings,
> Like watery words awash; like meanings said
>
> By repetitions of half-meanings. Am I not
> Myself, only half of a figure of a sort
>
> A figure half-seen, or seen for a moment, a man
> Of the mind, an apparition apparelled in
>
> Apparels of such lightest look that a turn
> Of my shoulder and quickly, too quickly, I am gone? (*CP* 497)

As both an active ghost and flat material trope, readers depend upon the figure, but there is no mystical pretension beyond the poem's walls. There is little to separate this angel from any other linguistic figure in the poem. He is, at once, as cold and distant as an inscription on a slate; yet intimately part of every metaphor: each sign constructed by the reader is the poet: the ghost in the machine as material letter and signified material. By paralleling "half-meaning" with "half-figure," the figure becomes an "apparition." But it is reflexively ironic (and oxymoronic) because as an "apparition apparelled" the ghost is clothed, which I think is Stevens' point. The apparition is brought down to earth through the word-play, "apparition apparelled in / Apparels. . . ." Within this hilarity, Stevens takes a traditional ethereal ghost figure (something that floats around with transcendent imprecision) and re-clothes it in new linguistic alliterative "apparel." In doing so, the spiritual wizardry of the figure is now performed anew in the materiality of language, thus grounded. Stevens is most effective at taking signifieds like this that are full of mysterious hocus-pocus, parodying them, and yet resignifying them as signifiers that still evoke bewilderment due to the rhetorical power of sound and image (the muse of "Key West" is another example). While the figure from "The Motive for Metaphor" is reluctantly signified a dominant and indeterminate "X" through the course of the whole poem, this ghostly subject is swiftly dressed in fitting clothes made of tailored words. These multiple layers of poetry depict a subject so expressive of itself that we can see why Stevens argues that the style of a poem, gods, and men are one (*OP* 262).[12] The poetry of "Angel Surrounded by Paysans" converses between a self-reflexive text and exterior references, while demonstrating how the poet coproduces that occasional relationship with the reader.

After co-opting the reader in a coproductive, dialogic poetry, Stevens writes several poems in the fifties that question epic narrative teleology. These late poems problematize characteristics of epic writing, such as possessive totality and linear definitions of knowledge (territory, language). "Prologues to What Is Possible," and "The World as Meditation" suggest that lyrical motivations drive epic routes. The maps of poetry and knowledge are drawn by muses. Stevens, though, is discontent with poetry's musical tailoring, and "The Sail of Ulysses" shows that the motives for muses need delineating.

"Prologues to What Is Possible" (*CP* 515), demonstrates the dangers of neglecting the motives involved in defining the figure or poem. In "Prologues," the main seafaring figure acquires tropes with rapid grandeur, and in the process he forgets about the factors propelling his boat. This voyager becomes increasingly "at sea," in both senses of the word:

> There was an ease of mind that was like being alone in a boat at
> sea,
> A boat carried forward by waves resembling the bright backs of
> rowers,
> Gripping their oars, as if they were sure of the way to their
> destination,
> . . . .

> The boat was built of stones that had lost their weight and being no
>   longer
> heavy / Had left in them only a brilliance, of unaccustomed
>   origin.. . . .
>
>   (*CP* 515)

The mariner's epic journey, his energy, is propelled through the simile of
the waves as rowers: "as if they were sure of the way to their destination"
suggests a multiplicity of impulses seemingly sure in their plot. The conditional simile contradicts the surety of the rowing, pointing to the way in
which a plotted direction often makes up for uncertainty. The material
"stones" comprising the boat are then abstracted into an "unaccustomed
origin." Their "brilliance" may be more anathema than praise; the traveler
also forges an increasingly singular identity that neglects his composition.
This singularity becomes a symbol, which for Stevens is often "a question
of identity" (*OP* 194).[13]

> He belonged to the far-foreign departure of his vessel and was part
>   of it,
> Part of the speculum of fire on its prow, its symbol, whatever it was,
> Part of the glass-like sides on which it glided over the salt-stained
>   water,
> As he traveled alone, like a man lured on by a syllable without any
> meaning / A syllable of which he felt, with an appointed sureness,
> That it contained the meaning into which he wanted to enter,
> A meaning which, as he entered it, would shatter the boat and leave
>   the oarsmen quiet . . .   (*CP* 516)

The monument on the prow, traditionally a symbol of grandeur, here slides
from a stately synecdoche to a metonymy in an undetermined relationship
with the traveler, the "glass-like sides of the boat," even the water. The
indeterminacy is then set in a metaphor of linguistic construction, "a syllable." The epic journey is the process of making meaning: not so much a
journey of topographical adventure, or a poem, not even a word, but a syllable in search of a metaphor.

The downsizing of focus here leads, in the second section of the poem,
to a "metaphor [that] stirred his fear." Whether or not the metaphor links
up with the "fire on the prow" is the point. In addition to the fear of
uncertainty and identity that the poet-voyager demonstrates, his epistemological insight obliterates those around him: the oarsmen, who may be fellow writers, mentors, family, friends, or simply tropes.[14] The oarsmen

become "all his hereditary lights." The metaphorical discovery is "a new and unobserved, slight dithering, / The smallest lamp, which added its puissant flick, to which he gave / A name and privilege over the ordinary of his commonplace. . . ." This illumination, the introduction of a new signification, is treated here in miniaturist idolatry—rather like a new trinket for a glass menagerie. There is a part of Stevens, the collector, who relishes such a thing, and a part of him, the skeptic or socialist, who despises it. Both these tones can be read here, especially in the "puissant flick," which juxtaposes French civility with American flippancy.

Stevens resolves these battles of tone, and, moreover, comes to terms with the epic ingredient within the lyrical gift:

> A flick which added to what was real and its vocabulary,
> The way some first thing coming into Northern trees
> Adds to them the whole vocabulary of the South,
> The way the earliest single light in the evening sky, in spring,
> Creates a fresh universe out of nothingness by adding itself,
> The way a look or a touch reveals its unexpected magnitudes.
>
> (*CP* 517)

These novelties—words or touches—are lyrical gifts exchanged between pairs (North and South, poet and reader). Yet the exchange epically brings the journey of one into contact with an other. "What is Possible" arises out of the anxiety of "Prologues" with the acceptance that each nomination, however arbitrary, is a novelty in a pre-set world of language only revitalized by new arrivals. Like numerous late Stevens poems, this one ends with a rhetorical appeal to human contact, thus bringing the epic, poetic, linguistic discussion into warmer environs. More than rhetorical tricks, Stevens' theories of poetry apply to ethical human interaction. For instance, the mariner's hierarchical symbolization neglects his crew and could be taken as a comment on authority; a warning about prioritizing ego over communication in collective endeavors. Or the seafarer could be seen as a visionary colonialist, blind not only to his destination, but also to his crew of countrymen.

The three final metaphors following the "flick which added to what was real and its vocabulary" all speak of communion, which indirectly invokes the reader. Earlier in the poem, the fearsome metaphor's arrival into the poet-traveler's repertoire was "Removed from any shore, from any man or woman, and needing none." If left in that state, the metaphor remains an isolated, stubborn symbol. The "fire on its prow, its symbol" is akin to

Yeats's gold bird in "Sailing to Byzantium," that is used "To keep a drowsy Emperor awake." Stevens' refusal of monumental fixtures extends to a re-examination of all poetries leading toward stasis, or any destination. The danger of the epic is its conquest, which here is brought down to the level of syllable. For Stevens, the only way around such inherent destructiveness is through the notion of gifts, exemplified by the communications in the final stanza of "Prologues to What is Possible."

"The World as Meditation," one of the later poems from *The Rock,* continues Stevens' inquiry into the epic and lyric dialectic. The poem is set in the storyline of Ulysses' return to Penelope, and unites masculine and feminine roles as they are typecast in this narrative paradigm. The poem begins by asking whether Ulysses "approaches from the east." While this question raises expectations, Penelope's home is domestically prepared, as "Someone is moving"

> On the horizon and lifting himself above it.
> A form of fire approaches the cretonnes of Penelope,
> Whose mere savage presence wakens the world in which she dwells.
>
> (*CP* 520)

We might assume that Ulysses' combustible spirit is the "savage presence," but the lady in waiting, Penelope, composes herself in her world, suggesting that she might be the agent of desire. Ulysses is either a god or an apparition; whatever the case, Penelope has an inordinate amount of control in this courtship:

> She wanted nothing he could not bring her by coming alone.
> She wanted no fetchings. His arms would be her necklace
> And her belt, the final fortune of their desire.   (*CP* 521)

Instead of being possessed in the story, the narrative becomes irrevocably hers:

> But was it Ulysses? Or was it only the warmth of the sun
> On her pillow? The thought kept beating in her like her heart.
> The two kept beating together. It was only day.   (*CP* 521)

In "The Idea of Order at Key West," written some 15 years earlier, the poet observes the woman as the "single artificer of the world" and then steps back with Ramon Fernandez to order and question human origins. In

"The World as Meditation," the destination of the narrative, Penelope, becomes its subjective center. She changes from being the poetic object to the motivational ego of the tale: the epic plot becomes the lyric narrative. Stevens' poem lyricizes the epic male journey. The poet enacts a marriage of genres through the narrative.

Well, almost. Stevens reports "She wanted no fetchings." Short of concluding that the mythic desire belongs to Penelope, the sun creeps in as the external influence. Opposite from the "first idea" sun idealized in "Notes Toward a Supreme Fiction," Penelope's "gold flourisher" has a strong but indeterminate bearing upon the desired figure of Ulysses. Stevens resists closure, as usual, by disallowing ownership and origins of truth (Penelope's, Ulysses's, the poet Stevens', or Homer's). "The thought kept beating in her like her heart" reinforces simulacrum through simile, followed by harmony, "The two kept beating together," cut short by time, "It was only day."

Within Stevens' transformation of Penelope from the epic object to lyric desirer, we can infer not only epic impulses, but also an everyday occurrence demonstrating vulnerable truths about human motivations:

> It was Ulysses and it was not. Yet they had met,
> Friend and dear friend and a planet's encouragement.
> The barbarous strength within her would never fail.   (*CP* 521)

The identity of the epic hero is shrugged off. The "planet's encouragement" speaks of a willful mythmaking driven by humanity's sentimental desire for romance. Penelope, possessing "barbarous strength," becomes a romantic heroine of lyric and epic persuasions. She is presented by the poet as a trite romantic character, and as a potent power because of, first, her domestic resilience, and second, her role as an alternative origin for this well-known myth of Western civilization. The poem ends with Penelope consoling herself in a language sure of itself but not of its desired referent:

> She would talk a little to herself as she combed her hair,[15]
> Repeating his name with its patient syllables,
> Never forgetting him that kept coming constantly so near.   (*CP* 521)

This lyricization of the epic expresses domestic triumph (however pejorative for Lentricchia) over masculine control. The poem enacts a dismantling of the tribal tale's plot by acknowledging myth as desire (in the displaced figures of the sun on her pillow, in her heart). The abstraction of the hero into Penelope's rhetorical suasion disengages the helmsman from controlling the plot. This reversal empties plot by turning the narrative into itself. In so doing, the tale of the tribe becomes a lyric narrative joining "patient syllables" within composed myth.[16]

Stevens was not the first to do this. In Joyce's *Ulysses,* Molly goes from being plotted to captaining her own vessel. In 1931's *Counter-Statement,* Kenneth Burke recognizes Joyce's reworking of the epic, which applies to what I'm suggesting about Stevens here:

> Perhaps the most elaborate re-individuation [of form] in all history is James Joyce's *Ulysses.* But whereas in most instances the purpose of the new individuations is to make changes which reproduce under one set of conditions an effect originally obtained under another set of conditions, in the case of *Ulysses* each individuation is given a strictly "un-Homeric" equivalent. The new individuations intentionally alter the effect. *Ulysses* is the Anti-Odyssey.[17]

Together with Pound's and Williams' approaches to the epic, we can observe the importance of "re-individuating" old forms (see Bernstein). In the *Cantos,* Pound tried to decreate the poetic ego to tell the tales of historic evolution. In *Paterson,* the narrator could not stand outside the city or the poem, for they were he. Regardless of the success or failure of these epics, the modernist revisions point to fundamental instabilities of such an authoritative genre. For Williams and Stevens, lyrical involvement disallowed the distance required for narrative objectivity, yet their poetry was made local. The poems lived as active occasions in their locales.

While "The World as Meditation" resuscitates lyric desire within epic mythmaking, 1954's "The Sail of Ulysses" returns to the familiar trope of the epic, and questions the paradigm of the quest. Its motivations prove to have bleak consequences, as the muse adopts the shape of a sibyl. This poem perhaps goes furthest into how the Odyssean journey has affected the English language that the poet must contend with.

The "Sail" of Ulysses suggests the voyager's method of transport, vehicle, poem or pen, catcher of wind, inspirational tool, motive for metaphor. This poem commemorates much of Stevens' career, as Ulysses not surprisingly *"read his own mind"* (*OP* 126). Rather than totalizing a long poem's chart of a long career, I will instead look at a few loose ends, that inevitably we'll want to tie together.

> There is a human loneliness
> . . . .
> The luminous companion, the hand,

> The fortifying arm, the profound
> Response, the completely answering voice
> That which is more than anything else
> The right within us and about us,
> Joined, the triumphant vigor, felt,
> The inner direction on which we depend . . .
> That which keeps us the little that we are,
> The aid of greatness to be and the force. (*OP* 126–127)

This excerpt from canto ii summarizes Stevens' muse as that dialogically intimate double, so common to the later poems. However, just when the request for a readerly "answering voice" seems integral, the poet asserts that the dialogue is answered "within." The nature of this force is not debated or pursued as much as it is teased out by the rest of the poem: some characterizations are "the true creator," "the thinker," "Apollo," "black constructions, such public shapes / And murky masonry" (which I infer as poetic and worldly inscription). The heavy, almost Yeatsian voice then moves toward revelation in canto v. The oracle, however, is typically pejorative: "There is no map of paradise." Since Stevens felt that heaven and hell had been done, his big ambition for poetry was forecasted by the notion that "the great poem of the earth remains to be written." Twentieth-century critics, such as Northrop Frye, too, connect "earthly paradise . . . with lyrical poetry" (Hosek and Parker 309). To admit "there is no map of paradise," Stevens again dismisses an available teleology (map) while asserting lyrical presence within an elusive epic context.

Following this epically inoperative assertion, Stevens does offer a second coming with the "great Omnium": a "litter of truths becomes / A whole, the day on which the last star / Has been counted" (*OP* 128). This plurality of truth portends to "have gone beyond the symbols / To that which they have symbolized." Stevens' typical poetic performance of the motives for metaphor here seems a hunt for origins after all. The seemingly external Omnium is roped back into interior compass in canto vii. Eluding an apparent self-divinity, the poet divulges a system that brings these philosophical-religious-semiotic-local inquiries together:

> The living man in the present place,
> Always, the particular thought
> Among Plantagenet abstractions,
> Always and always, the difficult inch,
> On which the vast arches of space
> Repose, always, the credible thought

> From which the incredible systems spring,
> The little confine soon unconfined
> In stellar largenesses—these
> Are the manifestations of a law
> That bends the particulars to the abstract,
> Makes them a pack on a giant's back,
> A majestic mother's flocking brood
> As if abstractions were, themselves
> Particulars of a relative sublime.
> This is not poet's ease of mind.
> It is the fate that dwells in truth.
> We obey the coaxings of our end.   (*OP* 129–130)

The "difficult inch" suggests a movement forward but, moreover, a "particular" grounding of idea—an inscription. This form of "law" adopts the marked creatures (words, contents of a "pack," the "brood") into abstract orders. As "particulars of a relative sublime," Stevens projects the abstractions themselves as larger tropes partaking in an unruly fate the poet has trouble with. The problem with this seemingly abstract house of law and order is not its abstraction but its fatal finality. Abstractions are made of particular laws. But the power of law to become collective fate scares the poet. A collection of laws becomes sublimely dominant, thus fatal. Many poems demonstrate how the process of signification becomes law: the "fatal, dominant X" from "The Motive for Metaphor"; the symbol of the mariner on the prow in "Prologues to What Is Possible." Michael Beehler comments on Stevens' performance of language, law, and abstraction in this poem:

> It is not a law as in natural law or universal principle but a procedure. . . .
> Each of its subsequent manifestations repeats a structure in which particulars are bent "to the abstract" and are made to organize themselves around that abstraction as though it were their natural center and origin. . . . Truths cannot be determined without this pattern of organization, but, for Stevens, it is the paradigm itself that has not ultimate justification. As an earlier poem asked, "where was it one first heard of the truth?" Its answer, "The the," interrupts the neutrality of the truth by returning it to the "dump" of images (*CP* 203). (Beehler 168–169)

Beehler articulates Stevens' resistance to the totality of abstract paradigms. However, "The the" also points to language's ability to arbitrarily define, which is the fate Stevens fears and makes us aware of. As the poet stands on history's dump of images, he must contend with the coaxed endings underneath him. Because this paradigm of manufacturing truth seems unjustified in its arbitrary fatal power, "The Sail of Ulysses" warns readers of the danger and potential that poetry has to coax fates for the future. However, instead of dwelling on permanence, Stevens demonstrates that language's "coaxings" continue to change laws because of the differences within each new particular combination of words. Such "coaxings" can be attributed to human will, and for Stevens are written in each "difficult inch," that belongs to "our end." Stevens' theory of poetry and life performs rhetorically by linking will and fate together in a coaxing language.

This poem's mystery tour has come full circle and one might think to a stop. Just as Stevens refuses to do away with Ulysses, neither will he neglect his feminine counterpart. Stevens opens the final canto with an old friend, who appears less a "completely answering voice" than a fanciful prop:

> What is the shape of the sibyl? Not,
> For a change, the englistered woman, seated
> In colorings harmonious, dewed and dashed
> By them: gorgeous symbol seated
> On the seat of halidom, rainbowed . . .   (*OP* 130)

The previous canto's "relative sublime" is concocted by abstractions in the same paradigmatic way that "the sibyl" is "englistered." Stevens propels his theory of the sublime through the verbalization of "englistered," thus making English language's tradition of the beloved a violent process. Within the alliterative "s," violence is the contrasted confectionery adorning the sibyl as if she were a doll. The sibyl becomes a violently "englistered" sign that is dressed by her linguistic accoutrements, in a similar manner as the "apparition" was "apparelled" in "Angel Surrounded by Paysans." With the sibyl, Stevens reverses a traditional pattern of exaltation and demonization. Stevens attributes beauty's violence to the writers of English literature, rather than to the bewitched woman. "It is the sibyl of the self," then locates this violence within. The poet further admits that art comes from a vulnerable lack:

> The sibyl as self, whose diamond,
> Whose chiefest embracing of all wealth
> Is poverty, whose jewel found
> At the exactest central of the earth
> Is need. For this, the sibyl's shape
> Is a blind thing fumbling for form . . .   (*OP* 130)

The sibyl, then, is the final manifestation of "the force" in the poem. As a sibylline character, she is another version of "X," or the "fluent mundo" crystallized in "Notes." All of them are part of Stevens' evolving poetics that work to re-articulate signifiers away from their darkened impoverished pasts.

As the poem moves toward closure, there is an uncommon acknowledgment: "As these depend, so must they use." This line follows examples of a woman and child that serve as rhetorical appeals to regeneration. The question remains as to who are the dependents and users. Stevens depends on others for his poetry, and likewise the poet wants his words to be put to use:

> The englistered woman is now seen
> In an isolation, separate
> From the human in humanity,
> A part of the inhuman more,
> The still inhuman more, and yet
> An inhuman of our features, known
> And unknown, inhuman for a little while,
> Inhuman for a little, lesser time." (*OP* 131)

The sibyl is an "ancient mouthpiece of God" and a "witch" *(O.E.D.)*. By making her an outdated figure sprung from the breasts of poets, Stevens comments on a damaging paradigm (to women and to poetry) by forwarding the she-devil as a signified human motive in need of demystification. Stevens has made this historically abstract figure particular. This fortune-teller is "known / And unknown" in order to be recognized, as are most of Stevens' metaphors. Her inhuman figure, trope, and tradition is decreated within the rhetorical coaxings of Stevens' lyrics.

The poem is framed within an epic narrative, closing as follows:

> The great sail of Ulysses seemed,
> In the breathings of this soliloquy,
> Alive with an enigma's flittering . . .
> As if another sail went on
> Straight forwardly through another night
> And clumped stars dangled all the way.   (*OP* 131)

This narrative epilogue incorporates a few previous elements of the poem. Having presented the sibyl's conventional "englistered . . . wealth [as] poverty," the poet then requests an end to the figure's "inhuman" mysticism in literature. Similarly, in canto v, the forecasted oracle of the Omnium ends a current astronomy with "the last star . . . counted." The epilogue's "enigma" suggests another second coming, "[a]s if" on its way here, in which the "flittering" offers an alternative route for poetry. As with "The Motive for Metaphor," this poem undermines symbolic definition and mastery by activating the conditional similes that constitute Stevens' open lyric. "The Sail of Ulysses" extends the semiotic inquiry to decreate the epic paradigm in literature. In deconstructing epic structures in language and literature, Stevens more significantly constructs motivations. In the tantalizing last line of the epilogue, Stevens projects stars as lyrical gifts that coax the reader into wanting to possess them for guidance. Once again, Stevens shows how human desire is taunted by the mysterious givings that beg questions of meaning and meaning's possessive reciprocal, knowledge.

Both the epic and lyric prove inadequate generic containers for Stevens' ambitions. Yet these modes of writing are finally indivisible because in the lyrical gift there exists an epic transfer of goods. Neither genre can collapse; they are part of hand-to-mouth existence.[18] Still, epic models of language depend upon possession, seizure, totality, cultural segregation, and ideals of destiny. Engaging readerly cooperation, Stevens' lyrics look to the future with the hope that ethical occasions contribute to "the intelligence that endures."[19]

In the next and final chapter I will continue to ask what sort of goods we get from Stevens' poetry. By turning to Fredric Jameson's *Postmodernism, or, The Cultural Logic of Late Capitalism,* I will reconsider Stevens' poetry in terms of postmodern marketplaces. Is the Insurance Executive's writing a gift to culture, or is it a sign of excessive Western wealth? By relating the poetry to Stevens' "Insurance and Social Change" essay, I ask whether this poetry provides its readers with a beneficial insurance policy for the future. Stevens' vocational essay and the postmodern context help to further implode binary oppositional interpretations of Stevens: this time, the big division between the executive and the poet. Yes, Stevens was secretive and compartmentalized, but his stereotypically partitioned world remains for his readers to cohere.

Chapter 7

Conclusion: The Necessary Abstracts of Market Belief and Social Democracy

This final chapter presents Stevens' poetics in relation to the postmodern capitalist state. Specifically, I bring Stevens into the context of Fredric Jameson's question about how belief informs "the market" in his book *Postmodernism, or, The Cultural Logic of Late Capitalism*. Jameson's inquiry resembles Stevens' suggestions about rhetoric seducing its audiences. Jameson analyzes popular behavior in the market, and wonders about belief driving the market. Stevens also wonders how human fate is decided, but within this question Stevens' poetry dramatizes rhetoric as a persuasive force in the lives of people. Although the writerly contexts differ between Stevens and Jameson, they share thoughts about human behavior as it is socio-politically determined in history.

Before developing this alignment further, I return to the critical genealogy set by Melita Schaum in *Wallace Stevens and the Critical Schools* in order to take stock of our location in the tradition of writing about Stevens:

Stevens may well develop further in his figure as a theorist of reading, continuing the exploration of generative, performative models of literature and language for which Altieri demonstrates philosophical and humanistic outcomes, and with which Davidson illustrates the fluid, operative processes of language and thought continued in the postmodern poetic enterprise. Stevens may also occasion a fruitful reexamination by historicist critics and, by the very intractability and complexity of his poetics, necessitate a deeper scrutiny of the aims and methods of the historicist project, taking into account cultural and ideological matrices surrounding [the poet] in the twentieth century. (181–2)

In this book, I have studied Stevens' language, following, among others, Davidson and Altieri. Schaum neatly summarizes how Altieri develops "the significance of the *as:* rhetorical producer of resemblances . . ." (179). Learning from Altieri and Brogan's attention to *significance* (the study of Stevens' language as it evolves into meaningful poetry), I have applied the "postmodern poetic enterprise" to the historical findings of Filreis and Longenbach. Their historicist projects display awareness of Stevens' treatment of history in poetry. I emphasize Stevens' use of language as a rhetorical force that writes history. De Man's theory of "rhetoricity" helps to focus on "the confusion of sign and substance" in language and literature. With reference to criticism on Stevens, I pinpointed a dialectical oscillation between Riddel's fondness for *creation* and Filreis' emphatic *argument,* formalism and polemics, as an indication of the much larger taxonomic divide that persists in Stevens criticism and Western culture. I excised this dichotomy in interpreting *Owl's Clover* and Stevens' rhetorical poetry in general.

This chapter further considers "cultural and ideological matrices surrounding [the poet] in the twentieth century" by comparing Stevens' ideas about rhetoric in history with an analysis of contemporary capitalist society. Jameson's chapter "Immanence and Nominalism in Postmodern Theoretical Discourse" systematizes twentieth-century modernism through postmodernism, especially in the contexts of historical hermeneutics and capitalism. Jameson's specific focus is the New Historicism of Walter Benn Michaels' *The Gold Standard and the Logic of Naturalism,* but in the tradition of postmodern bastardization, I am more interested in Jameson's ideas than in his commentary upon Michaels' text. In raising numerous conundrums, Jameson inadvertently broaches several criticisms of Stevens' poetics. To begin with, the following critique of modernism unintentionally reveals both an established view of Stevens' poetics, and some challenges that the poet is less known for meeting:

> This is the *modernist* moment: not merely the emergence of reflexivity about the process of fiction-making (the weakest of all accounts of modernism) but rather the dawning sense of that necessary failure that is now to be forestalled, or better still, to be transformed into a new kind of success and triumph, by reckoning the very impossibility of representation back into the thing itself[.] (*Postmodernism, or, The Cultural Logic of Late Capitalism* 216)

I read "Notes Toward A Supreme Fiction" into Jameson's judgment of "(the weakest of all accounts of modernism)." The above quotation from

Jameson develops just like many a Stevens poem: announcing the moment *in situ,* deconstructing the fallacy of the occasion, acknowledging "failure" as a limitation that is instead a potential ("the nothing that is"), and transforming it "into a new kind of success" by revitalizing the fiction as a corporeal understanding that ascribes function to "the thing itself" in the world. Or,

> At the earliest ending of winter,
> In March, a scrawny cry from outside
> Seemed like a sound in his mind.
>
> He knew that he heard it,
> A bird's cry, at daylight or before,
> In the early March wind.
>
> The sun was rising at six,
> No longer a battered panache above snow . . .
> It would have been outside.
>
> It was not from the vast ventriloquism
> Of sleep's faded papier-mache . . .
> The sun was coming from outside.
>
> That scrawny cry—it was
> A chorister whose c preceded the choir.
> It was part of the colossal sun,
>
> Surrounded by its choral rings,
> Still far away. It was like
> A new knowledge of reality.   (*CP* 534)

This is a system of belief that serves a healthy Zeitgeist. I use the word "belief" following from Stevens and Jameson, the latter of whom ties belief to the market. Jameson links the modernist moment (described by Wendy Steiner as a choice between "Collage or Miracle")[1] to corporate capitalism, citing Michaels:

> "Hence the corporation comes to seem the embodiment of figurality that makes personhood possible, rather than appearing as a figurative extension of personhood" (*Gold Standard* 205; quoted by Jameson). . . . Being immortal, the corporation also stills those fears of death and dying aroused as we have seen, by individual consumption. (216)

In the 1990s we became increasingly skeptical of corporate immortality, while at the same time corporate control has never been so powerful. Stevens' fearful prophesy precedes Jameson's analysis of belief in the corporate Zeitgeist:

> The way we work is a good deal more difficult for the imagination than the highly civilized revolution that is occuring in respect to work indicates. . . . [The workers] have become, at their work, in the face of the machines, something approaching an abstraction, an energy. The time must be coming when, as they leave the factories, they will be passed through an air-chamber or a bar for riot and reading. (*NA* 19)

I hope that "riot and reading" are still possible today, but I am not so sure. Stevens' factories are often offices now, and employees are systematically re-invigorated by the dead air-chambers of company fitness clubs. If we are lucky enough to live in a place like British Columbia, the company will consign us to a volleyball league and we will be able to consume fresh, or slightly polluted, air in a mountain setting that "stills those fears of death and dying" superbly. The corporation now acquires a religious role, fitting with Stevens' adage: "The final belief is to believe in a fiction, which you know to be a fiction, there being nothing else. The exquisite truth is to know that it is a fiction and that you believe in it willingly" (*OP* 189). The ability to be conscious of fictions is in jeopardy today; fictions are real by necessity and belief only becomes an issue upon a crisis of faith, such as "downsizing."

Jameson and Stevens are not the strange partners that they first seem. Stevens has firsthand knowledge of the corporation, Hartford Indemnity, that is. Rather than leading a double life, Stevens' job was to create fictions in the form of surety policies, and fulfill customer claims. In this respect, his vocation was fully modernist by Jameson's definition: fictional value in the form of money transformed failure, say farm drought, into success "by reckoning the very impossibility of representation back into the thing itself" (*Postmodernism* 216). The farm loses representational value when its grain or vegetable is jeopardized, but insurance replenishes monetary value back into the thing itself.

In addition to representing Jameson's modernism and capitalism, Stevens' vocations of insurance—claims man and poet—signify social democracy. Stevens offers claimants and readers values, or commodities, that are used when needed. The poet's insurance also resembles Canada's social system. Canadian citizens are heavily taxed so that they may be helped by medicare, pensions, unemployment, and welfare services. While Canada's social democracy is currently threatened by corporate takeover, it has until now fostered esteem in our national community.

In terms mixing Jameson and Stevens—social commodities, such as taxes and insurance premiums, appear to be "impossible representations" because they are abstract (dollar) signs dispensed without foreseeable economic return. Nevertheless, the abstract premium becomes successful when necessity calls upon the policy, and money returns to the self (the unemployed, sick, pensioners). Our system of social democracy *must be abstract* because insurance is a scripted idea holding potential for material return. The problem today is that citizens feel duped by an abstract system whose fictional potency is jeopardized—by the debt clock, a competing enemy fiction that appears to possess a more convincing material significance. Usury is now so thick that it has obscured the sight of an effective social system. Conservatives feel they will receive no significant return, as pensions diminish and national debt is placed upon the backs of younger generations. Consequently, the wealthy hoard their money in the form of the corporate governments in Ontario and Alberta, which protect rich interest and hang the masses out to dry. With this greedy panic or "national hysteria," hatred rises between classes and interest groups so that we get a nation of tribes (resembling many international conflicts) and the "impossible representations" of social democracy are slammed shut. The debate rages on about whether corporate or social democracy will be more expensive in the end, but in the meantime the rich increasingly rule by monopoly.

Stevens' 1937 essay, "Insurance and Social Change," considers issues of national and privatized social insurance, and concludes: "If private companies can continue to expand with profit, no question of nationalization, except in regulatory and certain social aspects, is likely to arise under our system" (*OP* 236). Stevens the capital realist plays devil's advocate to Stevens the idealist, who in the first half of the essay sounds as if he is speaking of the Canadian dream:

> The objective of all of us is to live in a world in which nothing unpleasant can happen. Our prime instinct is to go on indefinitely like the wax flowers on the mantelpiece. Insurance is the most easily understood geometry for calculating how to bring the thing about. (*OP* 234)

The realist of the insurance business then integrates some impinging "irrational elements," as evidenced by the following ironic parody that we are familiar with from his poetry: "There is no difference between the worm in the apple and the tack in the can of sardines, and not the slightest difference between the piano out of tune and a person disabled" (*OP* 234). This sounds brutal, but Stevens' impudence points to the necessary insurance of everything. The difference today is that many people insure their pianos instead of the disabled.

The necessarily abstract mode of the insurance business is exemplified when Stevens cites the science fiction method of H. G. Wells, suggesting that when "he passes from the international to the interstellar, we hug the purely local." Wells' "impossible representation" shows why *it must be abstract;* "it" being language, poetry, belief, work, insurance:

> In the same way it helps us to see insurance in the midst of social change to imagine a world in which insurance has been made perfect. In such a world we should be certain of an income. Out of the income we should be able, by the payment of a trivial premium, to protect ourselves, our families and our property against everything. (*OP* 234)

"Notes Toward" Canada, Hartford Indemnity, Holly, gated communities? Stevens fancies we drop a penny in a box on the way to work each morning, and so we do, through premiums. Stevens finds "what will suffice" ("Of Modern Poetry") in a democracy that must resist monopolization. Conversely, he recognizes that corporate business would rather avoid such costs: "Liability insurance, or civil responsibility business, as they call it, is not so attractive a subject for the monopolistically-minded politician . . ." (*OP* 235). That is another reason why we need to read Stevens. Even though Stevens sauntered in a corporate universe, his "civil responsibility business" resisted monopolies, just as his increasingly civic poetry resisted state monumentality.

Since "poetry is a form of resistance" (Stevens) and "resistance is the domain of theory" (de Man), let's develop further the tension between resistance and monopoly. In *Negation, Subjectivity, and the History of Rhetoric*, Victor Vitanza addresses linguistic lawmaking in terms of political economy, much in the same way Stevens resists monumental definition.

> Lyotard points out that Marxists and Capitalists, however, do not want to play the (just) game this way, the pagan way. (Nor, I would add, do Aristotelians.) Both systems of thought are informed by what Lyotard calls "the economic genre," which demands *litigation* at the expense of the *differend*—demands *litigation,* which in turn demands centralism and monopoly and the suppression of heterogeneity. (43)

Referring to Jean-Francois Lyotard's *The Differend,* Vitanza's assertion of *litigation* at the expense of "heterogeneity" resembles Stevens' "fatal . . . X," which detracts from "the motive for metaphor" by litigating it. The expression of the dominant sign in "The Motive for Metaphor" finalizes the fluctuating subject of that poem. In Stevens' *signification* the subject's *significance* immediately disappears because she no longer evolves. While Stevens' poem directs us to semiotic and ontological litigation, Vitanza and Lyotard suggest that difference is annulled by economical law.

We might expect Jameson's Marxism to agree with the influence of "the economic genre," but Jameson inserts a third factor, belief, into the reverberation between people and money. Jameson's stress on belief resembles Stevens' credo *it must be abstract* as a requisite for language that makes people think:

> the "market" bears the same relationship to individual subjects, with their desires and their commodity lust, as the charged term *belief* to the conscious, "theoretical" attempts (sometimes designated as "knowledge") to step outside that, to theorize or even change it. *Belief* is here the missing totalization, the other term you can never get out of, some ultimate and definitive form of ideology fixed for all time (or what Sartre called the "ordinary choice of being" [Stevens' humdrum!]): "the only relevant truth about belief is that you can't go outside of it, and, far from being unlivable, this is a truth you can't help but live. It has no practical consequences not because it can never be *united* with practice but because it can never be *separated* from practice" (*Against Theory* 29). But have we not gotten a little out of "belief" just by calling it "the market" and giving it that figuration? And in that case, which comes first? Is it the condemnation of human beings to "belief" in this absolute sense which generates the infernal dynamic of the market? Or is it the market which somehow "produces" today this odd concept of "belief"? Is not the very *separation of belief from knowledge* presupposed here itself an example of the production of a theory by way of the *artificial creation of two abstract identities* out of an inseparable reality? (*Postmodernism* 217; my emphasis)

Knowledge is made belief through rhetoric. Stevens' rhetorical poetry lets us not forget that knowledge *must be abstract,* therefore we need question what we believe. Whether money, fear, force, sex or government wields the power of rhetoric, we need to deconstruct the abstractly composed message by finding out about the agent whose power is bolstered by the rhetoric. Jameson would counter by saying "you can't get outside of" belief. The Clash sing:

I'm all lost in the Supermarket,
I can no longer shop happily,
I came in for that special offer,
Guaranteed Personality.

We can be conscious of external rhetorical pressure attempting to litigate belief.

"Whose spirit is this?" in "The Idea of Order at Key West" asks a similar question as Jameson does above about "inseparable reality." In seeking that answer, Stevens shows the muse to be an "artificial creation" that is part of producing a marketable belief in a composition that *asked, sought, and knew* (*CP* 129). The poet's business was deconstructing the ultimate Barbie doll of the ages. But in order to do that he had to sell her seductively to the reader; she's sold as an abstract figure from the first line of the poem; she's a believable fiction who is discredited only to be replaced by the poem's new abstract composition of the romantic quest, minus a trophy.

Just as the *asking, seeking, knowing* composition of "Key West" deconstructs the poet-muse dichotomy, the rhetorical methods of *Owl's Clover* demonstrate political polemics as monumental aesthetics, and vice versa. Jameson's rhetorical chicken or egg question about market knowledge and belief traverses similar ground to that covered by the dialectic of argument and creation exercised in *Owl's Clover*. Stevens showed that Statues and Marxist credos claim authoritative knowledge, and as such they are romantic beliefs imposed. Marxist arguments against romantic creation were shown in *Owl's Clover* to be tied up in monumental ideological compositions. In such conflation, the poem illustrates "an inseparable reality" of creation and argument, belief and market. This 1930s' reality is ruptured when one rhetoric, such as the State statue, marginalizes part of its market, the Old Woman, which results in a crisis of belief on her behalf. In other words, the Old Woman is made a distanced "abstract identity" by way of the elite artifact that categorically excludes her. The Statue is an "artificial creation" because its monumental elitism excludes her "reality." Therefore, monumental art, whether from the right or the left, acts in bad faith because it ruptures "inseparable reality" into factions. "The Old Woman and the Statue" in today's world are the homeless standing beneath the debt clock.

For these oppressive reasons, art must propose ideal knowledges that are marketable and believable for many audiences. The success of idealism (trying to improve life on earth) depends upon an abstract aesthetic/polemic that appeals across factions. There are many potential dangers in mass appeal, such as fanaticism, populism, and universalism. The challenge of poetry and criticism is to have wide appeal without diluted compromises, and conversely to strive for specific interests without excluding others in bad faith. This returns us to "some harmonious skeptic soon in a harmonious music." Mixing music and skepticism is rhetorical domain, as shown in *Owl's Clover* and Stevens' successive inquiries into war, evil, and fascism. Figures such as Nietzsche, Lenin, and Sumner Welles embody the danger of harmonious skepticism, but by rhetorizing these important figures of warning, Stevens urges readers to innovate abstract ethical ideals that can materialize into future examples for people. Historical pessimism led Stevens to exclaim in a letter that he needed a figure in history to admire. The later poetry composes necessary angels, or abstract shamans, whose humdrum characteristics forward considerations for readers who can then practice, teach, or market persuasive ethics without reverting to idolatry. (These days, the cult of celebrity is a frightening manifestation of corporatized idols.)

People who write about Stevens have increasingly turned to the poetry's ethical capacity "to help people live their lives" (*NA* 29). The ethical prompts that Michael Beehler makes by teaching Emmanuel Levinas together with Stevens, and those that Judith Butler suggests about a post-Hegelian Stevens who preserves difference, are the types of intelligence that must endure.

In 1985 Michael Davidson offered an ethical reading of Stevens while charting his influence on contemporary poetics. Davidson observed that Stevens' long poems differ from the modernist epic-collages of Pound, Eliot, and Williams. Neither does Stevens "appeal to some ultimate value (Joy, Truth, Beauty)" to reconcile opposites in Coleridge's Romantic way (Gelpi 146). Davidson states that Stevens'

> long, exploratory poem has become one of the primary models for contemporary poets in their attempt to move beyond the single, self-sufficient lyric to the "poem of life." Works such as A. R. Ammons' *Sphere,* Robert Duncan's *Passages,* Robert Kelly's *The Loom,* John Berryman's *Dream Songs,* John Ashbery's *Three Poems,* and James Merrill's *The Changing Light at Sandover* could be seen as variations on this mode. (Gelpi 146)

Davidson differentiates Stevens from "certain formalist models of high Modernism" (Gelpi 157), and his essay moves toward Stevens' poems that ask readers to consider signs as social products.

In this regard, poetry employs language as material content in capitalist culture, rather than as an art form that stands truthfully apart as New Criticism had taught. Davidson opens his essay with a definition of poetry that Robert Creeley quotes from Stevens:

> "Poetic form in its proper sense is a question of what appears within the poem itself. . . . By appearance within the poem itself one means the things created and existing there. . . ." Creeley adds: "Basic. Yet they won't see it, that it cannot be a box or a bag or what you will." (Letter to Charles Olson, April 28, 1950; Gelpi 141)

To depart from the register of male poets continuing the Stevens line, I turn to Jeanette Winterson as someone who expresses poetry, even though she writes prose. She admires T. S. Eliot, Virginia Woolf, and Wordsworth, and her concerns inadvertently (because Stevens is not mentioned) bring Stevens into the present. A chapter from her book of essays, *Art Objects,* is entitled "Imagination and Reality," and its epigraph reads, *"The reality of art is the reality of the imagination"* (133). Stevens' *The Necessary Angel: Essays on Reality and the Imagination,* and "Adagia," contain similar statements. The resemblance of these writers extends beyond adages to fine points in their essays. Stevens discusses how imagination and reality are effected by the workplace in "The Noble Rider and the Sound of Words":

> The way we work is a good deal more difficult for the imagination than the highly civilized revolution that is occuring in respect to work indicates. It is, in the main, a revolution for more pay. We have been assured, by every visitor, that the American businessman is absorbed in his business and there is nothing to be gained by disputing it. As for the workers, it is enough to say that the word has grown to be literary. They have become, at their work, in the face of the machines, something approximating an abstraction, an energy. The time must be coming when, as they leave the factories, they will be passed through an air-chamber or a bar to revive them for riot and reading. (*NA* 19)

Fifty years down the (not so) progressive road, Winterson cites this accelerated problem:

> Since our economy is now a consumer economy, we must be credulous and passive. We must believe that we want to earn money to buy things we don't need. The education system is not designed to turn out thoughtful individ-

ualists, it is there to get us to work. When we come home exhausted from the inanities of our jobs we can relax in front of the inanities of the TV screen. This pattern, punctuated by birth, death and marriage and a new car, is offered to us as real life.

Children who are born into a tired world as batteries of new energy are plugged into the system as soon as possible and gradually drained away. At the time when they become adult and conscious they are already depleted and prepared to accept a world of shadows. Those who have kept their spirit find it hard to nourish it and between the ages to twenty and thirty, many are successfully emptied of all resistance. (*Art Objects* 134–5)

Winterson, Stevens, Jameson, and many other writers today help us turn shadows into color by deconstructing the gray shades pulled down by corporate rule. Jameson displays optimism because he includes "belief" as a factor in market behavior. Belief entails conscious will, however, Winterson sees resistance emptied by age thirty. "Resistance" is an effective word to stress the intelligence that is necessary for the ethical writing we urgently require. Winterson's book title has the crafty double-reference to art óbjects and to the imperative that art objécts (stresses mine). Before I return to our necessary ethical resistance, here is more of Winterson's social diagnosis:

Money culture recognises no currency but its own. Whatever is not money, whatever is not making money, is useless to it. The entire efforts of our government as directed through our society are efforts towards making more and more money. This favors the survival of the dullest. This favors those who prefer to live in a notional reality where goods are worth more than time and where things are more important than ideas. (*Art Objects* 138)

Anyone working in a social institution today knows this only too well.

How to resist corporatization? I return to the necessity of the abstract: our ability to consider how corporate sponsorship functions in its composed environment, rather than just being seduced by its perks. Stevens' rhetorical poetry shows us that language is a "sign and thus a social product" (Davidson in Gelpi 158). The product is sold by the merchandiser in self-interest. This person is today considered a realist, of whom Winterson says: "The realist (from the Latin *res* = thing) who thinks he deals in things and not in images and who is suspicious of the abstract and of art, is not the practical man but a man caught in a fantasy of his own unmaking"

(143). Winterson's version of the realist sounds like a description of Ontario premier Mike Harris, who has torn apart social democracy for a nifty balance sheet:

> The realist unmakes the coherent multiple world into a collection of random objects. He thinks of reality as that which has an objective existence, but understands no more about objective existence than that which he can touch and feel, sell and buy. A lover of objects and objectivity, he is in fact caught in a world of symbols and symbolism, where he is unable to see the thing in itself, as it really is, he sees it only in relation to his own story of the world. (*Art Objects* 143)

When Winterson says the realist "is unable to see the thing itself, as it really is," I think she emphasizes an object's *significance* as it functions in the social world. Her use of the Latin *res* to contextualize the thing itself as it abstractly functions in the material world is echoed in Stevens' famous lines from "An Ordinary Evening in New Haven":

> The poem is the cry of its occasion,
> Part of the res and not about it.
> The poet speaks and the poem is,
>
> Not as it was: part of the reverberation
> Of a windy night as it is, when the marble statues
> Are like newspapers blown by the wind. He speaks
>
> By sight and insight as they are. There is no
> Tomorrow for him. The wind will have passed by,
> The statues will have gone back to be things about.   (*CP* 473)

By seeking the immediate "cry of its occasion," these words comprise the thing itself (an event in time) rather than objectifying the thing. The middle stanza's simile shakes "the marble statues" from being too obviously *significant* "things about" to the lively *significance* of scurrying newspapers, which blow in the wind like Bob Dylan's answer.

To become "Part of the res and not about it," whether that thing itself is the market or work or art, the individual must move in time rather than try to grab hold of it. An abstract practice of art involves participation, which ideally contributes to contemporary life in process. Winterson describes the artist's role as a "superconductor" in *Sexing the Cherry*. My general argument here for abstraction sounds abstract in the pejorative sense because the words appear to be about the res rather than part of it. However, abstract involvement is exemplified (again) in "Not Ideas About the Thing But the Thing Itself," which begins objectively, then abstractly becomes "Part of the res" itself:

> At the earliest ending of winter,
> In March, a scrawny cry from outside
> Seemed like a sound in his mind.
>
> He knew that he had heard it,
> A bird's cry, at daylight or before,
> In the early March wind.
>
> The sun was rising at six,
> No longer a battered panache above snow . . .
> It would have been outside.
>
> It was not from the vast ventriloquism
> Of sleep's faded paper-maché . . .
> The sun was coming from outside.
>
> That scrawny cry—it was
> A chorister whose c preceded the choir.
> It was part of the colossal sun,
>
> Surrounded by its choral rings,
> Still far away. It was like
> A new knowledge of reality.   (*CP* 534)

The knowledge of the sun in the third stanza is conditioned by deductive reason; the speaker knows "about" the sun rising from memory: "It would have been outside." This detached sleepy knowledge is pierced by the "scrawny cry" of "A chorister whose c preceded the choir." This bird is early in several ways: in the poem's basic narrative, the bird cries before the rest. More importantly, the early bird's "c" note precedes "the choir," and is therefore not part of an identifiable refrain. Since the scrawny cry is a "c," this letter's material significance distinctly outshines stale known entities such as the choir and the sun; it is an abstract demarcation in the poem. Because the scrawny cry exists as "Part of the res and not about it," this birdnote partakes in the composition of "the colossal sun." By way of its metonymical contribution, the comic letter "c" startles us.

The cry of the "c" adds to the rhetoric of awakening. It is an unexpected gift to a familiar occasion. Writing that instills life into tired situations not only invigorates us, the very life it creates resists corporate mind control. "Isn't a freshening of life a thing of consequence?" (*L* 293) asks Stevens. For this I look to contemporary poetry, and *The Best American Poetry 1994* volume, edited by A. R. Ammons. Reading this collection in search of surprises that make me think, perhaps even change my perception of the world, I find that some poems shock in an intentional manner verging on sensationalism. Conversely, some poems appear to me so discreet that they leave little impression. However, Ammons has selected a number of fine erotic poems that surprisingly teach ethics through the body's navigation of desire.

Catherine Bowman's "Demographics" and Janet Holmes' "The Love of the Flesh" both incorporate ideas about Western history into their poems' accelerating desire. While this is not new, Joyce's *Ulysses* and Stevens' "The World as Meditation" are previous examples, these contemporary poets propose ethics intimately within the courtship of the poems. Bowman's poem bombards the reader quickly, whereas Holmes' meditation patiently includes ethical inferences that can be linked to Levinas's philosophy of "the other." Here is Holmes' "The Love of The Flesh":

> Reality is not limited to the tactile:
> still, we touch our own faces, as if by the slide
> of fingers over cheekbones, eyelids, lips,
>
> we can check that we are not dreaming. This is
> the life of the body, the life of gesture,
>
> tangible, a palm against the skin.
> When I put my hand to your face it becomes a caress,
> but here, against my own, it is disbelief
> or wonder.
>
> The questions are hard, as when medieval scholars
> divvied up the body in debate
> as to where the soul hung its ephemeral hat—
>
> and those who plumped for the heart laboring its fenced-in field
> shouted down those others who felt God's messages
> precisely in the pit of the stomach,

while the ancients reasoned *the brain, the unromantic brain,*
and virtually every organ had its champion . . .

Their filigree of argument confounds me
just as, then,
the suddenness of love left me dazed:

for days they had to call me twice
to get a single answer—I was deaf
and breathless and stunned. It was not
as if the world were new and beautiful.

It was, instead, as if I had unlearned
how to use my hands
and feet. Where does the life of the body

leave off, the life of the spirit start? When
does the mouthful of air move beyond breathing
towards magic? We made

a spectacle of ourselves, dancing about
like clowns in huge shoes, goofy with happiness,
inarticulate in all but the lexicon
of sexual flesh;

and the soul, from its short-leased home
among the muscles, sent its respects,
or so we were told . . .

Even in *Paradise,* the light-filled spirits
long for their resurrection,
and Dante is surprised that they miss their bodies:

"Not only for themselves," he speculates,
"but for their mothers and fathers, and for the others
dear to them on earth,"

souls wistful for flesh, nostalgic
for their faraway, simple selves who walked about

and who, lifting and seeing their hands,
thought suddenly one day *These touch, caress, stroke;*
who found in the body a bridge beyond it

> and coined the word *beloved*. And thus we performed
> for ourselves the seamless changing over
> of element to element,
>
> body to air, solid to spirit, magic trick
> or miracle, without knowing the particular
> spell or prayer or luck that made it quicken.
>
> (Ammons 83–5)

"In ghostlier demarcations, keener sounds," concludes "The Idea of Order at Key West." Holmes, like Stevens, rejects oppositional methods of reason that objectify others for the sake of comfortably classified knowledge. Whereas in "Key West" Stevens transformed the otherly muse into the composed images in the poem, Holmes reverses the process by scripting *beloved* as transcendence itself. While both poems posit mystery within the transcendent claims of knowledge, Stevens displays the material construction of the muse, whereas Holmes carves a question mark between the symbiosis of body and spirit. She removes "therefore" from Descartes' "I think . . . I am."

Holmes' claim that the other cannot be known, only caressed, strongly resembles the philosophy of Levinas. Michael Beehler discusses and quotes Levinas in a manner that inadvertently describes "The Love of The Flesh":

> It is this original relation with the other as other that opens the ethical in human experience by wrenching that experience "out of its aesthetic self-sufficiency" and awakening the ego "from [the] imperialist dream" in which Western philosophy, as a history of the destruction of transcendence, has shut it up. (*Levinas Reader* 148; *Teaching Wallace Stevens* 270)

The middle of Holmes' poem, where she begins, "The questions are hard," traces some of "the imperialist dream" in terms of the ego's effort to classify human intelligence. The poem's end reissues the mystery of transcendence, but as a suspended question, rather than a claim of knowledge.

This discussion of knowledge, reason, and transcendence may sound mystical, but Holmes, Levinas, and Stevens all address our approach to others. Holmes' poem employs love to undermine "the imperialist dream" of reason. Taking love to the street as an ideology seems impossible when people cut in front of us in traffic or mug us. However, love is an abstract ideal—a form of resistance that must be practiced in an effort to better society—which Levinas writes about in words that echo "The Love of the Flesh":

The pathos of love . . . consists in an unsurmountable duality of beings. It is a relationship with what always slips away. The relationship does not *ipso facto* neutralize alterity but preserves it. The pathos of voluptuousness lies in the fact of being two. The other as other is not here an object that becomes ours or becomes us; to the contrary, it withdraws into its mystery. (*Levinas Reader* 49; *Teaching Wallace Stevens* 275)

Levinas's ideas apply to Holmes, to Stevens' "Re-statement of Romance," and to Sharon Olds' poem "The Knowing," which concretely exemplifies love in its physical manifestation:

Afterwards, when we have slept, paradise-
comaed, and woken, we lie a long time
looking at each other,
I do not know what he sees, but I see
eyes of surpassing tenderness
and calm, a calm like the dignity
of matter. I love the open ocean
blue-gray-green of his iris, I love
the curve of it against the white,
that curve the sight of what has caused me
to come, when he's quite still, deep
inside me. I have never seen a curve
like that, except the earth from outer
space. I don't know where he got
his kindness without self-regard,
almost without self, and yet
he chose one woman, instead of the others.
By knowing him, I get to know
the purity of the animal
which mates for life. Sometimes he is slightly
smiling, but mostly he just gazes at me gazing,
his entire face lit. I love
to see it change if I cry—there is no worry,
no pity, a graver radiance. If we
are on our backs, side by side,
with our faces turned fully to face each other,
I can hear a tear from my lower eye
hit the sheet, as if it is an early day on earth,
and then the upper eye's tears
braid and sluice down through the lower eyebrow
like the invention of farming, irrigation, a non-nomadic people.
I am so lucky that I can know him.

> This is the only way to know him.
> I am the only one who knows him.
> When I wake again, he is still looking at me,
> as if he is eternal. For an hour
> we wake and doze, and slowly I know
> that though we are sated, though we are hardly
> touching, this is the coming the other
> brought us to the edge of—we are entering,
> deeper and deeper, gaze by gaze,
> this place beyond the other places,
> beyond the body itself, we are making
> love.   (Ammons 146–7)

Olds challenges readers because intimacy never retreats. This poem succeeds because it thwarts the conventional detachment or skepticism in
socialized human behavior. It also treads the thin line between love and
possession. This couple belongs to each other but the speaker sustains "the
voluptuousness . . . of being two." When she states three times that she
knows him, the repetition strains for certainty while fortune predominates.
And then he wakes "as if he is eternal"—beyond human scope. Olds has the
speaker stepping over the boundary of what she can know. The repeated
lines about knowing him ring false in their certainty, and thereby demonstrate the small mistakes that reason exerts on love.

   Instead of extrapolating more ethics of the Levinasian variety from
"The Knowing," I return to the less intimate, and more rhetorically theoretical manner in which Stevens "preserves alterity":

> The eye's plain version is a thing apart,
> The vulgate of experience. Of this,
> A few words, an and yet, and yet, and yet—
>
> As part of the never-ending meditation,
> Part of the question that is a giant himself:
> Of what is this house composed if not of the sun,
>
> These houses, these difficult objects, dilapidate
> Appearances of what appearances,
> Words, lines, not meanings, not communications,
>
> Dark things without a double, after all,
> Unless a second giant kills the first—
> A recent imagining of reality,

> Much like a new resemblance of the sun,
> Down-pouring, up-springing and inevitable,
> A larger poem for a larger audience,
>
> As if the crude collops came together as one,
> A mythological form, a festival sphere,
> A great bosom, beard and being, alive with age. (*CP* 465–6)

"A few words, an and yet, and yet, and yet—" remind us of the aggregating metonymies Stevens uses to compose poetry: "Add this. It is to add." In the framework of Levinas, the indefinite article "an" can be seen to describe the subject, while "and yet" is the other. Stevens confronts the extreme difficulty of describing the other ethically in language. In "An Ordinary Evening in New Haven," the other is the object being described, whether that refers to a lover or the city's difficult houses. These "Dark things without a double" require "a second giant" who "kills the first" "eye's plain version" with new significance. Stevens acknowledges the need for language to transgress our solitary inarticulate sight in order to communicate with others. Recognizing that communication disrupts individuals, Stevens stresses, as he did in "Mozart, 1935," *Owl's Clover,* and "Description without Place," the need for "A larger poem for a larger audience." Stevens' ideal "harmonious skepticism" is sought here, but with cynicism. People are "crude collops," which are slices of meat or fried eggs and bacon *(OED)*.

Pursuing the poet's ideal, Stevens speaks in the third canto of the abstract desire required to materialize abstract love:

> The point of vision and desire are the same.
> It is to the hero of midnight that we pray
> On a hill of stones to make beau mont thereof.
>
> If it is misery that infuriates our love,
> If the black of night stands glistening on beau mont,
> Then, ancientest saint ablaze with ancientest truth,
>
> Say next to holiness is the will thereto,
> And next to love is the desire for love,
> The desire for its celestial ease in the heart,
>
> Which nothing can frustrate, that most secure,
> Unlike love in possession of that which was
> To be possessed and is. But this cannot

> Possess. It is desire, set deep in the eye,
> Behind all actual seeing, in the actual scene,
> In the street, in a room, on a carpet or a wall,
>
> Always an emptiness that would be filled,
> In denial that cannot contain its blood,
> A porcelain, as yet in the bats thereof.   (*CP* 466–7)

I think that strange last line refers to how desire can never be totally sated or denied. Passion spills from containment; the ever-batting eye seeks a hardened porcelain image. The point is that our desire looks for meaningful fulfillment, yet we find the last line of the poem tantalizingly cryptic. Love moves through time whereas possession monumentalizes it. Desire aggregates love, and Stevens' rhetorical poetry propels desire against static denials.

> It is not in the premise that reality
> Is a solid. It may be a shade that traverses
> A dust, a force that traverses a shade.   (*CP* 489)

Stevens' poetry confronts blunt barriers that are shades because they produce diminished definition: the ethereal romantic muse in "Key West"; the Statue, *To Be Itself* ideology, Imperialism, and traditional nostalgia in *Owl's Clover;* megalomania in "Life on a Battleship"; mastery over the sublime in "Esthetique du Mal"; centralized visions of power in "Description without Place"; and authoritative tales in the late Ulysses poems. Stevens' adage, "The world is a force, not a presence" (*OP* 198), points to the necessity of traversing the stolid presences that curtail human expression.

Notes

Preface

1. Helen Vendler, "Ice and Fire and Solitude." Rev. of *Wallace Stevens: Collected Poetry and Prose*. ed. F. Kermode, J. Richardson. New York: Library of America, 1997. *New York Review of Books,* Dec. 4, 1997: 39–42; Milton Bates, Review of *Wallace Stevens: Collected Poetry and Prose. Wallace Stevens Journal* 22:1 (Spring 1998): 89–93.
2. Alan Filreis, *Wallace Stevens and the Actual World* (Princeton University Press, 1991); *Modernism from Right to Left : Wallace Stevens, the Thirties and Literary Radicalism* (Cambridge University Press, 1994); James Longenbach, *Wallace Stevens: The Plain Sense of Things* (Oxford University Press, 1991).

Chapter 1

1. Pound's essay "The Promised Land" admires Thomas Hardy's elegiac writing as a bygone style that is inapporiate for the "communist age" of the 1930s (*Guide to Kulchur* 293).
2. For abstraction in Stevens' work, see Marie Borroff, "An Always Incipient Cosmos," in *Beyond New Criticism* (Hosek and Parker, eds.), Altieri's *Painterly Abstraction in Modernist American Poetry,* Macleod's *Wallace Stevens and Modern Art,* and Filreis's "'Beyond the Rhetorician's Touch': Stevens's Painterly Abstractions," in *American Literary History* (Spring 1992): 230–263.
3. Janet McCann concludes *Wallace Stevens Revisited: "The Celestial Possible"* by summarizing the history of criticism on Stevens. McCann cites Melita Schaum's valuable book, *Wallace Stevens and the Critical Schools,* which quotes the critical discrepancy between Aiken and Untermeyer in "the second decade of this century":

> Conrad Aiken and Louis Untermeyer argued, in the *New Republic,*
> issues of Europeanism versus Americanism and ivory-tower poetry
> versus socially conscious work. Basing his theory on universal stan-
> dards and distinguishing it from passing social concerns, Aiken
> advocated "absolute poetry" that "delivers no message, is imbued
> with no doctrine, a poetry that exists only for the sake of magic,—
> magic of beauty on the one hand, magic of reality on the other,
> but both struck at rather through a play of implication than
> through matter-of-fact statement. This sort of poetry is of course
> unmoral and unsociological." Aiken championed Stevens as a fine
> poet by this definition, which stands in contrast to that of Louis
> Untermeyer, who rejected Stevens as an art-for-art's-sake techni-
> cian, a sort of Andrea del Sarto of poetry who was capable of
> "mere verbal legerdemain." Untermeyer sought a sense of social
> involvement in poetry and believed that art should be "community
> expression" of a direct nature. (139)

I suggest that Stevens displays language's magic as it persuades society.

4. Filreis, *Modernism From Right to Left: Wallace Stevens, the Thirties and Literary Radicalism* (Cambridge University Press, 1994) 229; Joseph Riddel, *The Clairvoyant Eye* (Baltimore: Johns Hopkins University Press, 1965) 121.

5. Cook, *Poetry, Word-play and Word-war in Wallace Stevens* (Princeton: Princeton University Press, 1988), 120. Previous to the groundbreaking historical work of Filreis and Longenbach, a poststructuralist Stevens—deconstruct-ing aesthetic and philosophical structures—was cast in the work of Michael Beehler, Michael Davidson, Paul Bove, J. Hillis Miller, as well as critics who managed to adapt to deconstructive readings, such as Roy Harvey Pearce, and Joseph Riddel. Romantic, phenomenological, and, to be general, for-malist work by Helen Vendler and Harold Bloom predated those above and established Stevens' aesthetic reputation. To generalize further, formalist readings emphasize the complex literary aesthetics of Stevens' poetry, while downplaying external references and contexts. Longenbach and Filreis have recuperated this lost aspect of Stevens.

6. These words from Brogan's "'The Sister of the Minotaur': Sexism and Stevens" are found in the collection, *Wallace Stevens and the Feminine,* edited by Melita Schaum (Alabama University Press, 1994).

7. Beginning the list of critics with Miller, books on Stevens' semiotics are *The Linguistic Moment, Destructive Poetics, T. S. Eliot, Wallace Stevens and the Dis-courses of Difference,* and *Wallace Stevens and the Critical Schools.*

8. William Doreski points out in a helpful letter to me: "Stevens' essentially symbolist poetics conflict with an inherent skepticism. Therefore to undo his own symbolism Stevens works into his poetry a rhetoric of deconstruc-tion that undermines the symbolist tendencies." Stevens' early poems, such

as "Blackbird," resemble Stephane Mallarmé's Symbolisme, which greatly influenced the deconstruction of Derrida and Kristeva.

9. Maurice Merleau-Ponty, *The Primacy of Perception* (Northwestern University Press, 1985) 17–18.

10. Beehler, "Teaching the Ethical Lessons of Wallace Stevens," in *Teaching Wallace Stevens,* eds. Serio and Leggett (Tennessee University Press, 1994); Ziarek, *Inflected Language: Towards a Hermeneutics of Nearness; Heidegger, Levinas, Stevens, Celan* (SUNY Press, 1994).

11. "Difference," since the rise of postcolonial theory, has become a term primarily designating social difference, referring to the ability of people to live without being dominated by a social group or race. Derrida employs the term "differance" to refer to how the signified meaning of a word depends upon its surrounding signifiers in the text. "Differance" also implies language's process of deferral in which meaning always changes over time, according to context and usage. I will use the word "difference" as it has been widely used by many poststructural theorists.

12. I borrow the term "aggregate" from C. K. Stead's book *Pound, Yeats, Eliot and the Modernist Movement.* Stead uses "metonymical aggregation" to describe the juxtaposing images of early Eliot and Pound. I must stress that Stevens' metonymies aggregate rather than replace, whereas Stead originally employs his term to describe how Pound and Eliot's metonymic images tend to replace as well as aggregate, thus enacting juxtaposition. Stead cites Pound's "The Return" as an example. In the final lines, "Slow on the leash, / pallid the leash men!," "pallid" extends the lackluster motion of the men, and then the exclamatory sound of the second line juxtaposes their inertia by virtually whipping them into shape.

13. Davidson, "Notes Beyond the *Notes:* Wallace Stevens and Contemporary Poetics," in *Wallace Stevens: The Poetics of Modernism,* Albert Gelpi, ed. (Cambridge University Press, 1988).

Chapter 2

1. A. Walton Litz, in *The Introspective Voyager* (Oxford University Press, 1972), points out that "Farewell to Florida" was written in 1936, and introduces the second edition of the volume. In so doing, it departs from the creative period of *Ideas of Order.* Litz notes that "renouncing the gaudy South of *Harmonium* . . . falsifies" its "complexities" (168). However, my simplification indicates Stevens' overall turn away from the "Green barbarism turning paradigm" (*CP* 31) of Floridian romance in an effort to speak of his time and place. "After *Ideas of Order* the word Florida never appears again in Stevens' verse" (201).

2. Thomas F. Bertonneau reads these poems sacrificially in "What Figure

Costs: Stevens' 'The Idea of Order at Key West' (An Anthropoetics)" in *Wallace Stevens Journal* 19:1 (Spring 1995): 51–70.

3. "Tropism" is defined in the *O.E.D.* as a biological term for "turning (part of) an organism in a particular direction in response to external stimulus." The external stimulus is often the historical context of the tropes, the "wormy metaphors." Within a poem, the stimuli are colliding tropes in the confines of the poem.

4. "Date Line" (1934) in *Literary Essays of Ezra Pound,* T. S. Eliot, ed. (New York: New Directions, 1968), 74–75.

5. *Selected Prose of T. S. Eliot,* F. Kermode, ed. (New York: Farrar, 1975), 40–41.

6. To call a poet anti-poetic is easily taken as insult, especially by admirers of Williams. Stevens' essay "Williams" describes him as a romantic who tempers his sentimentality "with acute reaction." "His passion for the anti-poetic is a blood passion and not a passion of the inkpot. The anti-poetic is his spirit's cure. He needs it as a naked man needs shelter or an animal needs salt" (*OP* 213). Deeming the anti-poetic as "his spirit's cure" is a compliment that complements Stevens' quest to cure spirit in the 1930s. "Williams" was published in 1934.

7. Litz, 175.

8. Miller, *The Disappearance of God* (Cambridge: Harvard University Press, 1963).

9. Bloom, *The Poems of Our Climate* (Ithaca: Cornell University Press, 1977), 93.

10. Eleanor Cook, *Poetry, Word-play and Word-war in Wallace Stevens* (Princeton University Press, 1988), 131.

11. Hollander's 1980 essay can be found in *Wallace Stevens,* Harold Bloom, ed. (New York: Chelsea Modern Critical Views, 1985), 134.

12. A. Walton Litz, *The Introspective Voyager* (Oxford University Press, 1972), 193–195.

13. William Doreski's *Wallace Stevens Journal* publication, "Fictive Music: The Iridescent Notes of Wallace Stevens," was previously read at the 1994 MLA session, "Stevens and Narrative." Doreski suggests: "The process of re-inventing narrative as a musical gesture occurs in "The Idea of Order at Key West," in which a musical instrument, the human voice, sings independently of the natural order, inventing a "mimic motion" that does not imitate the human voice yet is intelligible, a voice of pure music" (3). Doreski's "fictive music" helps explain Stevens' way of thinking: "It remains an idea of order because it is necessarily abstract, not because it refuses imagery—it is an image—but because it is irrational, not anti-rational but beyond or aside from rationality" (5).

14. Cook elaborates on the poem's Romantic context: "' Whose spirit is this?' the listeners ask. Not the old spiritus-wind Romantic afflatus. It is enough

to make any wind gasp . . . as when giving up the ghost—a very apt thought. Stevens is testing his ghosts and spirits of many a year" (132).

15. David Walker's *The Transparent Lyric* (Princeton University Press, 1984) emphasizes the role of the reader in trying to answer the questions poised by the poem. Walker's discussion draws from earlier analyses made by Denis Donaghue and Frank Doggett (see Walker, pages 23–27).

16. Thomas Bertonneau agrees about the prevalence of metonymy here: "Wind, rain, horizon, and sound acquire the character of sparagmatic metonymies, like the remains of an immolation." *Wallace Stevens Journal* 19:1 (Spring 1995): 63.

17. Marie Borroff notes Stevens' habitual technique of contrasting Latinate sounding words with his rather alliterative American idiom in "An Always Incipient Cosmos," in Bloom, ed. *Wallace Stevens*. Although I am not pursuing this technique here, it is another form of the defacement of logic exercised by Stevens' music.

18. Mervyn Nicholson, "'The Slightest Sound Matters': Stevens' Sound Cosmology," *Wallace Stevens Journal* 18:1 (Spring 1994): 67.

19. See Charles Altieri, *Painterly Abstraction in Modernist American Poetry* (New York: Cambridge University Press, 1989). In addition to Altieri, Borroff, and MacLeod, Alan Filreis's article "'Beyond the Rhetorician's Touch': Stevens's Painterly Abstractions," details Stevens' inheritance of French modern art and his development of an Abstract Expressionist poetry. Filreis's article is especially rewarding in its explanation of Abstract art and Cubism as aesthetics that give viewers a keener appreciation of reality through sharp attention to sensory perception.

20. Perloff's "flat surface" term is applied to modern arts, such as the collages of Picasso and Braque, and textual overlays of Pound and Williams, all of which critique the notion of *depth* in art by making surface textures limit reference. Books by Glen Macleod and J. V. Brogan link Stevens to modern arts, with an emphasis on painting. Brogan, for instance, describes Stevens' poetry as Cubist in *Part of the Climate*.

21. Bloom, *Poems of Our Climate,* 101.

22. Bloom, *Poems of Our Climate,* 101.

23. Thomas F. Bertonneau's fine article, "What Figure Costs: Stevens' 'The Idea of Order at Key West' (An Anthropoetics)" is in the spring 1995 *Wallace Stevens Journal*. Bertonneau clearly argues that the sacrifice of Key West's singer is "what figure costs." He contextualizes this "immolation" in literary history, suggesting by way of a quotation from Stevens' "Two or Three Ideas": "It might be that '[t]o see the gods dispelled in mid-air and dissolve like clouds is one of the great human experiences' (*OP* 260); and this appears to be what has happened to the Floridian singer when she stops singing, thereby marking the end of a divine epoch. But what now?" (65). That epoch included Eliot and Pound, as Bertonneau points out. What is

unclear to me about Bertonneau's interpretation is exactly when he thinks "she stops singing." He appears to agree with Bloom that her song lasts throughout the poem. After quoting "for she was the maker," Bertonneau continues: "She fulfills the role of signifier, so to speak, and the whole world, from the immediacy of the beach to the 'mountainous atmospheres/ Of sky and sea' (*CP* 129) fulfills the role of signified" (62). However, the poem reads, "she was the maker. Then we / As we beheld her striding there alone," which indicates to me a change in agency in which the observers take responsibility for the music; the poetic voice admits that the muse was simply his instrument of composition. The muse was the poet's signified ghost of a signifier. The answer to the question "what now" is that, as Bertonneau himself points out, Stevens' poetry "ceases to be a matter of chance" and thus assumes responsibility as a secular ethical practice.

24. Bloom, *Poems of Our Climate,* 102.

25. Bloom holds on to the muse here after her exit: "Stevens' singer stops, but her lingering idea of order triumphs over both the pale unknowing Fernandez and the Stevens who knows too well the fear of a calm darkening among water lights" (103). For Bloom, "her lingering idea of order triumphs" likely because the muse reigns atop a romantic transcendent order. However, the poem composes the singing figure as a trope that no longer participates in Stevens' idea of order at Key West by the poem's end.

26. Some other examples are "Debris of Life and Mind," "Final Soliloquy of the Interior Paramour," and "Angel Surrounded by Paysans."

27. James Longenbach updates the lineage of pale Ramon in *Wallace Stevens: The Plain Sense of Things* (New York: Oxford University Press, 1991): "Stevens always insisted that 'Ramon Fernandez' was 'not intended to be anyone at all,' and, in a sense, like the 'Mr. Burnshaw' of 'Mr. Burnshaw and the Statue,' he is a caricature. Yet most of Stevens's readers will know that Fernandez was a critic familiar to Stevens from the pages of the *Nouvelle Revue Francaise,* the *Partisan Review,* and the *Criterion* (where he was translated by T. S. Eliot). . . . [In "I Came Near Being a Fascist"] Fernandez confessed that he had 'a professional fondness for theorizing, which tends to make one highly susceptible to original "solutions."' It was just that susceptibility that bothered Stevens and made him challenge Fernandez to answer a question to which he knew there was no certain answer" (161). In the context of Longenbach's commentary, notice that Stevens calls Fernandez "pale Ramon," thereby transferring the figure of the ghostly muse more firmly upon his directed reader.

28. In "Projecting Modernisms: Phantasmagoria and Consumer Culture," a paper read by Michael Davidson at The Recovery of the Public World conference for Robin Blaser in Vancouver, June 1–4, 1995, Davidson explained how phantasmagorias were originally nineteenth-century London magic lantern shows. With modernist figures such as Freud and Pound, ghostly

images became absorbed into thought. Fitting with the demise of external-
ized deities and the rise of subjective consciousness, in "Key West" Stevens
makes the muse phantom a subjective, or writerly responsibility to be taken
up in poetry.

29. Hollander notes Bloom's point that this poem is a debate "between the
    grackels [of "The Man on the Dump"] and Keats." Hollander proceeds:
    "The Keatsian nightingale may sum up a whole tradition for Stevens. There
    are in America neither larks nor nightingales of the kind that have aston-
    ished English poets for their invisible voices; there are only copies of them"
    (143). He also points to the double meaning of "refrain" as a repeated cho-
    rus that is presently refrained from song (144).

30. "Be thou" echoes Shelley's "Ode to the West Wind"; perhaps a comment
    from Stevens on the sort of Romanticism needed for social responsibility.
    Douglas Mao's dissertation, "Modernism and the question of the object,"
    argues the development of Stevens' voice for the masses.

31. Litz, *The Introspective Voyager*, 177. Litz also discusses poems rejected from
    Ideas of Order for their "light and playful tone," suggesting Stevens' determi-
    nation to move away from *Harmonium*.

Chapter 3

1. I apologize for the gender divisions according to subject matter, as many of
   these critics are well versed in both domains. For instance, the "Stevens and
   Politics" issue of the *Wallace Stevens Journal* contains Brogan's essay, "Stevens
   in History and Not in History: The Poet and the Second World War," and
   Schaum's essay, "Lyric Resistance: Views of the Political and Poetics of Wallace Stevens and H. D." (168–205).

2. Riddel is quoted from *The Clairvoyant Eye* (Baltimore: Johns Hopkins University Press, 1965), 121; Filreis, *Modernism From Right to Left* (New York:
   Cambridge University Press, 1994), 229.

3. As a deconstructive poem, *Owl's Clover* is politically theoretical. For example, in "The Resistance to Theory," de Man claims that "resistance is the
   domain of theory itself." Stevens says that poetry is a form of resistance.

4. Jane Tompkins' "The Reader in History: The Changing Shape of Literary
   Response" chronicles the way in which formalist critics from I. A. Richards
   through W. K. Wimsatt enclosed their readings in a rigid competition for
   objective truth, reacting against nineteenth-century deification and twentieth-century science. The essay is in *Reader-Response Criticism* (Johns Hopkins, 1980).

5. Although Baker identified consistencies between *Harmonium* and *Ideas of
   Order*, which would likely disturb Stevens owing to his poetry's efforts at
   change in the 1930s, Stevens was enthusiastic about Baker's analysis because
   of his psychological insights: "No one before has ever come as close to me

as Mr. Baker does in that article" (*L* 292). Baker's "Wallace Stevens and Other Poets," *Southern Review,* I (Autumn 1935): 373–96. I quote Baker from the reprinted article in *The Achievement of Wallace Stevens,* Brown, Haller, eds. (New York: Lippincott, 1962), 96.

6. Steinman, *Made in America* (New Haven: Yale University Press, 1987); Wilde's article is in *Wallace Stevens Journal* 20:1 (Spring 1996): 3–26.

7. Burnshaw, "Turmoil in the Middle Ground" in *The New Masses* (Oct. 1, 1935): 41, 42. Reprinted following Burnshaw's humorously objective recount of the events entitled "Wallace Stevens and the Statue," *Sewanee Review,* Summer 1961.

8. Stanley Burnshaw, "Turmoil in the Middle Ground," reprinted alongside "Wallace Stevens and the Statue" in *Sewanee Review* 69 (Summer 1961) 363.

9. See Terry Cooney's *The Rise of the New York Intellectuals,* or Judy Kutulas's *The Long War,* for detailed accounts of politics in the 1930s, as they take shape in literary journals of the Northeastern States.

10. This Imagist credo was coined by May Sinclair.

11. Stanley Fish's reading of *How to do Things with Words* clearly summarizes Austin's distinctions: Constative language is language that is, or strives to be, accountable to the real or objective world. It is to constatives—to acts of referring, describing, and stating—that one puts the question "Is it true or false?" in which true and false are understood to be absolute judgments, made independently of any particular set of circumstances. Performative language, on the other hand, is circumstantial through and through. "How to do Things with Austin and Searle: Speech-Act Theory and Literary Criticism." *Is There A Text in this Class?* Harvard University Press, 1980 (198).

12. Litz's Appendix C to *The Introspective Voyager* details edits made to the Alcestis Press *Owl's Clover.*

13. Burnshaw, "Wallace Stevens and the Statue," *Sewanee Review* 69 (Summer 1961): 359.

14. Burnshaw, 358.

15. Burnshaw, 359.

16. Burnshaw, 357.

Chapter 4

1. The vocabulary in "The Greenest Continent" is an *OED* treasure trove. "Athos" is a monastery in northeastern Greece that is the site of an autonomous theocracy; "effulgent" means radiant; "paladin" derives from Palatine, Charlemagne's champion knight, and a protector of ideals.

2. In a letter, Stevens calls "Mr. Burnshaw and the Statue" "a general and rather vaguely poetic justification of leftism; to the extent that the Marxians are raising Cain with the peacocks and the doves, nature has been ruined by

them" (*L* 295). In *Ariel and the Police,* Lentricchia compares Stevens' anti-imperialist politics with those of William James.

3. The grotesque night is expressed in "A Word with Jose Rodriguez-Feo," Stevens' Cuban confidant, found in *Transport to Summer:*

> As one of the secretaries of the moon,
> The queen of ignorance, you have deplored
> How she presides over imbeciles. The night
> Makes everything grotesque. Is it because
> Night is the nature of man's interior world?
> Is lunar Habana the Cuba of the self?
>
> . . . .
>
> [The spirit] says there is an absolute grotesque.
> There is a nature that is grotesque within
> The boulevards of the generals.
>
> . . . .
>
> The grotesque is not a visitation. It is
> Not apparition but appearance, part
> Of the simplified geography, in which
> The sun comes up like news from Africa.   (*CP* 333–4)

Here again Ananke is wrapped up in the exotic other, this time in dialogue with a human incarnation. But Stevens knows that the exotic other is part of his "new knowledge of reality" in dawn, even if it's more pronounced in the strangeness of a general or news from Africa.

4. Vendler, *On Extended Wings* (Cambridge: Harvard University Press, 1969), 80.

5. Filreis, *Modernism from Right to Left,* 235.

6. Grigson's magazine *New Verse* was known for its "vitriolic style of reviewing," which may account for the title of Grigson's review of Stevens, "The Stuffed Goldfinch." Stevens called Grigson a "propagandist" (*L* 309), then later praised him for being on to something, but finally added that Grigson would never produce anything of value if he remained part of a group. *Modernism from Right to Left,* 240–245.

7. The following edited part of the 1937 edition shows how much was sacrificed from canto ii:

> Buckskins and broadbrims, crossers of divides,
> For whom men were to be ends in themselves,
> Are the cities to breed as the mountains bred? For you
> Day came upon the spirit as life comes
> And deep winds flooded you; for these, day comes,
> A penny sun in a tinsel sky, unrhymed,
> And the spirit writhes to be wakened, writhes

> To see, once more, this hacked-up world of tools.
> In their cadaverous Eden, they desire
> The same down-dropping of fruit in yellow leaves.
> The scholar's outline that you had, the print
> Of poets, the Italian lives preserved
> For poverty are gaudy o to these.
> Their destiny is just as much machine
> As death itself. It will, it will be changed,
> Time's fortune near, the sleepless sleepers moved
> By the torture of things that will be realized,
> Will, will, but how and all of the asking how.
> These are not your lives, O free, O bold
> That rode your horses straight away.
>
> (*The Man with the Blue Guitar* 74–5)

Gone are: the first O's associated with the "buckskin," the "trundl[ing] children," the "heart in slattern pinnacles," the "horror . . . and loss," London and Paris publications, and their "trivial chance foregone," "the agony of dreams" and the "tell-tale muttering." In short, all the extremes have been shaved off. The parodies of pioneer Americana and Eurocentrism, as well as the severest human emotions, were all sacrificed for a muted poem with little rhetorical satire.

8. *Modernism from Right to Left,* 240.
9. *Modernism from Right to Left,* 245–246.
10. Roland Barthes writes:

> To write the body.
> Neither the skin, nor the muscles, nor the bones,
> nor the nerves, but the rest: an awkward, fibrous,
> shaggy, raveled thing, a clown's coat   (*Barthes by Barthes* 180)

11. Exceptions to Stevens' rather automatic and posed prose are the interwoven "Sister of the Minotaur" figure in "The Figure of the Youth as a Virile Poet," and the discussion of the styles of poetry, men, and gods in "Two or Three Ideas." The latter's prose sounds like Gertrude Stein, and the former follows Stevens' poetry's manner of resurrecting and overhauling stale tropes into contemporary applications.
12. *Modernism from Right to Left,* 246–7.
13. *Modernism from Right to Left,* 244.
14. I am being defensive here because the Statue in *Owl's Clover* has been interpreted as a symbol of art, nonpejoratively, rather than as the huge critique of Western monumentalism that I suggest. Stevens' views about the dumbing-down of democratic conformity strongly resemble those espoused by Jeanette Winterson in *Art Objects.*

15. Hullot-Kentor's essay can be found in *West Coast Line* 29:2 (Fall 1995): 148–157. It was delivered as a talk at the "Recovery of the Public World" Vancouver conference in honor of poet Robin Blaser. The information regarding psychiatric illness in 1994 can be found in Anthony LaBruzza and Jose Mendez-Villarubbia, *Using DSM-IV: A Clinician's Guide to Psychiatric Diagnosis* (Northvale: Jason Aronson Inc., 1994), 303.

Chapter 5

1. See Jacqueline Brogan's article, "'Sister of the Minotaur': Sexism and Stevens," *Wallace Stevens and the Feminine*, Melita Schaum, ed. (Tuscaloosa: Alabama University Press, 1993). Brogan discusses the poet's later verse as curative, especially with reference to the gender divisions that occupy Stevens' poetry. My next chapter will develop Stevens' gender negotiations in relation to lyric and epic paradigms.

2. The idea that art primarily influences people through musical forms is not new, and although I don't think many people want to recognize this, it's not logical. For more thorough ideas in this domain, see Lisa Steinman's chapter on Stevens and physics in *Made in America;* there are also new books by Anca Rosu and Theodore Sampson. See Kristeva's theory of drives and utterance in *Revolution of Poetic Language,* which is based on reading Mallarme, whose line from "Coup de Des," "dice thrown will never annul chance," relates to this argument for conduction over-determining repressive logic. Joyce's *Ulysses* also contains an image of blood moving through the mind in the Sirens section. Jeannette Winterson, in *Sexing the Cherry,* states: "artists are superconductors" (91).

3. Perhaps we need to think about the poem's audience before passing judgment. Our notions of tough-minded anti-sentiment have many informing factors in need of question. As Jill Conway's "Politics, Pedagogy, and Gender" suggests, there is something of an *esthetique du mal* in American education:

> Moreover, because of American public schools' identification with maternal functions, colleges and universities have distanced themselves from schools and stressed the "masculine" tough-mindedness of American scholarship. This difference remains an enduring puzzle for Europeans, who see both schools and universities in a continuum of intellectual endeavor, and who value intellectual playfulness. (*Norton Reader* 305)

Conway attributes some of this attitude also to the cold war, and much needless aggression has concomitantly expired. An example of a critic who engages in polemics but refrains from hard-headed poses is Alan Filreis. His criticism invaluably makes us aware of the many audiences Stevens addresses in the thirties and forties. And although I often do not agree with Filreis's interpretation of Stevens' poetry, he replaces value judgments with contextual applications. For instance, in addition to providing the historical applications for "How Red the Rose," Filreis acknowledges its anthologizability, and then states: "Yet I would argue that one searches more usefully for Stevens's response to the soldier's need for poetry about pain in the eighth canto, where a 'shaken realist / First sees reality' . . ." (*Actual World* 136).

4. Again, we can bring the many polarities involved in poetry back into Stevens' sexual merger: unitive and fragmentary, creation and argument, significance and signification are coalesced when the poet's personae display characteristics of both female and male stereotypes.

5. See Kristin Ross's *The Emergence of Social Space,* in which she argues that Rimbaud's poems both comment on Parisian culture of 1870, and speak in advance of the critiques that have since followed. Rimbaud and Stevens write poetry of excess.

6. Jacqueline V. Brogan explores the "as if" in Stevens' poetry in her book *Stevens and Simile.* This philosophical approach derives from Hans Vaihinger, and also resembles the Pragmatism of William James. Longenbach develops this in *The Plain Sense of Things.*

7. For a study of Stevens' drama, see Maureen Kravec, "'As at a Theatre': Wallace Stevens' Dramatistic Poetry," *Wallace Stevens Journal* '96.

8. Welles' speech is located in *Virginia Quarterly Review* 21: 4 (Autumn 1945): 483–96. Excerpts from the speech are contrasted with "Description without Place" at the end of this chapter. In *Wallace Stevens and the Actual World,* Filreis describes Welles as "Former undersecretary of state, author of the polemical *Time for Decision* (1944), theorist of postwar balance of power, vociferous proponent of the nascent United Nations organization. . ." (151).

9. Alan Filreis informed me that Welles' speech was part of the speaker's larger circuit.

Chapter 6

1. Bonnie Costello, "Narrative Secrets, Lyric Openings: Stevens and Bishop," *Wallace Stevens Journal* (Fall 95): 180–200.

2. Kenneth Burke, *Counter-Statement* (California University Press, 1968), 149. I will return to Burke's comments on *Ulysses* later in this chapter, as Burke's analysis of form is applicable to Stevens. I will suggest, through Burke, that Stevens' and Joyce's methods counter the structures within which they write. The Joyce and Stevens comparison seems limitless, and has been written about by Daniel Schwarz.

3. In *Destructive Poetics: Heidegger and Modern American Poetry* (New York: Columbia University Press, 1980), Paul Bove's poetics are theorized through

Stevens' poetry, such as "The Motive for Metaphor." Michael Davidson aligns Stevens' influence on postmodern poetry in A. Gelpi, *Wallace Stevens: The Poetics of Modernism* (Cambridge University Press, 1985).

4. Nietzsche, "Twilight of the Idols," also in "Thus Spake Zarathrustra," in *The Portable Nietzsche,* Walter Kaufmann, ed. (New York: Viking, 1968), 563, 326.

5. "X" can be read as the cross that bears a dominant fate. In a line eloquently sounding like one of Stevens'"Adagia," Charles Altieri writes, "the doctrine of Incarnation is in essence a theory of metaphor" (In Cook, *Poetry, Word-play and Word-war in Wallace Stevens,* 229). Cook cites Altieri's essay "Wallace Stevens' Metaphors of Metaphor," *American Poetry* 1 (1983): 45.

6. *Wallace Stevens and the Feminine* (Tuscaloosa: Alabama University Press, 1993), edited by Melita Schaum provides a wide range of reading in this area.

7. In *Ariel and the Police* (Wisconsin University Press, 1988), Frank Lentricchia sees Stevens' early lyrics of courtship, and their consequent termination, as significant to his developing poetics and psychology (see pages 168–176).

8. Brogan's essay is in M. Schaum, ed., *Wallace Stevens and the Feminine.* Schaum's book develops the scholarship initiated in *Wallace Stevens Journal's* "Stevens and Women" fall 1988 issue, where Brogan's essay first appeared.

9. Kristeva's Ph. D. thesis, *Revolution in Poetic Language* (1974), focuses on avant-garde literature as social change. Kristeva's theory reads Mallarme, and can be applied to Stevens' poetics. "From Symbol to Sign" is also found in *The Kristeva Reader,* ed. Toril Moi (New York: Columbia University Press, 1986).

10. In *Wallace Stevens and the Actual World* (Princeton University Press, 1991) Alan Filreis measures the success of Stevens as a war poet at home and on the front. "How red the rose that is the soldier's wound," a canto from "Esthetique du Mal," was one of few World War II poems that spoke to both soldiers and the poetry crowd in America. The success of the epilogue to the soldier in "Notes" is less certain.

11. As usual in Stevens criticism, poetic analysis brings us into collision with theory. Bakhtin's "dialogism" can be helpful in discussing negotiated meanings. However, Bakhtin criticized lyric poetry for an absence of dialogism, which could be found more readily in novels. Stevens' poetry answers Bakhtin's critique. It must be remembered that Bakhtin wrote within modernism, looking to the possibilities of the novel as a more expansive form. Daniel Schwarz recently employed Bakhtin in his study, *Narrative and Representation in the Poetry of Wallace Stevens* (New York: St. Martin's Press, 1993).

12. Stevens, "Two or Three Ideas," *Opus Posthumous,* ed. M. J. Bates (New York: Vintage, 1989). Although seeming a flippant comment, the argument of the essay is summarized in the following excerpt, sounding more like Stein than Stevens: "Thus, it might be true that the style of a poem and the gods them-

selves are one; or that the style of the gods and the style of men are one; or that the style of a poem and the style of men are one" (262).

13. In the symbolism linking the captain to his vessel, there exists an ancient etymology, of which Stevens was likely more than aware. The Phoenician word origin of "I" is a character that symbolizes "boat." This observation was noted by friend and editor, Glen Lowry.

14. Paul de Man discusses the way patterns of discovery exclude all that is not in focus in the appropriately titled book *Blindness and Insight* (Minnesota University Press, 1983). See in particular, "The Rhetoric of Blindness: Jacques Derrida's Reading of Rousseau."

15. In French, "combing" is "peigner," linking Penelope to the female protagonist in the "peignoir" of "Sunday Morning."

16. This reversal of objective dominance undermines genres, such as the epic, that are associated with masculine control. For a discussion of Stevens' ethical employment of Penelope, see Michael Beehler, "Penelope's Experience: Teaching the Ethical Lessons of Stevens" in *Teaching Wallace Stevens: Practical Essays,* Serio and Leggett, eds. (Knoxville: Tennessee University Press, 1994), 267–279:

    > Penelope's "patient syllables" do not determine or command the presentation of Ulysses in the here and now of *her* presence. Rather, beyond their content and in a patience that is an extreme passivity, they are an invocation to the other as *other,* and thus her "Repeating his name" is an act of remembrance ("Never forgetting him that kept coming constantly so near") testifying to the other's essential alterity. (276)

    Beehler argues that this poem exemplifies the ethics of Emmanuel Levinas. Resemblances between Levinas and Stevens are evident in the following words of Levinas, which Beehler puts in the context of Penelope's "caress" of Ulysses: "like a game with something slipping away . . . not with what can become ours or us, but with something other, always other, always inaccessible, and always still to come" (*Levinas Reader* 51). While these words certainly sound utopic, Levinas's supreme fiction shares with Stevens the resistance to seizure and destination. This "mode of being . . . is radically nonviolent and essentially non-self-sufficient, [the ethical relation is] 'being for the other' (*Levinas Reader* 149)." This line of discussion about Stevens' ethics arises again at end of this chapter.

17. Kenneth Burke, "Lexicon Rhetoricae" in *Counter-Statement,* 149. Although I've yet to find similar comments from Burke about Stevens' poetic form, Burke does place Stevens as the most recent innovator in a long line of Western philosophers including Kant, Hegel, Marx, and Santayana in *A Grammar of Motives* (New York: Meridian, 1962).

18. In "Narrative Secrets, Lyric Openings: Stevens and Bishop" *Wallace Stevens Journal* (fall 95), Bonnie Costello argues that Stevens' lyrics are "a way of

releasing the world from the distortions of causal logic, back into its secrets" (198). Costello also employs Mark Strand, who echoes Stevens' effort at using lyrical coaxings to open fate: "The absent narrative is the one, I wanted to say, in which our fate is written" (198). Stevens' lyrics ask us to look for the secrets missing from narrative teleology. Costello and I come to similar conclusions about the indivisibility of lyric and narrative dialogues: "But it is a dialogue and not a dialectic, for in the negotiations of lyric and narrative there are no final settlements" (199).

19. In addition to Beehler's essay, see Ewa Ziarek, "Kristeva and Levinas: Mourning, Ethics and the Feminine," in *Ethics, Politics, and Difference in Julia Kristeva's Writing,* Kelly Oliver, ed. (New York: Routledge, 1993). In the following quotations, the name of Levinas could be replaced by Stevens and remain an accurate and provocative statement, which echoes and extends my essay's end: "Levinas claims that by annulling the difference between the known and the knowing, the activity of thought both grasps and constitutes alterity on its own terms" (Ziarek in Oliver 64). At the end of "The Sail of Ulysses," Stevens makes a proposal that resounds in the following words of Ziarek and Levinas respectively: "In opposition to the myth of Ulysses returning home, Levinas proposes an encounter with alterity as an Abrahamic movement without return: *'A work conceived radically is a movement of the same unto the other which never returns the same'*" (Levinas, "The Trace of the Other" in Oliver 65).

Chapter 7

1. See Steiner's essay, "Collage or Miracle: Historicism in a Deconstructed World," in *Reconstructing American Literary History,* edited by S. Bercovitch (Harvard University Press, 1986).

Bibliography

Altieri, Charles. *Painterly Abstraction in Modernist American Poetry.* New York: Cambridge University Press, 1989.

Ammons, A. R., ed. *The Best American Poetry 1994.* Series Editor, D. Lehman. New York: Touchstone, 1994.

Arendt, Hannah. *The Origins of Totalitarianism.* New York: Harcourt, 1951.

Arensberg, Mary. *The American Sublime.* Buffalo: SUNY Press, 1986.

Austin, J. L. *How to do Things with Words.* New York: Oxford, 1965.

Barthes, Roland. *Roland Barthes by Roland Barthes.* Trans. Richard Howard. New York: Noonday, 1977.

Bates, Milton J. *Wallace Stevens: A Mythology of Self.* Berkeley: California University Press, 1985.

Beehler, Michael. *T. S. Eliot, Wallace Stevens, and the Discourses of Difference.* Baton Rouge: Louisiana State University Press, 1987.

Bercovitch, Sacvan, ed. *Reconstructing American Literary History.* Cambridge: Harvard University Press, 1986.

Bernstein, M. A. *The Tale of the Tribe: Ezra Pound and the Modern Verse Epic.* Princeton: Princeton University Press, 1980.

Bertonneau, Thomas F. "What Figure Costs: Stevens' 'The Idea of Order at Key West' (An Anthropoetics)." *Wallace Stevens Journal* 19:1 (Spring 1995): 51–70.

Blaser, Robin. *The Holy Forest.* Toronto: Coach House, 1993.

Bloom, Harold. *The Poems of Our Climate.* Ithaca, NY: Cornell University Press, 1977.

———, ed. *Wallace Stevens* (Modern Critical Views). New York: Chelsea House, 1985.

Bohm, David. *Wholeness and the Implicate Order.* Boston: Routledge, 1980.

Borroff, Marie. "An Always Incipient Cosmos." *Wallace Stevens* (Modern Critical Views). Ed. Bloom. New York: Chelsea House, 1985.

Bove, Paul. *Destructive Poetics: Heidegger and Modern American Poetry.* New York: Columbia University Press, 1980.

Brazeau, Peter. *Parts of a World: Wallace Stevens Remembered.* New York: Random House, 1983.

Brogan, Jacqueline Vaught. *Stevens and Simile.* Princeton: Princeton University Press, 1986.

———. "Stevens in History and Not in History: The Poet and the Second World War." *Wallace Stevens Journal* 13: 2 (Fall 1989): 168–190.

———. *Part of the Climate: American Cubist Poetry.* Berkeley: California University Press, 1991.

———. "' Sister of the Minotaur': Sexism and Stevens." *Wallace Stevens and the Feminine.* Ed. Melita Schaum. Tuscaloosa: University of Alabama Press, 1993: 3–22.

———. "Planets on the Table: From Wallace Stevens and Elizabeth Bishop to Adrienne Rich and June Jordan," *Wallace Stevens Journal* 19: 2 (Fall 1995): 255–278.

Brown, Haller, ed. *The Achievement of Wallace Stevens.* New York: Lippincott, 1962.

Burke, Kenneth. *Counter-Statement.* Berkeley: California University Press, 1968.

———. *A Grammar of Motives and A Rhetoric of Motives.* New York: Meridian, 1962.

———. *Language as Symbolic Action.* Berkeley: California University Press, 1966.

Butler, Judith. *Subjects of Desire.* New York: Columbia University Press, 1987.

———. *Gender Trouble.* New York: Routledge, 1990.

———. "The Nothing that Is: Wallace Stevens' Hegelian Affinities." *Theorizing American Literature: Hegel, the Sign and History.* Ed. Cowan, B., Kronick, J. G. Baton Rouge: Louisiana State University Press, 1991.

Chrisman, Laura and Patrick Williams, eds. *Colonial Discourse and Post-Colonial Theory: A Reader.* New York: Columbia University Press, 1994.

Conway, Jill. "Politics, Pedagogy, and Gender." *The Norton Reader.* New York: Norton, 1996.

Cook, Eleanor. "The Decreations of Wallace Stevens." *Wallace Stevens Journal* 4.2 (1980).

———. *Poetry, Word-play and Word-war in Wallace Stevens.* Princeton: Princeton University Press, 1988.

Cooney, Terry A. *The Rise of the New York Intellectuals: Partisan Review and Its Circle.* Madison: Wisconsin University Press, 1986.

Coyle, Beverly and Alan Filreis, eds. *Secretaries of the Moon: The Letters of Wallace Stevens and José Rodríguez Feo.* Durham, NC: Duke University Press, 1986.

Davidson, Michael. "Notes Beyond the *Notes:* Wallace Stevens and Contemporary Poetics." *Wallace Stevens: The Poetics of Modernism.* Ed. A. Gelpi. London: Cambridge University Press, 1988.

De Man, Paul. "The Rhetoric of Blindness: Jacques Derrida's Reading of Rousseau." *Blindness and Insight.* Minneapolis: Minnesota University Press, 1983.

———. "The Resistance to Theory." *Modern Criticism and Theory.* Ed. D. Lodge, New York: Longman, 1988.

Derrida, Jacques. "Structure, sign and play in the discourse of the human sciences." *Writing and Difference.* Trans. Alan Bass. Chicago: Chicago University Press, 1978.

———. *Given Time: I. Counterfeit Money.* Trans. Peggy Kamuf. Chicago: Chicago University Press, 1992.

Dickie, Margaret. *Lyric Contingencies: Emily Dickinson and Wallace Stevens.* Philadelphia: Pennsylvania University Press, 1991.

Doreski, William. *The Modern Voice in American Poetry.* Gainesville: Florida University Press, 1995.

———. "Fictive Music: The Iridescent Notes of Wallace Stevens." *Wallace Stevens Journal* 20:1 (Spring 1996): 55–75.

Eagleton, Terry. *Literary Theory.* Oxford: Basil Blackwell, 1983.

Eliot, T. S. *Selected Prose of T. S. Eliot.* Ed. Frank Kermode. New York: Farrar, Straus and Giroux, 1975.

Ellmann, R. and R. O'Clair. *Modern Poems.* New York: Norton, 1989.

———. *Collected Poems 1909–1962.* London: Faber, 1963.

Filreis, Alan. *Wallace Stevens and the Actual World.* Princeton: Princeton University Press, 1991.

———. "'Beyond the Rhetorician's Touch': Stevens's Painterly Abstractions." *American Literary History* (Spring 1992): 230–263.

———. *Modernism from Right to Left : Wallace Stevens, the Thirties and Literary Radicalism.* London: Cambridge University Press, 1994.

Fish, Stanley. "How to do Things with Austin and Searle: Speech-Act Theory and Literary Criticism." *Is There A Text in this Class?* Cambridge, MA: Harvard University Press, 1980.

Gelpi, A., ed. *Wallace Stevens: The Poetics of Modernism.* London: Cambridge University Press, 1985.

Goldwater, M., R. Smith, and C. Tomkins. *Jennifer Bartlett.* New York: Abbeville Press, 1989.

Hobbs, Michael. "Stevens' Gunman Lover: Readers in the Rock." *Wallace Stevens Journal* 18:2 (Fall 1994): 157–169.

Hoerner, Fred. "Gratification and Its Discontents: The Politics of Stevens' Chastening Aesthetics." *Wallace Stevens Journal* 18:1 (Spring 1994): 81–105.

Hosek, C. and P. Parker, eds. *Lyric Poetry: Beyond New Criticism.* Ithaca, NY: Cornell University Press, 1985.

Hullot-Kentor, Robert. "Past-tense: Ethics, Aesthetics and the Recovery of the Public World." *West Coast Line* 29:2 (Fall 1995): 148–157.

Hunter, Sam and John Jacobus. *Modern Art.* New York: Harry N. Abrams, 1985.

Jakobson, R. "The metaphoric and metonymic poles." *Modern Criticism and Theory: A Reader.* Ed. Lodge. New York: Longman, 1988.

James, W. *Writings of William James.* London: Cambridge University Press, 1966.

Jameson, Fredric. *Marxism and Form.* Princeton: Princeton University Press, 1972.

————. *Postmodernism, or, The Cultural Logic of Late Capitalism*. Durham, NC: Duke University Press, 1991.

Jarraway, David. *Wallace Stevens and the Question of Belief*. Baton Rouge: Louisiana University Press, 1993.

Joyce, James. *Ulysses*. Ed. H. W. Gabler. London: Penguin, 1986.

Kenner, Hugh. *The Pound Era*. Berkeley: California University Press, 1971.

————. *A Homemade World*. New York: Knopf, 1975.

Kravec, Maureen. "'As at a Theatre': Wallace Stevens' Dramatistic Poetry." *Wallace Stevens Journal* 20:1 (Spring 1996): 27–46.

Kristeva, Julia. *The Kristeva Reader*. Ed. Toril Moi. New York: Columbia University Press, 1986.

Kutulas, Judy. *The Long War: The Intellectual People's Front and Anti-Stalinism*. Durham, NC: Duke University Press, 1995.

Laguardia, David. *Advance on Chaos*. Hanover, RI: Brown University Press, 1983.

Leckie, Ross. "A New Knowledge of Reality: Wallace Stevens' Use of Metaphor and Syntax as Modes of Perception." Diss. University of Toronto, 1989.

Lentricchia, Frank. *Ariel and the Police*. Madison: Wisconsin University Press, 1988.

Levinas, Emmanuel. *The Levinas Reader*. Oxford: Blackwell, 1989.

Litz, A. Walton. *The Introspective Voyager*. New York: Oxford University Press, 1972.

Lodge, David. *Modern Criticism and Theory*. New York: Longman, 1988.

Longenbach, James. *Wallace Stevens: The Plain Sense of Things*. New York: Oxford University Press, 1991.

Lyotard, Jean-Francois. *The Differend*. Trans. G. Van Den Abbeele. Minneapolis: Minnesota University Press, 1988.

MacLeod, Glen. *Wallace Stevens and Modern Art*. New Haven: Yale University Press, 1993.

————. "The Influence of Wallace Stevens on Contemporary Artists." *Wallace Stevens Journal* 20.2 (Fall 1996): 139–180.

Mailloux, Steven. *Rhetorical Power*. Ithaca, NY: Cornell University Press, 1989.

Marx, Karl. *The Portable Karl Marx*. Ed. E. Kamenka. New York: Viking, 1983.

Mauss, Marcel. *The Gift: The Form and Reason for Exchange in Archaic Societies*. Trans. W. D. Halls. London: Routledge, 1990.

McCann, Janet. *Wallace Stevens Revisited: "The Celestial Possible."* New York: Twayne, 1995.

Merleau-Ponty, Maurice. *The Primacy of Perception*. Evanston, IL: Northwestern University Press, 1985.

Miller, J. H. *The Disappearance of God*. Cambridge: Harvard University Press, 1963.

————. *The Linguistic Moment: From Wordsworth to Stevens*. Princeton: Princeton University Press, 1985.

Mitchell, W. J. T., ed. *Against Theory*. Chicago: Chicago University Press, 1985.

Monroe, Robert Emmett. "Figuration and Society in 'Owl's Clover.'" *Wallace Stevens Journal* 13.2 (Fall 1989): 127–149.

Nelson, Cary. *Repression and Recovery: Modern American Poetry and the Politics of Cultural Memory, 1910–1945*. Madison: Wisconsin University Press, 1989.

Nicholson, Mervyn. "'The Slightest Sound Matters': Stevens' Sound Cosmology." *Wallace Stevens Journal* 18:1 (Spring 1994).

Nietzsche, F. *The Portable Nietzsche*. Ed. W. Kaufmann. New York: Viking, 1968.

North, Michael. *The Final Sculpture: Public Monuments and Modern Poets*. Ithaca, NY: Cornell University Press, 1985.

Oliver, Kelly, ed. *Ethics, Politics, and Difference in Julia Kristeva's Writing*. New York: Routledge, 1993.

Pearce, Roy Harvey. *The Act of the Mind*. Baltimore: Johns Hopkins University Press, 1965.

Perlis, Alan, "Wallace Stevens' Poems and the Effacement of Metaphor." *Wallace Stevens Journal* 10.2 (1986).

Perloff, M. *Poetics of Indeterminacy: From Rimbaud to Cage*. Princeton: Princeton University Press, 1981.

———. *Dance of the Intellect*. New York: Cambridge University Press, 1985.

———. *Poetic Licence: Essays on the Modernist and Postmodernist Lyric*. Evanston, IL: Northwestern University Press, 1990.

Pound, Ezra. *Guide to Kulchur*. New York: New Directions, 1952.

———. *Selected Poems of Ezra Pound*. New York: New Directions, 1957.

———. *Literary Essays of Ezra Pound*. Ed. T. S. Eliot. New York: New Directions, 1968.

Quinn, Sister Bernetta. "On Stevens' Catholic Conversion." *Renascence* 41:4 (Summer 1989).

Richardson, Joan. *Wallace Stevens: The Later Years, 1923–1955*. New York: William Morrow, 1988.

Riddel, Joseph. *The Clairvoyant Eye*. Baltimore: Johns Hopkins University Press, 1965.

Rieke, Alison. *The Senses of Nonsense*. Ames: Iowa State University Press, 1992.

Ross, Kristin. *The Emergence of Social Space: Rimbaud and the Paris Commune*. Minneapolis: Minnesota University Press, 1988.

Schaum, Melita. *Wallace Stevens and the Critical Schools*. Tuscaloosa: Alabama University Press, 1988.

———, ed. *Wallace Stevens and the Feminine*. Tuscaloosa: Alabama University Press, 1993.

Schwarz, Daniel. *Narrative and Representation in the Poetry of Wallace Stevens*. New York: St. Martin's Press, 1993.

Serio, John, and B. J. Leggett, eds. *Teaching Wallace Stevens*. Knoxville: Tennessee University Press, 1994.

———. *Wallace Stevens: An Annotated Secondary Bibliography*. Pittsburgh: Pittsburgh University Press, 1994.

Stead, C. K. *Pound, Yeats, Eliot and the Modernist Movement*. London: Macmillan, 1986.

Stein, Gertrude. *Selected Writings of Gertrude Stein*. Ed. Carl Van Vechten. New York: Vintage, 1990.

Steinman, Lisa. *Made in America: Science, Technology and American Modernist Poets*. New Haven, CT: Yale University Press, 1987.

Stevens, Holly, ed. *Letters of Wallace Stevens (L)*. New York: Knopf, 1966.

Stevens, Wallace. *Collected Poems (CP)*. New York: Vintage, 1982.

———. *Opus Posthumous (OP)*. Ed. M. J. Bates. New York: Vintage, 1989.

———. *The Necessary Angel (NA)*. New York: Vintage, 1951.

———. *Collected Poetry and Prose of Wallace Stevens*. Ed. Frank Kermode and Joan Richardson. New York: Library of America, 1997.

Strand, Mark. *Reasons for Moving, Darker, and The Sargentville Notebook*. New York: Knopf, 1992.

Tompkins, Jane, ed. *Reader-Response Criticism*. Baltimore: Johns Hopkins University Press, 1980.

Vendler, Helen. *On Extended Wings*. Cambridge: Harvard University Press, 1969.

———. *Words Chosen out of Desire*. Knoxville: Tennessee University Press, 1984.

Vitanza, Victor J. *Negation, Subjectivity, and The History of Rhetoric*. Buffalo: SUNY Press, 1997.

Voros, Gyorgyi. *Notations of the Wild: Ecology in the Poetry of Wallace Stevens*. Ames: Iowa State University Press, 1997.

Walker, David. *The Transparent Lyric: Reading and Meaning in the Poetry of Stevens and Williams*. Princeton: Princeton University Press, 1984.

Walsh, Thomas F. *Concordance to the Poetry of Wallace Stevens*. Philadelphia: Pennsylvania University Press, 1963.

Weinfield, Henry. "Wallace Stevens 'Esthetique du Mal' and the Evils of Aestheticism." *Wallace Stevens Journal* 12:1 (1989).

Welles, Sumner. "The Vision of a World at Peace." *The Virginia Quarterly Review* 21:4 (Autumn 1945): 481–496.

West, Cornel. *The American Evasion of Philosophy: A Genealogy of Pragmatism*. Madison: Wisconsin University Press, 1989.

White, Hayden. *The Content of Form*. Baltimore: Johns Hopkins University Press, 1987.

———, and Margaret Brose, eds. *Representing Kenneth Burke*. Baltimore: Johns Hopkins University Press, 1982.

Wilde, Dana. "Wallace Stevens, Modern Physics, and Wholeness." *Wallace Stevens Journal* 20:1 (Spring 1996): 3–26.

Williams, Raymond. *The Politics of Modernism*. Ed. Tony Pinkney. London: Verso, 1989.

Williams, William Carlos. *The William Carlos Williams Reader*. Ed. M. L. Rosenthal. New York: New Directions, 1966.

———. "Comment: Wallace Stevens." *Poetry* 87:4 (Jan. 1956): 234–39.

Winterson, Jeanette. *Sexing the Cherry*. London: Vintage, 1990.

———. *Art Objects*. London: Vintage, 1995.

Woodward, Kathleen. *At Last, The Real Distinguished Thing: The Late Poems of Eliot, Pound, Stevens, and Williams.* Columbus: Ohio State University Press, 1980.

Ziarek, Ewa. "Kristeva and Levinas: Mourning, Ethics and the Feminine." *Ethics, Politics, and Difference in Julia Kristeva's Writing.* Ed. Kelly Oliver. London: Routledge, 1993.

Ziarek, Kryzysztof. *Inflected Language: Towards a Hermeneutics of Nearness; Heidegger, Levinas, Stevens, Celan.* Buffalo: SUNY Press, 1994.

Index

Abstract Expressionism, 2, 3, 44–45
Adagia, 15–16, 22, 30, 127, 132, 192, 198
"Add This to Rhetoric," 18–22, 30, 105, 130
Altieri, Charles, 2, 9, 44, 189–190
Ammons, A. R., 61, 66, 146, 202
"Anecdote of the Jar," 27, 98
"Angel Surrounded by Paysans," 93, 107, 121, 133, 167, 175–178, 186
"Anglais Mort a Florence," 34–36, 71
Aristotle, 21, 61, 88, 103
"Artificial Populations," 106, 173
Ashbery, John, 61
"Auroras of Autumn, The," 108, 167
Austin, J. L., 79, 117
"Autumn Refrain," 31, 51–52

Baker, Howard, 59
Barthes, Roland, 22, 108, 142
Bates, Milton, xi
Beehler, Michael, 4, 5, 11, 61–62, 144, 185, 197
Bernstein, Michael Andre, 168, 183
Blaser, Robin, 145
Bloom, Harold, 16, 31, 37, 46–48, 56–57
Bohm, David, 120–121
Borroff, Marie, 2, 45
"Botanist on an Alp (No. 1)," 72

Bove, Paul, 5, 11, 174
Bowman, Catherine, 202
Brahms, 31, 34, 35
Brogan, Jacqueline Vaught, ix, 4, 8, 15, 21, 29, 56, 104, 144–145, 173, 190
Brown, Merle, 57
Burke, Kenneth, 22, 61, 81, 117, 121, 169, 183
Burnshaw, Stanley, 16, 57–58, 67–69, 75, 79–83, 146, 152
Butler, Judith, 2, 11–14 , 27, 197

Cezanne, Paul, 15
Champlain, Samuel de, 86
Church, Barbara, 115, 165
Church, Henry, 115, 124, 151, 156, 175–176
Clash, The, 195–196
Coleridge, Samuel Taylor, 4, 10, 114, 197
"Comedian as the Letter C, The," 27
"Connoisseur of Chaos," 14–15
Costello, Bonnie, 4, 167
Cook, Eleanor, 4, 14, 41, 57, 79
Creeley, Robert, 198
Cubism, 8, 15, 99

"Dance of the Macabre Mice," 53
Dante, 90, 142

Davidson, Michael, 25, 149, 168–169, 174, 189–90, 197–199
"Debris of Life and Mind," 177
Deleuze, Gilles, 12
de Man, Paul, 14, 18, 30, 60, 117–119, 130–131, 145, 190, 194
Derrida, Jacques, 5, 10, 59, 117, 130, 174–175
Descartes, Rene, 4, 23, 110, 118, 127–131, 145, 204
"Description without Place," xi, 23–24, 30, 61–62, 103, 110, 112, 117, 121, 123, 136–137, 149–165, 207
Donne, John, 100
Dos Passos, John, 81
Dr. Jekyll and Mr. Hyde, The Strange case of, 2
"Duck for Dinner, A," 85, 88, 96–106, 111, 126, 159
Dylan, Bob, 200

Eagleton, Terry, 5, 149
Eberhart, Richard, 147
Eliot, T. S., 4, 24, 33, 62, 73, 86, 100, 115, 117, 118, 130, 167, 197, 198
Emerson, Ralph Waldo, 5, 13, 100
"Esthetique du Mal," xi, 23, 105, 112, 121, 123, 129–130, 136–150, 158, 208

"Farewell to Florida," 16, 28–30, 48, 93
Fernandez, Ramon, 41, 48–50, 181
"Figure of the Youth as a Virile Poet, The," 25, 172–174
Filreis, Alan, xi, 2–4, 56–57, 66–68, 75, 87, 97, 100, 102–103, 106, 112–113, 126, 137–141, 147, 156, 190
"Final Soliloquy of the Interior Paramour, The," 177
Freud, Sigmund, 8, 110, 150–151
Foucault, Michel, 11, 59, 117
Frye, Northrop, 184

"Glass of Water, The," 8–9
"Greenest Continent, The," 60, 85, 88–96, 107, 111, 127, 129–130, 140
Grigson, Geoffrey, 100, 103

Hamlet, 33
Hartford Indemnity & Insurance Co., 135, 192
Harmonium, 16, 27, 28, 35, 59, 60, 65, 86
Hegel, 11–13, 27, 131
Heidegger, Martin, 11, 174
Hemingway, Ernest, 81, 139
H. D., 115
Hitler, Adolf, 83, 111
Hoerner, Fred, 144, 149, 162
Hollander, John, 37–38
Holmes, Janet, 202–205
Homer, 24, 165, 167, 169
Hullot-Kentor, Robert, 119

"Idea of Order at Key West, The," 16, 25, 28–31, 37–52, 59, 65, 69, 74, 86, 89, 99, 106, 108, 121, 158, 162, 176, 181, 196, 204, 208
Ideas of Order, 16, 27–55, 59, 60, 67, 75, 152
"Imagination as Value," 42, 115
"Insurance and Social Change," 188, 193–194
"Irrational Element in Poetry, The," 2, 31–34, 64, 71, 106–108, 135

Jackson, Andrew, 114
Jameson, Fredric, 188–196, 199
Joad, Dr., 120
Joyce, James, 4, 24, 33, 139, 167, 169, 174–175, 183, 202

Kant, Immanuel, 144
Keats, John, 31, 51–52, 98
Kenyon Review, The, 137
Kermode, Frank, xi, 57
Kingston, Maxine Hong, 61
Konstantinov, 23, 140–142, 152
Kravec, Maureen, 121
Kristeva, Julia, 117, 144, 174

Lacan, Jacques, 172
Latimer, Ronald Lane, 27, 71
Leggett, B. J., 11
"Le Monocle de Mon Oncle," 27

Lenin, V. I., 103, 141, 152, 154, 156–157, 162, 164, 197
Letters, 24, 59–60, 71, 72, 83, 96, 123–125, 146, 151–152, 165, 202
Lentricchia, Frank, 182
Levinas, Emmanuel, 11, 197, 202, 204–207
"Life on a Battleship," 23, 95, 123–137, 150, 154, 208
Litz, A. Walton, 38, 53
Longenbach, James, xi, 2, 3, 56, 87, 123–126, 132–134, 145, 150–151, 156, 165, 190
Lyotard, Jean-Francois, 195

MacDonald, Dwight, 141
MacLeish, Archibald, 81
MacLeod, Glen, 2, 45
Mallarme, Stephane, 22, 174
"Man and Bottle," 23
"Man on the Dump, The," 176, 185
Man with the Blue Guitar, The, xi, 1, 11–12, 20, 112–113, 123–124
Marlatt, Daphne, 61
Marvell, Andrew, 100
Marxism, 22, 27, 58–60, 68–85, 115–116, 124, 126, 149, 195–196
Marx, Karl, 22, 149, 162
McLuhan, Marshal, 62
Mauron, Charles, 116
Merleau-Ponty, Maurice, 9–11, 13
Michaels, Walter Benn, 190–191
Miller, J. Hillis, 5, 12, 36
Milton, John, 89–90
"Mr. Burnshaw and the Statue," 27, 58–60, 67–86, 90, 94, 97, 104, 111, 126, 130
Monroe, Robert Emmett, 55
Moore, Marianne, 34, 115
Morse, Samuel French, 80, 101
"Motive for Metaphor, The," 167, 169–172, 174–175, 178, 185, 188, 195
"Mozart, 1935," 30, 53, 126, 129, 207
Mussolini, Benito, 83, 96, 111

New Criticism, 59, 198
New Masses, 67, 72, 79–80

Nicholson, Mervyn, 43
Nietzsche, Friedrich, 11, 30, 36, 97, 103, 142, 148, 152, 154–157, 164, 171–172, 197
"Noble Rider and the Sound of Words, The," 109, 111, 113–122, 135, 143, 192, 198
"Not Ideas about the Thing but the Thing Itself," 191, 201–202
"Notes Toward a Supreme Fiction," 6–7, 10, 20, 45, 51, 113, 128, 132, 134, 136, 150–151, 155, 175–176, 182, 190

Odyssey, The, 24, 128, 133, 167, 181–188
"Of Modern Poetry," 47, 79, 121, 129, 148, 194
"Old Woman and the Statue, The," 56–57, 62–70, 78, 79, 85, 88, 89, 94, 97, 106, 119, 196
Olds, Sharon, 205–206
Olson, Charles, 168, 198
"Ordinary Evening in New Haven, The," 169, 200, 206–208
Ondaatje, Michael, 61, 81

"Parochial Theme," 12
Partisan Review, 123–124, 133
Parts of a World, 9, 23, 133, 150
Pearce, Roy Harvey, 56
Perloff, Marjorie, 118
"Peter Quince at the Clavier," 87
Picasso, Pablo, 15, 19
Plato, 45, 114, 117, 126
Poe, Edgar Allan, 31, 101
Pound, Ezra, 1, 4, 24, 32–34, 115, 118, 130, 136, 167–168, 183
"Prologues to What Is Possible," 24, 67, 89, 172, 178–181, 185
Proust, Marcel, 33
Pynchon, Thomas, 117–118

Ransom, John Crowe, 137–138
Rahv, Philip, 123–125
"Re-statement of Romance," 13–14, 205
Richardson, Joan, xi

Riddel, Joseph, 3, 4, 11, 56–57, 190
Rimbaud, Arthur, 123, 160
"Rock, The," 167, 181
Rodman, Sergeant, 147
Roethke, Theodore, 50
Ross, Kristin, 160

"Sad Strains of a Gay Waltz," 31, 52–53
"Sail of Ulysses, The" 24, 172, 178,
    183–188
"Sailing After Lunch," 35–37
Sartre, Jean-Paul, 147
Schaum, Melita, 4, 5, 56, 189–190
Serge, Victor, 140–141
Shelley, Percy Bysshe, 47, 70–71
Simons, Hi, 68
"Snow Man, The," 27
"Sombre Figuration," 85–86, 106–113,
    129, 132, 133
Spivak, Gayatri, 60
Stalin, Joseph, 83, 125
"Statue at the World's End, The,"
    80–83
Stein, Gertrude, 15, 33–34, 150
Steiner, Wendy, 117–118, 191
Steinman, Lisa, 4, 62, 120
Stevens, Holly, 2
Stevens, Elsie Kachel Moll, 25, 124,
    130, 134, 172
Strand, Mark, 136
"Sunday Morning," 22, 27, 90, 143

"Thirteen Ways of Looking at a
    Blackbird," 5–8, 27, 59
"Two or Three Ideas," 93, 157
Tompkins, Jane, 60–61
Transport to Summer, 23, 112, 150

van Gogh, Vincent, 22
Vendler, Helen, xi, 56, 95, 136, 142,
    145–146, 148
Virginia Quarterly Review, The,
    163–165
Vitanza, Victor, 194–195
Voros, Gyorgyi, 13

Wallace Stevens Journal, ix, 56
"Well Dressed Man with a Beard,
    The," 29
Weil, Simone, 6, 7
Weinfield, Henry, 145–146, 148
Welles, Sumner, 24, 122, 149, 152, 159,
    162–165, 197
Wells, H. G., 194
Whitman, Walt, 5, 100, 174
"Whole Man, The: Perspectives,
    Horizons," 115
Wilde, Dana, 62, 120
Williams, Oscar, 147
Williams, William Carlos, 33–34, 113,
    115, 118, 162, 168, 183
Wilson, Edmund, 156
Winterson, Jeanette, 61, 198–200
Woolf, Virginia, 198
"Woman That Had More Babies Than
    That, The" 23, 115, 123–124,
    132–136, 149–150
Wordsworth, William, 4, 10, 15, 16, 22,
    29, 31–32, 37, 117, 140, 146, 198
"World as Meditation, The," 24, 172,
    178, 181–183, 202

Yeats, W. B., 22, 66, 92, 108, 181

Ziarek, Krzysztof, 11